"The story of how Ian Gawler came to discover the great benefits of meditation is as inspiring as it is remarkable. I have known Ian for many years, and this instructive and accessible book is just the latest example of his passion for sharing the gift of meditation, and showing what a powerful and transformative effect it can have in every aspect of our lives."   —Sogyal Rinpoche, author of *The Tibetan Book of Living and Dying*

"A rich and skillfully nuanced introduction to the varied landscape of meditation practice and its healing and transformative potential. This book will be of great benefit to people interested in mindfulness-based approaches to working with stress, pain and chronic illness, as well as to anyone with a longing to recognize and inhabit the full dimensionality of the human heart and live with greater authenticity, well-being, clarity and kindness."   —Jon Kabat-Zinn, author of *Arriving at Your Own Door* and *Letting Everything Become Your Teacher*

"Meditation is as universal as art, and there are many manifestations of this form of creativity. Some are superficial and others plumb the depths. In an inclusive way Ian Gawler and Paul Bedson introduce people to the basic ideas of meditation which prepare the reader for the choice of practice that suits them best."
—Father Laurence Freeman, OSB, Director,
World Community for Christian Meditation

"*Meditation: An In-Depth Guide* offers an engaging journey into the benefits of developing a practice of focusing your mind to promote both mental and physical well-being. The authors have woven into clear prose helpful illustrations that create an inviting step-by-step plan for a 'mindfulness-based stillness meditation' that clearly illuminates the concepts at the heart of this mental training. We now know that we can use the focus of our attention to alter the connections in the brain, helping us to more effectively modulate our emotions, our thoughts and even our bodily functions. Developing the clarity of mind that this book and its wise authors offer will provide many readers who heed its advice an accessible way to create mindful states that, with regular practice, can become the powerful traits of well-being and equanimity in their lives."
—Daniel J. Siegel, M.D., author of *The Mindful Brain* and *Mindsight*

"This is a most important book, coming with the enormous authority of Ian Gawler's personal story of overcoming terminal cancer with the aid of meditation. This book explains in clear and simple language, sometimes having the rhythmic quality of the meditation process itself, the complex way toward the 'liberation of the utilitarian mind.' This is a book that can change your life."
—Russell Meares, Emeritus Professor of Psychiatry, University of Sydney

"The key to success in our lives is right inside us: our own mind. Ian and Paul show us in detail how to access it, to unravel its contents, and to gradually shape it—and thus ourselves—into the marvelous thing it can become."
—Robina Courtin, Tibetan Buddhist nun

"This book will be of great value to anyone with an interest in meditation but particularly to those who are new to the practice, for whom the experience of reading it will be akin to being taken by the hand and guided surely, clearly and confidently by two practitioners with a wealth of love and experience in the art."

—Dr. Craig Hassed, Deputy Head,
Department of General Practice, Monash University

"The power of the mind is untapped. We know that within the world of Olympic Games in our endeavors to go further, higher and faster, we discover new ways to unleash ourselves through the power of the mind. And we are only at the beginning. That is clear. Ian Gawler and Paul Bedson bring a fascinating insight into the powers of meditation and the benefits thereof. A fascinating read."

—John Bertrand, A.M., skipper of
Australia II, winner of the America's Cup

"More and more, scientific research is providing us with evidence of the benefits of meditation; however, this information is of little use without the insights of master practitioners. This volume distills the wisdom of two of our most experienced meditation teachers and practitioners into a comprehensive and clearly readable guide that will benefit the novice and the expert alike. If you want to learn from the best teachers around, this is the book for you."

—Professor Nick Allen, Department of
Psychology, University of Melbourne

"As a businessman I highly recommend this fabulous book as a business tool. I have meditated for twenty years according to Ian and Paul's approach. I started when it helped heal me of terminal cancer. I have kept going as it has transformed my business life: more creative, more productive, more fun and a whole lot less stress. You must read this!"

—Michael Rennie, Managing Partner,
McKinsey & Company, Australia and New Zealand

MEDITATION

ALSO BY IAN GAWLER

Books

You Can Conquer Cancer
Peace of Mind
Meditation: Pure & Simple
Imagery and Visualisation (revised edition of
The Creative Power of Imagery)

CDs

Ian Gawler has prepared three series of CDs for meditation, health
and well-being. Those relevant to this book are:
Meditation: A Complete Guide
Relaxation for Everyone
Deepening Your Meditation
Meditation: Pure & Simple
Mind-Body Medicine
Effective Pain Management
Meditation Live: A Meditation Workshop

Details of the work of Ian Gawler and Paul Bedson, and information
on how to obtain their resource materials and on the Gawler Foundation, are available at www.gawler.org.

MEDITATION
AN IN-DEPTH GUIDE

DR. IAN GAWLER
AND PAUL BEDSON

JEREMY P. TARCHER/PENGUIN
a member of Penguin Group (USA) Inc.
New York

JEREMY P. TARCHER/PENGUIN
Published by the Penguin Group
Penguin Group (USA) Inc., 375 Hudson Street, New York, New York 10014, USA •
Penguin Group (Canada), 90 Eglinton Avenue East, Suite 700, Toronto, Ontario M4P 2Y3, Canada
(a division of Pearson Penguin Canada Inc.) • Penguin Books Ltd, 80 Strand, London WC2R 0RL, England •
Penguin Ireland, 25 St Stephen's Green, Dublin 2, Ireland (a division of Penguin Books Ltd) •
Penguin Group (Australia), 250 Camberwell Road, Camberwell, Victoria 3124, Australia
(a division of Pearson Australia Group Pty Ltd) • Penguin Books India Pvt Ltd, 11 Community Centre,
Panchsheel Park, New Delhi–110 017, India • Penguin Group (NZ), 67 Apollo Drive, Rosedale,
North Shore 0632, New Zealand (a division of Pearson New Zealand Ltd) •
Penguin Books (South Africa) (Pty) Ltd, 24 Sturdee Avenue, Rosebank, Johannesburg 2196, South Africa

Penguin Books Ltd, Registered Offices: 80 Strand, London WC2R 0RL, England

Original edition published in Australia by Allen & Unwin Pty Ltd. 2010
First published in the United States by Jeremy P. Tarcher/Penguin 2011
Copyright © 2010 by Dr. Ian Gawler and Paul Bedson

Most Tarcher/Penguin books are available at special quantity discounts for bulk purchase for
sales promotions, premiums, fund-raising, and educational needs. Special books or book excerpts
also can be created to fit specific needs. For details, write Penguin Group (USA) Inc.
Special Markets, 375 Hudson Street, New York, NY 10014.

Library of Congress Cataloging-in-Publication Data

Gawler, Ian.
Meditation: an in-depth guide / Ian Gawler and Paul Bedson.
p.   cm.
ISBN 978-1-58542-861-8
1. Meditation—Therapeutic use.   I. Bedson, Paul   II. Title.
RC489.M43G39   2011   2011006803
615.8'52—dc22

Printed in the United States of America
5   7   9   10   8   6   4

Book design by Phil Campbell

Neither the publisher nor the authors are engaged in rendering professional advice or services to the individual reader.
The ideas, procedures, and suggestions contained in this book are not intended as a substitute for consulting with your
physician. All matters regarding your health require medical supervision. Neither the authors nor the publisher shall be
liable or responsible for any loss or damage allegedly arising from any information or suggestion in this book.

While the authors have made every effort to provide accurate telephone numbers and Internet addresses at the time of
publication, neither the publisher nor the authors assume any responsibility for errors, or for changes that occur after
publication. Further, the publisher does not have any control over and does not assume any responsibility for author or
third-party websites or their content.

The symbol that appears on the cover and inside this book is the glorious endless knot. According to Tibetan Buddhist tradition, it is one of the eight auspicious symbols and is the sign of interdependence, of how everything in the universe is interconnected. Also known as the endless or eternal knot, it is a symbol common to many ancient traditions.

To all who are searching
for a path to freedom, peace and happiness.
The path begins where you are.
The first step is inward.
May you find freedom, peace and happiness . . .
your own true nature.

CONTENTS

MEDITATION

INTRODUCTION

THE GIFT OF MEDITATION

Meditation is the process of getting to know your own mind.
—SOGYAL RINPOCHE

This is the book to read when you need to know how to meditate.

The truth is we live in troubled times. Many of us find it easy to get caught up in doubts and fears regarding our personal safety, relationships and well-being. Others have serious illness to deal with—physically, emotionally and mentally. On a community level, our society, our culture, our knowledge is changing incredibly fast. Globally, our physical environment is so threatened that our very survival on this planet is precarious. It is clear that large numbers of people are suffering at the hands of uncertainty, driven by anxiety, busyness and fear.

At the same time, it is not all gloom and doom. We do live in an age of incredible possibilities, and for many there are unprecedented freedoms and myriad opportunities to explore the apparent delights and experiences of the material world. However, many are coming to the realization that while there are real pleasures to be found and experienced, the satisfaction that comes from doing these things—from having and buying these things—is only temporary. Often the conclusion follows that while having lots of things can be "nice," it is short on lasting happiness.

It is no surprise then that many people are looking for something more substantial to hang on to, something that can provide real peace and contentedness amid the external turmoil. Many are seeking stability, healing and meaning, as well as wishing to connect the spiritual threads in their lives. Here is the good news: there is a solution. There is real potential within us.

Many people are coming to realize that on a personal level, the most useful, the most practical and the most effective thing that we can do for our own health, for healing and for our well-being, is to meditate. Ancient traditions, including all the great religions, have the practical experience that demonstrates meditation's rightful place at the heart of the spiritual path; and modern research demonstrates a vast array of physical and psychological benefits that accompany the regular practice of meditation.

People often know why they need to meditate, but many questions follow: How do we meditate? How do we get started? How do we develop our practice of meditation? How often do we need to do it? When do we do it? Where? Can it be harmful? How do we deepen our practice? Will it help us to heal? Will it lead to enlightenment? How do we know if and when we are doing it right?

You might even be wondering whether you are wise to even ask such questions. Well, yes, you are! The intention of this book is to answer these questions and to provide you with a comprehensive, clear and in-depth guide to the practice of meditation.

MINDFULNESS-BASED STILLNESS MEDITATION

Part I of this book provides a detailed guide to our recommended main method for meditation practice, which we call Mindfulness-Based Stillness Meditation (MBSM). Part II elaborates on other applications of meditation that are useful adjuncts to this main practice.

Learning to meditate using Mindfulness-Based Stillness Meditation is very simple. The main reason why this book is so thick is that we have explained each step in great detail. Hopefully you will find this detail informs your practice of meditation, clarifies how to proceed and answers any questions that you might have. But as you read, keep in mind that it is actually very easy. In Mindfulness-Based Stillness Meditation there are four key steps. Each one is helpful in its own right and each one flows naturally into the next. Each is easy to learn, easy to apply and should make logical sense to you.

The four steps of MBSM are preparation, relaxation, mindfulness and stillness. *Preparation* is to do with all the practical details of where you meditate, the posture you adopt, the attitude you need; all the things that relate to how you set yourself up to begin your meditation practice. When we get into a relaxed space in which to practice and take up an appropriate posture, we relax quite naturally—quite effortlessly—and the meditation begins to flow.

However, MBSM recognizes that we may need more help to proceed. We may well benefit by learning to relax more formally and thoroughly. So, in the second step, *relaxation*, we learn how to do this. We take time to learn how to relax our body and our mind.

As we relax more deeply our mind becomes clearer, more settled, and we become more aware. We flow on into a state of increasing *mindfulness*. So, in the third step of MBSM we give our attention to developing this mindfulness more fully and completely. What mindfulness means is that we simply learn to pay attention to our present moment experience, free of judgment and free of reaction. In doing so, we learn to let go of worrying about the past and being anxious about the future. We let go of excessive thinking and bring our attention to the here and now—another easy step to learn that has wonderful benefits in its own right. And remember, the effects are profound but it is a very simple process.

But there is more! As we become more mindful, as we learn to give our attention more fully to whatever we are doing in the present moment, we notice a fundamental truth: there is activity in our life and there is *stillness*. Just as the sky has its ever-present blue canopy, there are clouds that come and go; so when we meditate using this MBSM process, as we become more mindful, we notice that our mind has this ever-present stillness accompanied by a constantly changing parade of thoughts. So we learn to recognize and to rest in that stillness. We let go of our normal engagement with thinking and flow quite naturally from mindfulness into stillness. And then we experience the true essence of meditation, the true essence of the nature of our mind.

The delightful fact of MBSM is that each of its four steps is really beneficial as an individual unit, and each flows into the next. Each step—preparation, relaxation, mindfulness and stillness—is easy to learn and has the potential to lead into deep meditation in its own right.

You may take up meditation to manage stress or to heal physically or mentally, to find more peace and balance in your life, to be more efficient at work or to perform better at sports, or to be a nicer person. All these things are real possibilities as a consequence of regular meditation, and it makes good sense to begin meditation with any of these intentions in mind. But the reason why meditation is the greatest gift you can give yourself—or, if you can, give to another—is that meditation introduces us to our innermost nature, the truth of who we really are. And with this comes a deep inner knowing, a recognition of our own fundamental goodness. All the great spiritual traditions tell us this is so—that in our heart, in our essence, we are fundamentally pure and whole. Meditation provides the opportunity, the technology, to test this proposition.

While meditation has myriad well-proven benefits for our health, our healing and our well-being, the real gift of meditation is that it helps us to get to know ourselves better. And in doing so, brings a deep confidence and contentment; a sense that we are fundamentally okay, that life makes sense. And what we are left with is a joyful good humor and an easy smile; the essence of meditation.

DEFINITION OF *MEDITATION*

While these days a multitude of people are either learning and practicing meditation or discussing and writing about it, the word *meditation* does seem to present two very real difficulties in modern-day usage.

First, *meditation* is used in a generic sense to cover a wide range of mental activities, much as in the way the word *travel* is used to describe a wide range of physical activities. We can say we will travel from one city to another, but that says nothing about the detail. Will we travel by car or by plane? Will we get there as quickly as possible, or will we meander along the way? Just as there are many ways to travel, there are many different ways to meditate. Therefore when people say they are "meditating" they could be involved in any one of a wide range of activities.

This leads us to the second difficulty, and that is the actual definition of *meditation*. These days it seems that many books, teachers and individuals discuss meditation at length without defining it. So what is "meditation"?

In its simplest and most general sense meditation is a mental discipline involving attention regulation. More specifically, the broad act of meditation can be subclassified according to the processes it involves or the outcomes it leads to. This definition was developed and is used by the Australian Teachers of Meditation Association (ATMA) and the Gawler Foundation. While in the Appendix we present and discuss various traditional and modern definitions of meditation, we choose this as our definition for its accuracy and relevance to modern life.

Meditation is a mental discipline. It is clearly to do with the mind and it requires discipline to develop and maintain a practice. However, as our definition suggests, there are many different ways to meditate and many possible outcomes of meditation.

The processes and outcomes of meditation

The *process* of meditation is simply what we do while we are meditating. Attention regulation, which is essentially a fancy way of describing concentration, can be directed to various objects such as the breath or body, a mantra, a thought or prayer, a visualization or mental image, a physical object, a sense of being, or stillness. These in turn can be used to cultivate various *outcomes*, including therapeutic outcomes, cognitive changes such as improved concentration, non-attachment to experiences, stillness of mind and an attitude of acceptance. Other outcomes include meditative states or traits such as undistracted awareness, transcendence of thought, oneness, spiritual insight and enlightenment. Meditation can also be identified by the physical effects it produces, such as physiological, biochemical, hormonal, immunological or neurological changes. All of this will be explained in detail as we move through the book.

Bringing the definitions to life

The aim of this book is to help you to develop a personally satisfying and sustainable practice of meditation. To do this you need to strike a balance between learning the theory and practicing the technique. Doing this in conjunction leads to knowledge and skill and gives us the wings to fly.

The intention of this book, therefore, is to build on this definition of meditation, clarifying the theory and bringing it to life by detailing techniques that have direct relevance to the modern world.

THE HISTORY OF MEDITATION

Currently, meditation is going through quite a renaissance. However, one of its great strengths is its longevity. The earliest written records of meditation being practiced come from China and are dated around 5000 BC. In India, written records of meditation first appeared about 1500 BC, and in the West, in Greece, about 750 BC. So it seems that practice of meditation stretches back into antiquity.

From such early beginnings meditation has been practiced continuously in virtually all cultures. While meditation practice is often associated primarily with Eastern cultures and religions, it is apparent that it is a widespread and long-lasting phenomenon. What this tells us is that meditation has been well tried and tested.

Consider this: In just the last few centuries many of the great minds of the West have taken to their laboratories and studied physics, chemistry and the workings of the physical world. Very useful! But for thousands of years, countless great minds in the East took to their deserts or their caves, went into the laboratories between their ears and studied the workings of their minds. The mind science they learned was handed down from generation to generation, often by word of mouth, but also in written form. As a consequence, we know in great detail what meditation has to offer, how to practice it, what pitfalls to look out for and how to use this mind science to our best advantage. Meditation is a very safe and reliable technology. This is of particular significance and relevance when it comes to using meditation as a therapy.

Of course, during meditation's genesis, and even up until quite recent times, it was a practice that was singularly focused upon spiritual realization. During the 1800s meditation in the West was largely the domain of Christian contemplatives and a few adventurous explorers of the occult, spiritualism, mental healing and transcendental experience. This all changed when the first World Parliament of Religions was held in Chicago in 1893. This single event was epoch-making. For the first time major spiritual leaders from the East gathered and presented something of their experience, knowledge and presence to a large audience of influential Westerners. The ramifications were widespread and continue to be felt. The Interfaith Movement began, and at the same time a serious interest in the study and practice of meditation was sparked in the Western world.

While the 1950s saw a few pioneers (such as Alan Watts, who published his bestseller *Psychotherapy East and West* in 1961), until the early 1960s meditation in the West remained largely the domain of spiritual seekers. Most meditation was being taught and practiced within the context of either a Hindu yogic, Sufi, Buddhist or Taoist framework. Then came the Age of Aquarius. The Beatles went to India, met the Maharishi and brought Transcendental Meditation (TM) back to the West. Psychedelic drugs burst out of the experimental laboratories of psychiatrists and the CIA and flooded the streets. Vietnam galvanized a generation, the counterculture flourished and people were intent on expanding their minds. Very quickly meditation in the West was popularized, and perhaps even stigmatized to a degree, as the domain of the hippies.

Meanwhile, as an unexpected and positive side effect of what was otherwise a tragedy of epic proportions, when the communists invaded Asia a wave of highly realized spiritual refugees fled persecution and escaped to the West. While His Holiness the Dalai Lama is the best known of these, many other luminaries suddenly became directly available to Western audiences.

MEDITATION AS A THERAPY

Then the penny dropped. Beginning as a trickle in the 1960s and expanding into full flow in the seventies, innovative doctors and psychologists began to realize that meditation had specific therapeutic applications. This coincided with the beginnings of mind-body medicine.

Up until this time the health of the mind had been regarded in most medical circles to be quite unrelated to the health of the body. Likewise the capacity of the mind to influence healing had been largely ignored. This general lack of professional interest in these subjects was exacerbated by the fact that the philosophy and techniques of analytical Western science seemed far removed from the apparently mystical and mysterious world of the mind and meditation. This was in the days before the development of advanced EEGs, functional MRIs, PET scans and other technically sophisticated techniques, which in more recent times have allowed for empirical examination of the brain's anatomy and function even while it operates. It is not surprising then that very little academic research was being published before the 1970s on mind-body medicine in general or meditation specifically. Documenting the advent of meditation as a therapy, therefore, begins with popular books on the subject.

The first significant book focusing on meditation as a therapy would appear to be Dr. Ainslie Meares's *Relief Without Drugs*. First published in 1967 in the United Kingdom, it appeared in fairly rapid succession in the United States and in Meares's home country of Australia. The book created a publishing sensation and was translated into many languages. Perhaps Dr. Meares is the true founder of therapeutic meditation.

In the 1970s many more seminal authors appeared. The psychologist Larry LeShan had spent the 1960s delving into parapsychology and went on to become a founding pioneer in psycho-oncology, applying his psychotherapy training to the betterment of people affected by cancer. His book *How to Meditate*, intended for a general audience, was published in 1974 and became a standard reference for many years.

In the following year another landmark book emerged, this time out of Harvard. Herbert Benson, a cardiologist and convert to TM, published his scientifically based, runaway bestseller *The Relaxation Response*. Benson advocated a more secular version of TM, detailing a simple mantra-based meditation technique.

Then, in 1978, Carl Simonton and Stephanie Matthews published *Getting Well Again*, which broke more new ground as it applied Stephanie's training as a performance psychologist to enhance Carl's work as a radiation oncologist. Carl and Stephanie focused on teaching their patients imagery techniques to complement and facilitate radiotherapy treatment. They reported positive results and their research findings rapidly opened the doors to developments in the study and practice of the therapeutic use of imagery.

Through the 1970s and 1980s many excellent books were published on meditation in general. In the therapeutic arena, Pauline McKinnon, an Australian patient of Dr. Meares, who used his methods to recover from agoraphobia in 1983, published her own work based on his techniques, *In Stillness Conquer Fear*. Ian Gawler's first book, *You Can Conquer Cancer*, with its emphasis on meditation and cancer recovery, was released in 1984, followed by his more specific books on meditation, *Peace of Mind* in 1987, *Meditation: Pure and Simple* in 1996, and *The Creative Power of Imagery* in 1997.

The next major wave of interest in meditation seems to have been propelled by Jon Kabat-Zinn's first book, which detailed the use of mindfulness in the therapeutic setting. *Full Catastrophe Living* was published in 1990 and catalyzed huge interest in mindfulness among both the lay public and the scientific research community.

In 1992, Sogyal Rinpoche published his spiritual classic *The Tibetan Book of Living and Dying*, which to date has sold over two million copies and has been translated into over thirty languages. This book established that works written by traditionally trained spiritual leaders who can understand and speak in the vernacular of the West could become major bestsellers in the popular market. As a consequence, mainstream publishers entered this arena and many great books subsequently appeared.

Now to the beginning of the twenty-first century and a series of breakthroughs in neurological research that are well summarized in

Norman Doidge's book *The Brain That Changes Itself.* Doidge is a research psychiatrist who has documented revolutionary discoveries in the new and incredibly exciting field of neuroplasticity. Doidge collated recent clinical and research findings that clearly demonstrate that our brain changes both its physical structure and function according to how we use it. This knowledge supplants the long-held view that while the brain grows and develops up until the age of about eight years, from then on it remains anatomically static with no potential for new growth. The realization that this is not so and that the brain can regenerate has tremendous potential for those hoping to recover from major head injuries or disease, while at the same time showing how repetition reinforces function and changes anatomy. Put simply, the more we do something, the more our brain adapts physically to facilitate us doing it better. The catch is that this applies equally to bad habits as to good ones, so the whole notion of how we use and train our mind takes on even greater significance. Indeed, this new field of neuroplasticity also clearly confirms the old adage "Use it or lose it" and has great implications for a healthy and mentally active old age. Put simply, what we do more of we get better at, and as we do so our brain actually changes its physical shape to make everything easier, more consistent, more reliable and more possible.

The year 2007 was a vintage year for mind science breakthroughs. In *The Mindful Brain* Daniel Siegel, psychiatrist, educator and leader in the field of mental health, introduced recent research identifying what have been termed "mirror neurons." These specialized cells are located within particular areas of the brain, notably the frontal and parietal cortex as well as the superior temporal area. They form a system that appears to have the capacity to mirror internally what we as people are experiencing externally. This ability seems to be directly related to our potential to feel empathy, to resonate emotionally with somebody else and to imitate a wide range of practical behaviors. In other words, mirror neurons may well have a prime place in allowing us to tune in to what others are doing and feeling. As we experience, so we feel and so we do. Siegel points out that our capacity to tune in to our own internal states is crucial in determining our capacity to tune in to those of others.

If we want to develop empathy with others, we are wise to develop empathy with ourselves. One effective way to develop this empathy is by practicing the Mindfulness of Emotions exercises outlined in chapter 9.

In relation to healing, mirror neurons are another emerging area of research that point to many possibilities. First, when it comes to developing or changing to healthy habits, role models may well play a crucial role. It is common knowledge among lifestyle-based therapists that authenticity is essential if effective therapeutic relationships are to develop. The therapist needs to genuinely display the qualities and lifestyle advocated, and in so doing provide a sound template to mirror. It is the same with meditation. The traditional role of the teacher has been to demonstrate the experience of the meditation directly via their presence. Again, mirror neurons allude to the benefit of spending time with experienced teachers and the benefits that are likely when we learn how to merge our minds with theirs. Mirror neurons add a scientific rationale to the age-old tradition of having a guru, as well as the more recent phenomena of mentors and role models.

Scientific research

When TM came from India to the West it brought two exceptional benefits. It provided a reliable meditation technique that was relatively easy to teach and to learn, while organizationally TM had a strong commitment to research. By 1990, David Orme-Johnson and his colleagues at Maharishi University of Management in Iowa had compiled and edited 508 scientific studies on the therapeutic benefits of TM. Of these studies about one-third were from peer-reviewed scientific journals, TM conferences and TM's own publications. TM continues to lead the way as it studies its own specific mantra-based style of meditation and how this technique benefits physical, psychological, social and spiritual aspects of life. One of TM's leading advocates, Herbert Benson, established the Benson-Henry Institute for Mind Body Medicine at Harvard and continues to have a powerful effect in catalyzing research.

Another wave of extraordinary and groundbreaking research has been prompted by His Holiness the Dalai Lama. An accomplished scholar as well as a towering spiritual figure, His Holiness has a long-standing interest in science generally and, of course, the mind in particular. He has said, "A general stance of Buddhism is that it is inappropriate to hold a view that is logically inconsistent. This is taboo. But even more taboo than holding a view that is logically inconsistent is holding a view that goes against direct experience."

The Dalai Lama was instrumental in establishing the Mind and Life Institute, which is devoted to meetings and collaborative research between scientists and Buddhist scholars and meditators. This interaction between modern science and ancient wisdom has resulted in regular dialogues since 1987 between His Holiness and others such as Daniel Goleman, the author of *Emotional Intelligence*; Matthieu Ricard; neuroscientist Richard Davidson and Jon Kabat-Zinn. Many popular bestsellers have come directly from these dialogues, such as *Healing Emotions* (1997) and *Destructive Emotions: And How We Can Overcome Them* (2003), both edited by Daniel Goleman. Then there are more recent works by the new generation of young Tibetan teachers, such as Yongey Mingyur Rinpoche and his excellent books *The Joy of Living* (2007) and *Joyful Wisdom* (2009). Furthermore, leading scientists like Davidson were prompted by the Dalai Lama to commence scientific investigations on long-term meditators. This has led to major research being published in academic journals as well as popular books like Norman Doidge's.

The development of academic research has been underpinned by the pioneering and ongoing influences of Michael Murphy and Steven Donovan, and the famous personal development center they established in 1961, the Esalen Institute. Many of the pioneers in mind-body medicine and meditation in the West were either nurtured at Esalen or passed through it, and Murphy and Donovan themselves have provided their own wonderful contribution to this field with their work *The Physical and Psychological Effects of Meditation*. Along with an excellent introduction and a review of meditation, Murphy and Donovan have compiled a comprehensive bibliography of the scientific research on meditation published around the world. First released in 1988, an updated edition was published in 1996, and now this resource is available free online at www.noetic.org/research/medbiblio/biblio.htm, courtesy of the Institute of Noetic Sciences (IONS), whose mission is "advancing the science of consciousness and human experience to serve individual and collective transformation." This online bibliography is regularly updated, and in 2010 included well over four thousand scientific articles.

No wonder, then, that meditation has been so widely accepted by the medical mainstream. The body of research evidence is huge and powerfully attests to meditation's many benefits in the prevention, management and treatment of a wide range of physical and psychological conditions. This evidence base is arguably more extensive than that relating to many well-accepted treatments carried out daily in medical practices around the world.

Avenues for future research

The research currently available on the health benefits of meditation is extensive and convincing. However, it is important to point out that often the word *meditation* is used quite loosely in the arena of medicine, just as it is more generally. Surprisingly, much of the published research on meditation gives scant attention to the type of meditation practiced or even how much meditation the subjects who were studied actually completed. Of even greater significance is that currently there is no widely accepted or used measure that quantifies the depth or quality of meditation people actually do practice. This poses real problems for empirical research. When attempting to evaluate and compare meditation research outcomes, often it is not clear if we are comparing apples with apples. This is somewhat akin to publishing research saying that a new antibiotic was tested in the treatment of pneumonia, without specifying what type of antibiotic, how much of it was administered in each dose and how often each dose was taken.

Clearly the evolution of meditation as a therapy is at a point where more specific research is needed. What type? How much? How often? Are specific methods preferable for specific conditions and outcomes? These are all challenging and fertile areas for future investigation.

THE FOCUS OF THIS BOOK

The history of meditation is impressive, but it is a busy modern world in which we live. Meditation resided for thousands of years almost exclusively in the domain of spiritual practice. Delightfully, however, it is clear that meditation has so much to offer that is very relevant for our modern lives, whether or not we are spiritually inclined. It is a very practical technique. So while there are many different ways to meditate, our aim here is to draw on the knowledge of the great traditions, along with current scientific research and a wealth of practical experience, to present key meditation techniques that, in our experience, offer so much.

Part I focuses on the main practice we recommend and which we call Mindfulness-Based Stillness Meditation. As explained earlier, this technique incorporates four easy-to-learn steps that flow on quite naturally from one to the next: preparation, relaxation, mindfulness and stillness. For each step we provide clear instruction on the techniques, along with commentaries that cover the theory behind the techniques, experiences you might encounter along the way, benchmarks you can use to check your progress, stories of people who have used these techniques, common obstacles to be aware of (along with their antidotes) and, finally, how to integrate the benefits of each technique into daily life.

Part II looks at other applications and techniques with which we can train our minds and how to use meditation in response to particular needs. The chapters in this section cover meditation for health, healing and well-being; meditation to transform pain; affirmations and imagery; contemplation; analytical meditation; and meditation for the spiritual path. The book concludes with a brief summary of what to do, how to do it and the possibilities that flow from the regular practice of meditation.

ABOUT THE AUTHORS

In most traditions, up until very recently, meditation teachers would avoid speaking of their personal experiences. However, we live in times where sharing personal stories is regarded as helpful. While there is the risk of the ego creeping in, accounts of personal histories and development can be inspiring and instructional.

While we the authors come from quite different backgrounds, began meditating in different circumstances and followed different early paths, the range of our experiences may well be reflective of the diversity of meditation practice in modern times. Importantly, we have both had great teachers—really great teachers. This has inspired both our personal practice and our own work as teachers.

In fact, between the two of us we have been meditating for over seventy years and have introduced meditation to well over 100,000 people. This has given us an amazing opportunity to find out what happens when people in the modern world set about practicing meditation, what works and what to avoid. Providing some sense of who we are, where we come from and, particularly, some detail regarding our own teachers may also help to show you that meditation is a path. You progress by learning a little, doing some practice, learning some more and practicing again. The two wings of the bird—learning and practice.

In the past, most people would have learned meditation directly from a teacher. The novice would check out the teacher, often quite thoroughly, while at the same time the teacher would check out the new student. If there was agreement, the lessons would begin. These days many people learn directly from books. Nonetheless, it is still wise to check out who is behind the books and what their bona fides are. The stories that follow, therefore, are offered in the spirit of providing an opportunity to check us out.

IAN'S STORY

I first began meditating out of a very real need inspired by a life-threatening illness and the urge to heal. While I had been interested in religion and spiritual matters from an early age, it was only when faced with this sense of urgency that my casual interest in meditation was galvanized into action.

Born into a comfortable upper-middle-class family who went to church on Sundays, I loved the sense of community that was to be found at the church. I loved joining in on the singing of the hymns and I loved the stories. In particular, I loved the parables, as they seemed to offer something quite real in response to the uncertainty every young person has regarding how to lead a good life. In retrospect it was a luxury to have the comfort of a happy family to grow up in and the opportunity to reflect on such things.

And then, when I was twelve, my mother died, suddenly and unexpectedly and in strange circumstances. The night after her death, I remember, I lay alone in bed, forlorn and crying, but thankful that at least I still had my dog to comfort me. And then, about a week later, dear old Bimbo the Wonder Dog went missing. Two days later as I pedaled my bike home from school, I found him. He was stiff, bloated, legs outstretched. Not much marked but very dead. Run over and killed and left lying at the side of the road.

These powerful events challenged my worldview of the time. In my own boyish way, I had taken the Sunday school stories and lessons to mean that life involved a fairly simple and reasonable deal. Be a good boy, go to church, say your prayers, do the right thing and life will treat you kindly. Well, I knew I had been no saint, but I also knew I had not done anything terribly wrong. So how come my mother was dead? And when I sought comfort in my close companion Bimbo the dog, why was he too suddenly taken from me? These two events, occurring as they did in such rapid succession, made no sense at all. Where was the sense of justice? Where was the reason? The meaning?

Instead of turning me off religion, spirituality or even life itself, these two deaths only served to make me more curious, more questioning and more determined to find answers. Clearly the simplistic "Sunday school" notion I had formed of life did not fit my own circumstances. So now I became preoccupied with the meaning in life. I wanted to know the truth about what it was to be a human being. Where do we come from? What are we doing here? Where is life taking us and, most important, who am I really? But most of all I wanted to know what is the purpose of life. My life in particular. Several years went by with no real answers forthcoming, yet I maintained the search. Just having the question, actively looking for answers, dwelling on the possibilities and living with the mystery of the question seemed comforting in itself and made life okay.

When I was fourteen, my father remarried and we all moved interstate. I went to a new school that provided a vast array of opportunities across academic, sporting and artistic fields. Then it hit me. Whatever else life provided, it also brought the opportunity for experience. In fact, a wide range of experiences. From what I could observe, from what I could reason, it was as simple as this: as living beings we could experience life itself. Fueled by this deduction, my newfound purpose in life became to experience as many things as possible. I read avidly. I joined in many of the school's extracurricular activities. I had a go at anything.

Even a bad experience became a good one. Everything became interesting. Everything *was* interesting.

A glimpse of another reality

Then in late high school I experienced for the first time an altered state of consciousness that changed everything. As is often the way, this direct experience occurred quite unexpectedly. It was just getting dark. A cold, somewhat damp and gloomy wintry night. Aged seventeen, in uniform, at the end of the school day, I was walking into the city to buy a book. It was five p.m. As I made my way into the city center, a mass of humanity was walking toward me. The streets were damp from the rain, and light glistened and bounced off every surface. Suddenly my whole perception changed. Rather than being aware of all these individual people moving toward me, it was as if they all merged into one, coalescing into a single unit of interconnected humanity. There was an all-pervading sense of their oneness. In this moment, in a very real way, these people were no longer a bunch of individuals; they provided me with the direct experience of the unity of mankind. It was a timeless moment. I stood immersed in the feeling. A glimpse of a deeper truth, a moment of euphoria. It lasted but a few seconds. Yet nothing was ever the same. It was a direct experience that at a profound level all people are interconnected.

Yet at the same time, even during that wonderful—that is, full of wonder—experience, I was aware that I was observing all of this, but that I was not a part of it. I was aware of this oneness, this deep sense of spiritual connection between all of my fellows in that city streetscape, but I felt apart from it. There was me, the observer, and then there was the experience, that which I observed.

Nevertheless, this realization was genuinely mind-blowing. Now I had a whole new sense of what the purpose of life could be. For me, that purpose now became: How can I experience that oneness again and how can I be a part of, rather than separate from, that oneness? So, still a question and the mystery of an unknown answer. But the sense that an answer was available. Someone, somewhere must know more about what that oneness really was and, more important, know how to be able to experience that oneness. To learn about that oneness, to experience it directly—that surely must be the purpose of life.

Following this experience the focus of my reading changed. I moved on from the life experiences and insights of Hemingway, Steinbeck, Sartre and the classics, to explore the realm of philosophy, the esoteric and the mystic. What a blast! So many extraordinary ideas. Such a rich world of treasures so readily available in the wisdom traditions of the world.

And always mention of this thing called meditation. Over and over the word came up, spoken of with reverence, gratitude and even awe. Clearly meditation was at the heart of the spiritual quest—that quest to arrive at the knowledge, the experience of oneness, and the realization of who we really are. But then there was the rub. As a young scientist now studying to become a veterinarian, I found it both puzzling and frustrating to observe how many of the books with a spiritual theme that were available back in the 1970s spoke lovingly of meditation but gave no details. No definition. No method.

Then I attended a series of lectures by Dr. Raynor Johnson, physicist, Master of Queen's College at Melbourne University and author of *The Imprisoned Splendour*, a book on the ancient wisdom traditions. These teachings proved to be a revelation for me, pulling together many of the disparate pieces of reading I had been dipping into, and linking elements of Christianity, Hinduism, Buddhism and many mystical traditions. As a scientist himself, Dr. Johnson provided a logically compelling life view that made great sense to me. And he spoke of meditation. Here was my big chance.

At the end of one of Dr. Johnson's talks I approached him. "How do you meditate?" I asked. He seemed a bit perplexed by the question and tried to evade answering it. But I had been looking for an opportunity like this for a good long time, so I persisted. He suggested I try a mantra, and when I probed further, he explained to me what this was exactly—a sound or group of words, maybe a prayer that you repeat over and over to focus the mind. When I asked what mantra he used he replied that it is not thought appropriate to tell another person the mantra you are using. I tried a different tack and asked him what I might use. He suggested the Lord's Prayer repeated over and over. And that was it. The conversation was clearly finished and Dr. Johnson moved away. But I had my first real practical lead.

Thereafter, while still a student, and then as a young veterinary graduate, I would occasionally pause for just a few minutes to repeat my newfound mantra. Spectacularly little happened. I had no idea what to expect, but between my laziness, capacity for distraction, intense sporting activity and busy working life—that is, amid the normal level of chaos, contradictions and busyness of modern life—there was not enough in this rudimentary introduction to hold me, to commit me to a regular practice of meditation.

And then, quite consciously, I put my spiritual life on hold. I had what seemed like a really good idea at the time: work hard, get comfortable, buy land and a house, settle down and start a family, set up a great veterinary practice focusing on horses, small animals and surgery, and then, when everything is just right, take up the spiritual path again. But life intervened. What I initially thought was an athletic training injury turned out to be a highly malignant bone cancer. On January 8, 1975, my right leg was amputated through the hip joint.

Everything changed. It was as if the person I had been up to the age of twenty-four died during that operation. Yet I was still conscious. It was like dying and being reborn into a wholly new physical body. No longer the decathlon athlete, no longer capable of being the equine veterinarian. A twenty-four-year-old on crutches. Shunning an artificial leg for ease of mobility. Wearing a kaftan for comfort. With a need to reinvent a whole new life, and discovering an urgency with meditation.

Before going to the hospital to undergo the amputation, I had selected two previously unread books to bring with me. The first was the *Bhagavad-gita*, an Indian spiritual classic that helped deepen the paradigm of spiritual understanding I was developing. The second book, *Meditation in Action* by the great Tibetan teacher Chögyam Trungpa, provided less detail on how to meditate and more on Buddhist philosophy—in a way that I struggled to comprehend at the time. But from the book, it seemed that in order to meditate one was advised to sit cross-legged on the floor for about thirty minutes a day and think of nothing. I was a beginner. That is what I got from the book. So I attempted to do as instructed.

The sitting was easy. But then, not thinking for half an hour . . . you must be joking! As an athlete, I had become adept at training my body and having it do what I told it to do. So I told it to relax and stay still. And it did. However, I quickly realized that until this point in my life I had done almost no effective training of my mind, and that this mind of mine had ideas of its own.

But I persevered. Every day for half an hour I sat and attempted to still my mind. There was one minor breakthrough: almost a year after beginning this practice I had an experience of a bright light turning on in my head. This light was clearly not of the physical world, it was brief and it was interesting. And the phenomenon was accompanied by a deep sense of well-being. However, as soon as this light appeared I tried to analyze it. What was it? Where had it come from? What did it mean? Was this what meditation was all about? And almost immediately the light disappeared.

Shortly after this experience the cancer returned. Time to meet with my first real meditation teacher.

My first teacher

Dr. Ainslie Meares was a psychiatrist and world authority on hypnotherapy from Melbourne, Australia. A deep interest in pain management led him to travel the world visiting cultures that managed pain through the use of the mind. It was during one such visit, to Kathmandu in Nepal, that he was introduced to meditation.

Shiva Puri Baba was an ancient and revered Hindu saint. Many years before Dr. Meares met this widely respected holy man, Shiva Puri Baba had become a close friend, confidant and teacher of Queen Victoria in England. Then in the early 1960s, this venerable sage gave Dr. Meares a perspective on pain that literally changed his personal and professional life. Responding to questions about how he managed pain, Shiva Puri Baba quite simply stated, "I experience pain, but it does not hurt." Pain without hurt! How could this be? And could it be taught as a genuine and practical way of alleviating pain? Again, when asked, the sage had a simple answer: "To experience the truth of this, you must learn to meditate."

Soon after, Dr. Meares made the arduous trip back to Melbourne to begin experimenting, with himself as guinea pig. Before long Dr. Meares was able to have major dental surgery performed on himself involving scalpels, chisels and hammers but no anesthetic and no pain. He was convinced that he was on to something of major medical significance.

Quickly moving on past the realm of pain management, Dr. Meares realized that to meditate was to enter into a state of deep physiological rest. He developed a reliable way to relax physically, to calm the mind and to flow on into a consciously aware state beyond thoughts. Deeply relaxed. Deeply at peace. Essentially still. Motionless in body and mind. A specific form of meditation based on stillness. What Dr. Meares reasoned was that in this deeply relaxed, calm stillness, the body regressed to a state of profound inner balance that established and maintained good physical health. But he realized that there was more on offer than just the obvious physical benefits. The type of meditation that he developed flowed on to provide balance in emotion, mind and even spirit.

Dr. Meares's first book on meditation, *Relief Without Drugs*, was groundbreaking. Published in 1967, it circulated around the world to popular acclaim. But his colleagues were nonplussed. Often misunderstood in those early pioneering days, sometimes even derided, Dr. Meares decided to deregister himself as a medical practitioner so that he could convert his psychiatric practice to a meditation-based practice and escape any ire or ramifications from the Medical Board.

How times have changed. Currently there are more than four thousand research papers published in peer-reviewed medical journals from all around the world attesting to the physical and psychological benefits of meditation. The rate of publication for new research findings on meditation is rising rapidly as interest widens among the medical profession and the general public. Dr. Meares would be delighted to know that recent surveys show meditation has one of the highest approval ratings from doctors for the so-called complementary therapies.

Dr. Meares was a genuine pioneer in the therapeutic application of meditation. He was probably the first major medical identity to work seriously and consistently with meditation. In all, he published thirty-two books, many on the theme of meditation, and twenty-three articles in major medical journals specifically examining the links between the mind, meditation and cancer.

Meditation and cancer

In 1975, just before my cancer secondaries appeared, Dr. Meares bravely announced to the medical world that he believed intensive meditation may in fact reverse cancer. "Bravely" is correct. At that time, many in the medical world condemned him for what they believed to be an outrageous claim.

For me, Dr. Meares came as a lifeline. I had osteogenic sarcoma—bone cancer—widely spread throughout my body. Back in the 1970s, all the medical texts said that this aggressive cancer was fast-moving and uniformly fatal once it had reached the stage I was in. Medically I could be expected to live for three to six months, and modern medicine at that time had nothing but pain relief to offer me.

On first meeting Dr. Meares, I was struck by his hypnotic presence. He spoke slowly and quietly. In a measured tone he explained how, based upon his experience as a psychiatrist, he felt that the chronic stress that cancer patients tend to bottle up inside of them leads to significant physiological changes in the body. He postulated that this alters the levels of an array of hormones circulating in the body, especially cortisol. This in turn affects the body's immune system and its capacity to resist or eliminate small cancers when they form, thus allowing them to develop into clinical disease. "When we meditate," he told me, "our body relaxes, and the mind goes with it. As we become calmer, the calm flows into our daily life. More calm. Less stress. Cortisol levels go down. Our body defenses go up. Our body is what does the healing."

It made perfect sense to me. Intense meditation. Perhaps the chance to heal. Certainly the chance to explore my interest in meditation itself. By "intense," Dr. Meares meant three hours of meditation a day. So over the next six weeks I met with him regularly to learn and practice his style of meditation. I really enjoyed the sessions and felt the benefits of them. I made time to do five hours a day. I had no time to lose.

For a while things went well. I was also following a strict dietary regime and exploring all the other complementary and alternative therapies of the day. Three months later, the cancer had not grown at all. This in itself seemed like a minor miracle. Then pain became an increasingly major and debilitating issue. I did not have the skills at the time or the capacity to manage it. I left my contact with Dr. Meares and went off around the world seeking answers.

The tale of the adventures that followed is well told in Guy Allenby's biography of my life, *Ian Gawler: The Dragon's Blessing*. I managed to stay alive long enough to experiment with most cancer treatments, medical, non-medical and fringe. What helped me the most, in my view, was what can best be described as the lifestyle activities that I developed and maintained—food, exercise, healthy emotions and meditation, along with the support of my first wife.

Apart from Dr. Meares, the two most notable people from that time who helped me to develop meditation were Mr. Terte and Sai Baba. Mr. Terte was a shamanistic healer whom I met in the Philippines and received a great deal of benefit from. Regarding meditation, he gave me a passage from the Bible, instructed me to learn it and then to repeat it over and over like a mantra while contemplating its meaning. I did this faithfully for about eighteen months, maybe two years, on a daily basis, and was amazed at the depth of wisdom revealed to me through this practice of contemplation.

Then I met Sai Baba, the holy man and Avatar of India. An avatar is, by definition, a living embodiment of the Divine. When I heard that there may be a Divine incarnation living in my time on this planet, I certainly did not want to miss the opportunity of a meeting. And I believed that surely such a person would be a profound healer. The lure was irresistible. Now one could say, as Christians do, that man is made in God's image, and therefore, each one of us has an element of the Divine within us. Sai Baba agrees with this proposition. "The only difference between you and me," I heard him say, "is that while we are both Divine, I know that I am and you do not!"

There was no doubting Sai Baba's presence. You could tangibly feel him from many, many feet away. However, despite the buildup and my expectations of a full-on mystical experience, the reality of that first and fateful meeting with him was that it was all rather matter-of-fact. "You are already healed, don't worry," was the synthesis of what he had to say to me. The meeting itself and its impact had a huge significance in the context and course of my illness, yet the message was simple and down to earth. Stop worrying; accept that you are doing what is needed to heal. Persevere and get well.

And I did. Eighteen months later I was found to be cancer-free. The first of my four children was born at the same time. I was back working as a veterinarian. Dr. Meares recorded my case in the *Medical Journal of Australia* in 1978. The media got ahold of my story and soon people were contacting me from all over, seeking help with illness.

In 1981, after three years of answering countless letters and telephone inquiries, and even having people turn up at my veterinary practice seeking cancer advice, I decided to really test the proposition that what had helped me might also help others. Very soon I was teaching Dr. Meares's theories on meditation to large groups of people affected by cancer—patients, their families and friends, and even a growing number of health professionals. I was leading people experientially in meditation sessions using Dr. Meares's stillness-based style. All of this among an innovative and comprehensive lifestyle-based self-help cancer-support-group setting.

These groups turned out to be the first of their kind in Australia, and among some of the very first in the world. The demand for them steadily grew and a not-for-profit organization developed to support the work. Currently the Gawler Foundation employs around fifty staff and conducts residential and non-residential programs for people affected by cancer or multiple sclerosis, as well as wellness programs and numerous meditation retreats.

Seeking new methods
Once the meditation teaching began in 1981, however, it soon became apparent that while the Meares technique worked exceptionally well for many people, a significant number found it unhelpful and unsatisfying.

There are two styles of teaching meditation. One is where you teach a method and expect the students to adapt to that method, a sort of one-size-fits-all approach. The other possibility is that you teach an individual with the expectation that the method will be adapted to that particular person. I have always preferred the latter approach.

So, back in those early days, I reasoned that there must be more ways to learn, and hence to teach, meditation. So through the 1980s I had this wonderful project. Seek out as many and varied a range of teachers of meditation as possible. Ask them questions, read their books, study their methods. Sit with them. Practice meditation with them. Find out what else is useful and how it may be possible to help more people.

As well as reading widely, I also had the good fortune to meet many masters in meditation. I met the wonderful Christian mystic Father Bede Griffiths. I sat in Zen sessions with the Japanese master Hogan-San and the extraordinary Jesuit Zen master (yes, that is correct, a Jesuit and Zen master in the one person!) Father Ama Samy. I went to teachings with His Holiness the Dalai Lama, and studied with the mystics Paul Solomon and the Reverend Mario Schoenmaker. I met with many others who taught and practiced meditation, always asking them: What do you do? Who did you learn from? What did you learn? How do you teach?

Then I got really lucky. In 1984 I met the great Tibetan lama Sogyal Rinpoche. "Rinpoche" is an honorific title, a bit like "cardinal" in the Catholic Church. It translates as "precious one," and this is how the holder of such a title is often referred to. Rinpoche was born in eastern Tibet and raised like a son by one of the greatest Buddhist masters of that time. With the Chinese invasion, he escaped to India and, as a refugee, attended a Catholic school, learning firsthand about the Christian tradition. From there, Rinpoche traveled on to England, studied comparative religion at Cambridge University, and became deeply acquainted with the emerging field of hospice care for people who were dying.

I was attracted to attend Rinpoche's first talk in Melbourne because he was speaking on the subject of understanding death and helping the dying. Many of the people who came to me for help at the time were facing death, and I knew that the Tibetans really value the moment of death as a great opportunity for two immediate reasons. First, while believing in reincarnation, Tibetans are of the view that the state of your mind at the moment of death has a major impact on what sort of life you will be reborn into. But more important, they believe that at the moment of death your consciousness leaves your body and there is a gap before it gets caught up in whatever comes next. And in this gap, at the moment of death, when the spirit is free of the body and not yet attracted to anything else, is actually one of the very best chances that we have to become fully enlightened. So I was interested to hear what this highly respected young lama might have to say on the subject. I felt it likely I could learn something for myself and, more importantly, something that might be of practical use to those people I was helping who might go on to die of their illness.

In that first meeting with Sogyal Rinpoche there was what I can only describe as an instant recognition of him as a genuine and major spiritual leader. Nobody needed to tell me. There was no need for a formal introduction, a history or an explanation. Just an instant recognition that here in this young Tibetan was authenticity personified. He was part of an authentic lineage—a line of teachers who had used the spoken word to pass teachings down from master to student in a continuous, unbroken line from the Buddha himself. Rinpoche spoke with gentle authority and crystal clarity of these authentic teachings. Ancient teachings that he eloquently brought to life in current times through his intimate knowledge of the Western mind and its modern context. And he was funny. Really funny. He had a great sense of humor.

As I listened, I was deeply awed. Awed first by what he had to say, but then awed by another remarkable phenomenon. I felt like I was remembering. Remembering something that had lain dormant inside me for a long time. Something I knew from long ago and had somehow forgotten, put aside or passed over. Now it was like a reawakening of memory. Rinpoche spoke with such clarity on how to use your mind, how to train the mind, how to meditate. His understanding of how the mind works, his capacity to explain all of this and the logic and the precision of detail around techniques was staggering. And yet I felt this almost weird familiarity with it all.

Now, I had grown up a good Christian boy. During my illness, it had been Christ and Christianity from which I had drawn inspiration, strength and direction. Sure I had overlain this with my understanding of Eastern concepts like karma and reincarnation, but I felt that these principles were existent in the early days of the Christian church and it all made sense within the context of my own understanding of mystical Christianity.

In Sogyal Rinpoche I had met someone who had the capacity to be my personal spiritual teacher. But this posed a real dilemma. I came from a Christian background, not a Tibetan Buddhist one. Through my healing experiences I also had a profound connection to Sai Baba. I still highly valued my relationship with Father Bede, Hogan-San and others. But here in Rinpoche was the undeniable possibility of a real teacher. Someone I could learn from directly, talk to, interact with. Someone to really commit to, someone to accept as a personal guide on the spiritual path.

Almost immediately the voices started clamoring in my head: "Beware of false idols," "Thou shall have no other gods but me," "What of the loyalty you have to both the traditions and the people that have been so helpful and meaningful in your life so far?" . . . and on and on.

His Holiness the Dalai Lama recommends strongly against people changing their religion. Conversion in any tradition is a serious and fraught proposition. His Holiness recommends doing all we can do to find what we are seeking within the tradition we have grown up in. While he recognizes the value of Buddhism as a mind science and while he is keen to share with people from all traditions the philosophy that is within Buddhism, he does not encourage individuals to change their religion or to convert to Buddhism.

Still, I went to retreats to learn what I could from Rinpoche during his early days in the West when not many others attended. I helped to organize some of those retreats in the 1980s, and I had the blessing of getting to know him somewhat while receiving the most profound and direct teachings on meditation and the spiritual path.

Rinpoche is a Dzogchen master. *Dzogchen* translates as "the great perfection" and is regarded as the highest form of Tibetan Buddhist meditation practice. A feature of this tradition is that it is the teacher's function to provide a direct introduction to the essence of meditation by his presence and through the use of a specific method.

For me there were two remarkable things about that time. First, it was amazing that Rinpoche gave such profound teachings, the highest teachings, so openly and so freely to those of us who were in fact such real beginners. But more extraordinary, he came annually to lead retreats in my home state of Victoria, and when he returned, I would be one of the few who turned up from the previous year. What were the others thinking? Or doing? Did they miss it? Did they not realize what was on offer? I was amazed.

Yet I too was still dabbling around the edges. Trying to work out if I did want to commit as a student, trying to work out what my connection to Rinpoche really meant. Realizing that devotion to the teacher was a major element on this spiritual path, and struggling to clarify in my own mind what devotion meant. What was the relationship between a spiritual teacher and a student? What was I committing to? My sense is that Rinpoche appreciated my reserve, my caution. He told me once that people who jump in quickly full of fire and passion often go cold and move on to whatever comes next. He said that there is nothing wrong with taking your time, being deliberate and making a considered commitment.

All this began in the 1980s and continued into the 1990s. I was receiving so much from Sogyal Rinpoche's teachings that was helpful to me personally, as a teacher of meditation, and in the work I was doing generally. The steady but slow progression toward deeply accepting Rinpoche as "my teacher" was built upon my Christian foundation. It did not supplant that foundation, it added to it.

Now, as it happens, the Tibetans do not actually call themselves Buddhists. They call themselves *nangpas*. *Nangpa* is a Tibetan word that translates as "one who seeks the truth within." So this is me as I am now, a truth seeker who is profoundly grateful to have a strong connection to one of the world's great living spiritual teachers, the Tibetan master Sogyal Rinpoche.

But I need to acknowledge my other great teacher—or should I say teachers, those from whom I have learned so much through attempting to teach. Over the years I have been fortunate to receive so much feedback on what works in practice and what does not. Just writing my previous books on meditation provided a huge learning in itself. The first, *Peace of Mind*, began with the intention of providing a short workbook for people attending my meditation classes. It soon burgeoned into a full text covering the broad scope and key practices of meditation. *Meditation: Pure and Simple* went deeper into techniques for physical relaxation and what turned out to be a really useful process that I developed for moving into the stillness beyond everyday thoughts. Then *The Creative Power of Imagery* delved into the more active meditation teachings that utilize the power of the mind.

Also there has been the opportunity to work with great colleagues, including this collaboration with Paul Bedson. As you will now read, Paul has his own story to tell of the spiritual path and his journey into meditation. Paul is one of those remarkable and, I would suggest, amazingly intelligent people who, instead of following all the potential lures and distractions of modern life, sought as a young man to tread the tortuous path in search of the truth. His search is all the more commendable as it was not propelled, as mine was, by the urgency of serious illness. Paul went off in search of his own truth.

PAUL'S STORY

> *The privilege of a lifetime is being who you are.*
> —JOSEPH CAMPBELL

I am telling the story of my meditation journey for several reasons. Primarily to explain how my understanding and experience of meditation has developed from a wide variety of teachings and traditions, and also to acknowledge the wonderful teachers I have met along the way. Third, there is the need to recognize the mysterious role of serendipity and grace in such a journey.

I was inspired to learn that a lateral thinker like Sigmund Freud once exclaimed, "Everywhere I go, I find that a poet has been there before me!" Poetry and metaphor can lead us into places that the thinking mind struggles to access and enter. So let me begin this account of my meditation journey by using a somewhat poetic voice.

Looking back, I now see the path that has unfolded on this meditation journey, the path that has brought me to this place, here today. My journey was navigated by the compass of grace, the guidance of many valued teachers and the good fortune to have listened to the "still, small voice" inside my heart—the voice of Spirit. This meditation journey has revealed an intimate love affair with the life within me, outside of me and beyond, into the silent, nameless realms of awe and mystery. Like whispers echoing from a silent core.

Meditation has given me a deep reverence for the Divine, as it reveals itself in this ordinary life that we share. It has been a humbling process: learning to let go, learning when to trust and when to wait and see. Learning what I do not know, what I cannot know and what I do not need to know. Basically, learning how to "mind my own business."

And it has been an empowering process: learning that I have direct access to the source of creativity and goodness that sustains all life. I have learned that we are all One, that we are all connected, and therefore, my choices, my words and my deeds, my *being*, has an impact on all beings. This life does matter; I am important and special.

My childhood was a mixture of loneliness, academic achievement, sporting success and some spiritual experiences. I was a sensitive soul born into a footballer's body.

My first meditation experience was at the age of eighteen. Carmel, the mother of my best friend at high school, was a yoga teacher. I expressed interest and Carmel invited me along. Her yoga class was conducted in an old run-down wooden building in Sydney's Chinatown. When I entered the room, I was greeted by a circle of about eight middle-aged women. Each woman was holding a small teapot; the spout was inserted into one nostril, and in their other hand was a small bowl. The women were pouring water into one nostril and it was coming out of the other and filling the bowl. I felt very uncomfortable, as if I had walked in on some secret women's business! I wanted to turn and run back down the stairs, but Carmel enthusiastically welcomed me and explained that they were practicing a nasal cleansing technique called *jala neti*. I stayed for the class, enjoyed the stretching postures, and was particularly captivated by the Yoga Nidra that occurred toward the end of the class. We all lay down on the floor and thoroughly relaxed the whole body, then Carmel suggested images for us to visualize: a full moon, a red rose, a baby's face, a starlit sky, waves lapping on a beach. I could see the images vividly, and accompanying the images was a deep feeling of wonder, awe and peace within me. This was my first experience of the power and potential of the mind—and I was hooked.

After Carmel, my next meditation teacher was a flute-playing hippie who could see devas (or nature spirits) and painted them in watercolor. His name was Bodo. I was nineteen years old and Bodo was thirty. He had spent many years studying theosophy, in particular the esoteric writings of Alice A. Bailey. Our meditation group consisted only of myself, my girlfriend Kate and Bodo. In a candlelit basement in the inner-city Sydney suburb of Glebe he taught us to chant Aum, to recite an inspirational prayer called "The Great Invocation" and to meditate by softly gazing into a candle flame. He also taught us about chakras, auras and astral traveling. My mind was filled with hopes and imaginings of psychic experiences, Kundalini arising and channeled wisdom.

These early experiences on the meditation journey left me with expectations that something profound should happen while meditating and that this would fill me with bliss and insight. If only I could meditate in the right way, then "it" would happen and I would be awakened to another, more spiritual reality. Bodo's free spirit, his colorful personality, his creativity, spontaneity and his esoteric teachings inspired me; however, I never did reach Bodo's level of "psychic powers." My unfulfilled hopes and dreams propelled me into the next step on the journey.

At the age of twenty-one, I stumbled into a group of earnest spiritual seekers who were studying the challenging and confronting teachings of G. I. Gurdjieff, a Greek-Armenian mystic who taught throughout

Europe and America in the early twentieth century. We practiced "The Work," which referred to working on oneself according to Gurdjieff's principles and instructions. The Work involved a series of self-awareness exercises that Gurdjieff called "self-remembering." We practiced being mindful, for example trying to be aware each time we walked through a doorway that we were actually walking through a doorway. The intention was to wake up from what Gurdjieff called a robotic and mindless way of being. These exercises gave me my first experiences of mindfulness, being in the present moment and letting go of the importance of thinking—waking up from daydreaming.

Paradoxically, Gurdjieff's philosophical writings were so obtuse and bewildering that they generated in me a desire to understand intellectually the nature of All and Everything. I was also studying existentialist philosophy at university at the time and my mind was spinning with the exhilarating and exhausting desire to understand the Truth. Fortunately, as well as studying Gurdjieff's writings, we also learned sacred dances and practiced Sufi breathing and chanting exercises called *zhikr*. I experienced the sacred dances and music as both poignant and inspiring; they gave me an embodied sense of spirituality that was a real blessing. The zhikr exercises gave me an early appreciation of the importance of breath, movement and sound in taming the philosophy student's mind and touching his heart and his spirit.

The gifts imparted through this stage in the journey were the experiences of present moment awareness, or mindfulness as it is commonly known, a respect for the power of conscious breathing, and an intuitive sense that physical embodiment and spirituality are intimately connected and not at all separate. Body, breath, emotions, mind and spirit are all steps in one sacred dance.

Yet the role of meditation, and particularly sitting meditation, was still unclear and confusing for me. I knew of its importance but my thinking mind was still very dominant and my expectations of meditative "experiences" were still very strong. In retrospect, I can see that I was trying way too hard; my idea was that spiritual attainment required hard work. I was also hoping for too much, too soon. My journey was to be (and still is) composed of baby steps—beautiful small steps that I can relish and have the time to integrate into my everyday life in a way that can be described as extraordinary ordinariness. I had not yet learned to be patient, to be present and to let go of expectations.

The search for a teacher

As a student of Gurdjieff's teachings, I read many accounts of his confrontational style in dealing with his students. He would embarrass, humiliate and belittle his students at times to make them aware of their ego attachments and to shock them out of unconscious habits. At other times he was full of benevolence and deep wisdom. I began to realize that I needed to find a living master who could challenge me when necessary, and inspire and encourage me when needed. So, like many of my generation, I went "in search of Secret India" to find a spiritual teacher to guide me on my meditation journey.

Two encounters propelled me with big strides between the many other small steps along the way. The first was at a Tibetan monastery, Kopan, in Nepal, where in 1978 I participated in a retreat and an initiation with Lama Thubten Yeshe and Lama Zopa Rinpoche. Although the Mahayana Buddhist style of meditation, using chanting and visualization, did not really appeal to me, the lamas were inspirational. They were embodiments of the two wings of Buddhism—that is, wisdom and compassion—with a third wing, humor, thrown in for good measure. In their good-natured, warm-hearted presence I could feel a nonverbal transmission of goodness that has stayed with me ever since.

My second encounter, in western India, was to be life-changing, and it provided a new depth to my experience of meditation. In an ashram in Pune, I met Bhagwan Shree Rajneesh (later known as Osho) and became a disciple of this amazing guru. This was the direct contact with a living master for which I had been searching. Bhagwan Rajneesh had created meditations to suit the hyperactive Western body and mind—dynamic meditations that move the physical body and release suppressed emotion before sitting in stillness meditation. Cathartic breathing, shaking, dancing, yelling and jumping released stress and naturally led to a more relaxed body, a calmer mind and a more open heart. Bhagwan encouraged us, "When you don't have a mind, you have a heart. When you don't have a mind, only then your heart starts pulsating, and then you have love. No mind means love. Love is my message."

These dynamic meditations were extremely liberating for this former philosophy student and "serious" seeker on the spiritual path. They actually broke down my need to philosophically understand each step along the way, and they humbled my thinking mind and brought me back to direct experience and raw emotion. They taught me to trust feelings and to integrate emotion into the meditation journey. In Pune, I laughed, cried and released a whole lot of unconscious limiting beliefs and pent-up emotional baggage from my past. I began to love myself and sense the goodness in myself and in life.

Bhagwan's guidance and the ashram environment gave me the spiritual inspiration and psychological safety to shed many layers of old, dead skin and to emerge with a less-defended heart. The challenge would be to bring this openness out of the ashram and into the "real" world. The dynamic meditations worked extremely well in a group context with the support of the *sangha* (the spiritual community), but I found them difficult to continue back home, by myself, in the West. For my time with Bhagwan I will always be most grateful and I will hold him with the deepest respect as my guru. The encounter with this living master prepared me for the next steps.

Coming home

By the time I returned to Australia, aged thirty-three, I had experienced many spiritual teachers and spiritual practices. Now I was looking for a regular daily practice to help me deal with the "real" world, to nourish my spirit and to keep my heart open and my feet firmly planted on the path. I needed a regular practice that was direct and simple—not too philosophical or esoteric—and that embraced and integrated body, mind, emotions and spirit (the steps in my journey so far).

At a vipassana meditation retreat in the Blue Mountains I was taught mindfulness meditation, and it was like being thrown a lifeline.

Practicing mindfulness meditation was like a homecoming; my meditation journey finally brought me back to my own being, my own direct experience and to the true Self. In the words of T. S. Eliot:

We shall not cease from exploration,
And the end of all our exploring
Will be to arrive where we started
And to know the place for the first time.[1]

Mindfulness meditation is defined by Jon Kabat-Zinn as: "Paying attention in a particular way: on purpose, in the present moment and non-judgmentally."[2] I found in mindfulness meditation a simple yet profound practice of patience, presence and compassion. Through this simple practice I began to experience that simply being, with less and less doing, released the spiritual sweetness and nourishment that I had been searching for. Peak experiences, psychic insights, energy surges were all interesting and played their part along the way, but mindfulness practice was grounded, steady and reliable. What is more, I could feel its direct impact on my day-to-day life. At last, I learned to "just sit" with an attitude that in Zen practice is called "beginner's mind"—free of expectations, dreams, hopes and judgments. (This will be explored further in chapter 1.)

I began teaching meditation in 1990, and as a teacher, I learned more about meditation practice. I learned how to communicate the essentials of meditation theory and practice: the right attitude to bring to meditation, the difference between thinking and awareness, between doing meditation and allowing it to unfold, and trying too hard and not trying hard enough. Through teaching meditation, I learned so much about the nature of thinking and the ways in which thinking dominates our attention, and about the stress response. I began to understand how meditation could be used for physical, emotional and spiritual healing. Then, in my next step as a therapist and meditation teacher, I came to the Gawler Foundation in the Yarra Valley, Victoria, and began to teach meditation with Ian Gawler.

Ian's experiences of meditation with Ainslie Meares largely shaped his method of teaching, one that gives emphasis to the direct experience of the meditation. Ian would guide the meditation students through a process of deep physical relaxation, and then simply encourage them to "let go . . . more and more . . . deeper and deeper." The instructions were delivered in a slow, calm, hypnotic tone of voice that invariably induced a calmness of mind. This approach to meditation was simple and direct and, for those who could flow with it, there was the possibility of experiencing a profound stillness.

However, some were unable to "get it" because, by its very nature, this approach lacked structure; it was too simple! Others found it effective when guided by the instructor or when listening to a CD, but found it difficult to access the stillness on their own. I was often reminded of a beautiful teaching metaphor used by Bhagwan Shree Rajneesh, who said: "Meditation requires a delicate balance. It is like drilling a hole in a pearl to string it on a necklace. Too much pressure on the drill and the pearl will shatter, not enough pressure and the drill will not penetrate into the pearl." With a structured approach to meditation, the practitioner will often try too hard, be too focused and expect too much, and the pearl shatters. With an unstructured approach the practitioner can drift into sleep, daydreaming or flights of imagination, and the drill doesn't penetrate.

From working together, Ian and I began to learn from each other. We shared our meditation experiences and journeys and, by a process of synthesis, Mindfulness-Based Stillness Meditation emerged.

Our heartfelt wish is that these collective experiences of meditation will clearly guide you to peace, healing and your own homecoming to realize the truth of who you really are, to realize your true nature.

PART 1

MINDFULNESS–BASED STILLNESS MEDITATION

CHAPTER 1

INTRODUCING MINDFULNESS-BASED STILLNESS MEDITATION

The past no longer is.
The future has not yet come.
Looking deeply at life as it is
in the very here and now,
the practitioner dwells in stability and freedom.
—THE BUDDHA

It is often useful in starting a journey to have a map of the route and some prior knowledge of the terrain. In a Zen story, the Sixth Patriarch, Huineng, was famously reported as saying:

Truth has nothing to do with words. Truth can be likened to the bright moon in the sky. Words, in this case, can be likened to a finger. The finger can point to the moon's location. However, the finger is not the moon. To look at the moon is to gaze beyond the finger, right?

We hope to guide and inspire you, but these words and techniques, however concise and accurate, can only ever be "fingers pointed to the moon." It is your patience, perseverance and practice that will reveal the moon. After all, what you are looking for, the essence of meditation, is within you all the time; it is only eclipsed, hidden by the shadow of excessive thinking. So having acknowledged the limitations of words and conceptual thinking, let us use them to our best advantage. We will start with some distinctions and definitions of the terrain of meditation.

DIRECT AND GRADUAL APPROACHES TO MEDITATION

Broadly speaking, there are two basic approaches that we can use for meditation: the direct approach and the gradual approach.

The direct approach

The essence of meditation is characterized by deep relaxation accompanied by an open awareness. In this state both our body and our mind are relaxed; there is a sense of natural ease and an innate stillness. As a consequence, there is nothing we need to do. The direct approach to meditation, therefore, is less about doing something in particular and more about simply being. All we need "to do" is to let go and be still. This is what we mean by using no method. In this approach, a technique is considered to be a hindrance that only keeps the mind busy and focused. The Zen teachers say that no effort is needed; it is effortless. Just sit. The famous teacher Krishnamurti said, "No device is needed, no method is needed." Ian's first teacher, Ainslie Meares, was a great advocate of this direct, no-method approach.

Here are some guidelines for using the principle of the direct approach to just sit in meditation. As an experiment, read the guidelines for "just sitting" and practice them for five to ten minutes.

THE DIRECT APPROACH: "JUST SITTING"

Prepare the environment so you will not be disturbed for the period of time you are giving to "just sitting."

Sit with your back straight and body relaxed. Meditation is about being relaxed and at the same time being alert; so make yourself comfortable, but not too comfortable.

Gently close your eyes. You might like to take a deeper breath or two to help you to settle into your posture.

Give yourself mental permission: there is nowhere else that you need to be right now and nothing else you need to do. Now is the time to simply be . . . to be yourself.

Allow yourself to open to this moment . . . its sounds, its smells, feelings, thoughts. . . . Allow whatever comes into this moment to just be. . . . No struggle, no effort. . . . Nothing has to change or be achieved. . . . Nothing need be resisted.

Just sit and be free to be yourself.

Give yourself complete space and freedom to just sit. . . . Just this . . . just sitting.

Let these moments simply unfold. . . . Enjoy the space. . . . Be simple. . . . Be free.

So, how was "just sitting" for you? Easy? Peaceful? Busy?

With this direct approach, some people report intermittent moments of peace from an otherwise very busy mind. Some report just the very busy mind. For others the direct approach seems to take them directly into stillness. Some people do just sit in a disarmingly simple way and meditate. For them, the direct approach is all they need. No real method. Just relaxing into this very moment.

There is no doubt that this approach is helped by being in the company of a charismatic and accomplished teacher who has their own genuine experience of meditation and can convey something of this experience through their presence.

However, for many people the direct approach is confusing, frustrating, unreliable or simply unworkable. The no-method approach can leave people in states of sleepiness, dreaminess or imagination. These states may feel relaxed but they are not meditation.

What many people need is the benefit of a more structured, more gradual approach. Many of us need a method; we need to learn a technique. Then practice it. Then learn some more. Practice some more, and so on. On and on until, like learning to drive a car, we can eventually just do it. We go through that normal beginner's phase where we learn all the different elements. We practice until the gears begin to flow smoothly, and we arrive at the place of natural simplicity. And then we just do it.

The gradual approach

This approach provides a path with clearly defined steps and guidance on how to proceed. Due to the way our minds work and the deeply ingrained habits of thinking, most people do benefit from this more structured, gradual approach—at least to begin with.

But while meditation techniques can be extremely useful and reliable, it should be remembered that they, too, are "fingers pointed to the moon." No technique makes meditation happen; in fact it may be helpful to regard a meditation technique as being like a series of stepping-stones designed to take us from one state of mind to another. The essence of meditation begins when the techniques stop. So while techniques are very useful in their own right, they are most useful when we go that extra step beyond them. The "doing" of the technique is only a framework for the "being" of meditation. Every method is just a device, a means. It is creating the right environment in which the essence of meditation happens by itself.

Meditation is sometimes referred to as "creating a space for grace." We cannot do it or force it; we can only create the space in which it appears. This is why most meditation techniques are actually methods for doing less, expecting less, judging less and being more spacious and open. The doing facilitates an undoing and a letting go. Osho said of meditation methods:

> Meditation, and all meditation devices, can do one thing: push you away from your negative hindrances. It can bring you out of

the imprisonment that is the thinking mind, and when you have come out, you will laugh. It was so easy to come out, it was right there. Only one step was needed. But we go on in a circle and the one step is missed . . . the one step that can bring you to the center. You go on in a circle on the periphery, repeating the same thing; somewhere the continuity must be broken. That is all that can be done by any meditation method.[1]

As we will explore, a structured, gradual approach to meditation can be useful and reliable in breaking "the imprisonment that is the thinking mind."

THREE STYLES OF MEDITATION

There have been many, many techniques and applications of meditation. Different meditative disciplines encompass a wide range of physical, psychological, mental and spiritual practices that may emphasize different goals—from the achievement of expanded states of consciousness, to greater focus, creativity and healing, or simply a more relaxed and peaceful frame of mind.

Generally speaking, meditation is a process of mind training, and the various techniques of meditation can be best classified according to their focus and methodology. In this book we have classified meditation into three main streams or styles: meditation utilizing attention, meditation utilizing intention and meditation utilizing inquiry.

1. Meditation utilizing attention

Generally called mindfulness meditation, this is an alert yet passive style of meditation that involves the self-regulation of attention toward one's moment-to-moment experience. We simply pay attention to our breath, our body, our emotions and our thoughts. Mindfulness is passive in that it does not cultivate conscious thinking. This is the method we will explore in Part I of this book.

2. Meditation utilizing intention

Intentional meditation is directed toward a particular outcome for the meditator and/or others, and this type of meditation includes practices called imagery, invocation or prayer. The outcome may be healing, well-being, peace or release from suffering. Intentional meditation is more active than mindfulness in that it carries a wish, a hope or a goal, and uses conscious, creative thinking in the form of images, words and emotions like gratitude, compassion, enthusiasm and empathy to achieve the desired outcome.

Meditation utilizing intention (imagery) will be explained in Part II of this book.

3. Meditation utilizing inquiry

Generally called contemplative or analytical meditation, an inquiry is an investigation of a particular issue using questioning and listening. The meditator consciously asks a question, thinks about it deliberately and then listens for a response from their own inner wisdom. The questioning may be as simple as "What do I need to do in this situation?" or as profound as "Who am I?" This form of meditation has both active and passive aspects; the questioning is active whereas the listening is more passive. The questioning is in the form of words, ideas and concepts; the answer or the insight arises from the analysis and the listening.

Meditation utilizing inquiry (contemplation) will be explained in Part II of this book.

AN OVERVIEW OF MINDFULNESS-BASED STILLNESS MEDITATION

From our collective experience as students, practitioners and teachers we have formulated a gradual approach to meditation utilizing attention. We have called this meditation path Mindfulness-Based Stillness Meditation (MBSM). We wholeheartedly recommend that MBSM becomes your main meditation practice. In itself, MBSM is a complete practice with many benefits. It is also a very beneficial foundation for practicing the other styles of meditation using intention and inquiry.

As mentioned in the Introduction, MBSM has four steps: preparation, relaxation, mindfulness and stillness. We will examine each of these in turn.

Step 1: Preparation

Preparation involves establishing comfort and ease. We create a conducive external and internal environment for meditation by preparing the location, our posture and our attitude (see chapter 2).

Step 2: Relaxation

A tight or tense body often accompanies a busy and restless mind. We use relaxation techniques to create more spaciousness in the body, which helps in calming the mind and bringing our attention into the present moment (see chapters 3 and 4).

Step 3: Mindfulness

Mindfulness is paying attention to what is happening around and inside of us each moment, without judging or attempting to change anything. We notice whatever sounds come to our attention. We notice the sensations in the body, the feeling of the breath moving in and out. We notice any emotions and thoughts. We surrender our attention to the present moment.

In later chapters we explain how mindfulness can be practiced by using a narrow focus of attention such as Mindfulness of Breath (chapters 5 and 6). Then a more open and inclusive practice can be developed through Mindfulness of Body (chapters 7 and 8), Mindfulness of Emotions (chapters 9 and 10) and Mindfulness of Thoughts (chapter 11).

Step 4: Stillness

Gradually, by just paying attention without reacting, we become aware of a stillness. Sounds, sensations, even emotions and thoughts just come and go. Free of judgment. Free of reaction. We notice a background of stillness against which sounds, sensations and thoughts come and go, appear and disappear. We become aware of that still and silent presence that is just noticing the movement of sounds, sensations and thoughts. In this stillness, awareness is open and undistracted. Stillness is not a static nothingness; it is an alive, alert and non-reactive presence (see chapters 11 and 12).

Liberation of the utilitarian mind

To function in life, our minds must be able to concentrate. Through schooling, we train our children to focus their minds because without the ability to concentrate they will not be able to cope with life. Concentration enables us to narrow and focus our attention on a specific object or task. Without the ability to concentrate, we would be constantly "spaced out" and unable to perform even the simplest of everyday functions. We could even be overwhelmed by too much information. Walking down the street and crossing the road could be disastrous without the ability to concentrate. Concentration makes it possible to direct our attention toward defining and achieving our goals and is thus a vital function of the utilitarian mind—the goal-oriented, problem-solving aspect of our mind. This narrowing of attention is necessary for survival, but the utilitarian mind is not the whole picture. When we narrow our focus of attention to become particularly conscious of one thing, we simultaneously become unconscious of so many other parts of our present moment experience. With a narrow focus of attention, we use only a small part of the mind's potential.

Concentration, the narrowing of mind, is therefore a means for survival and achieving goals, but not for a relaxed quality of life. Walking along the beach, for example, becomes much more enjoyable when we are open to smelling the sea air, feeling the warmth of the sun, hearing the sounds of the seagulls and feeling the soft sand beneath our feet. A concentrated mind with a narrow focus of attention would miss out on most of the delight. Expansive experiences of open awareness bring welcome relief from the narrow focus of the utilitarian mind. Being stuck in the utilitarian mind can lead to a flat, two-dimensional, excessively logical and functional existence. Even simple expansive experiences like walking along the beach with an open awareness are healing and restorative; they relax the mind and nourish the heart and soul.

Overuse of the utilitarian mind creates a chronic narrowing of awareness that detracts from the joy of life, reduces performance and limits our capacity to release stress and to heal. When we remain in narrow-focused attention, constant thinking plays an exaggerated and dominating role in our mind. We miss out on rich and rewarding experiences that are filled with sensual and emotional textures. The narrow focus of the utilitarian mind, when overused, can also distance us from feelings of compassion and empathy; distance us from others and from nature. We get stuck in our head. This is one reason why so many people in our contemporary world, despite advances in transport and communication, feel isolated and anxious.

Being too goal-oriented and focused goes hand in hand with being busy, driven and worried. We can lose the ability to be more open and more present, and to have freedom and space in our minds and our lives. Our quality of life is vastly improved by developing flexible attention so that we can move freely and responsively from narrow-focused concentration to open-focused awareness. Open-focused awareness does not have to be "spaced out"; it is a state where we are alert, relaxed and mindful. We will discuss this further in chapter 6, "Habits of Thinking and Awareness," when we investigate the stress response and excessive thinking. Mindfulness meditation can lead us from narrow-focused concentration to open awareness and into spaciousness and stillness. Mindfulness can liberate the utilitarian mind.

Thich Nhat Hanh, a Vietnamese Zen monk, poet and author, summarized the essence of mindfulness in these words:

Mindfulness is a part of living. When you are mindful, you are fully present. You can get in touch with the wonders of life that can nourish you and heal you. And you are stronger, you are more solid in order to handle the suffering inside you and around you. When you are mindful you can recognize, embrace and handle the pain, the sorrow in you and around you . . . you'll be able to transform the suffering in you and help transform the suffering around you.[2]

Focused and open mindfulness

Having said all this, it may seem somewhat paradoxical that when we begin to learn and practice mindfulness it is often most effective to narrow our focus of attention on some part of our present moment experience—for example, the breath. First we develop narrow-focus mindfulness, and then we learn a more open mindfulness that is inclusive of all of the components of our present moment experience. Beginning with the narrow focus of attention helps to develop the qualities of mindfulness: presence, acceptance, patience and perseverance. How to do this is described in detail in chapter 5.

From this narrow-focus practice of mindfulness, we then learn how to open our attention to be inclusive of the other aspects of our present moment experience: body sensations, emotional feelings and thoughts. The same qualities of mindfulness—presence, acceptance, patience and perseverance—are brought to our body, emotions and thoughts. We practice being more fully present in the moment, without goals and without judgments. We reclaim the disowned and forgotten (unconscious) parts of ourselves. Mindfulness of body, emotions and thoughts is described in detail in chapters 7–12.

As we continue to practice these techniques we develop an open and undistracted awareness that is not dominated by thoughts and reactions. We reach a subtlety of awareness wherein we increasingly become aware of awareness itself. This state has been called meta-cognition. In this awareness, we experience the stillness, spaciousness and silence that is our own true nature. At this point, words, concepts and ideas become somewhat limited, just "fingers pointed to the moon." Chapters 11 and 12, on stillness, will point you toward the luminous light of your original "face," the essence of who you really are.

Effort and effortlessness, doing and allowing

Mindfulness is not commonly the default position of our attention. The default position is the "normal," thinking mind. The default position of an untrained mind is usually daydreaming, worrying, judging and rehearsing (or anticipating). In Buddhist philosophy this is sometimes referred to as "monkey mind." The monkey mind is constantly busy, jumping from one thing to another; it is the active aspect of mind; the inner chatter of the thinking mind.

MBSM requires that we bring some discipline to this monkey mind, yet too much discipline destroys the lightness and spontaneity of the practice. Too much discipline creates an inner struggle. And too much discipline covers a hidden agenda of expectations, craving and aversion, which will undermine the qualities of presence, patience and acceptance.

MBSM requires a good deal of perseverance yet with a light touch and a kind heart. Paul recalls the wise old Chinese saying "Gently, gently, catch a monkey!" and comments how in his own meditation practice he often reminds himself to lighten up: "I lift the corners of my mouth in a subtle Buddha-like smile and stop taking myself too seriously." Just try it now. Soften your gaze and lift the corners of your mouth; smile subtly and feel the difference. The utilitarian mind relaxes with a subtle smile.

Seriousness in meditation often accompanies expectations of what we hope to achieve, and these expectations will create struggle and self-judgment. The depths of meditation can only be reached with a lightness and openness of mind, not through seriousness. One of Paul's qi gong teachers used to walk among his students, smiling and saying, "Just forget yourself." He encouraged his students to forget the doer, forget the destination, in order to give full attention to the present moment . . . and smile.

The "project" of learning and practicing MBSM is different from any other learning task or challenge. There is what seems at first to be a real paradox involved. The harder you try to still the mind, the more active it becomes. Yet clearly a certain degree of effort and application is required to get started with meditation. Remember Osho's metaphor: Meditation is like drilling a hole in a pearl to string it on a necklace. Too much pressure and the pearl cracks; not enough pressure and the drill will not penetrate the pearl.

Discipline as a personal kindness
Discipline is often required to avoid laziness or busyness and to make time to meditate. To be kind to ourselves, a degree of effort may be

required in preparing the external environment and even in relaxing the body. So this initial stage of mindfulness meditation requires a certain degree of effort and application.

We can think of this initial effort as creating presence or choosing to be present. Since the "normal" mind is preoccupied with thinking and paying little attention to present moment experience, we need to choose to be present. We need to break old attentional habits in order to create new ones. This does require some effort. It is like choosing to play with your children—it may involve some discipline to put aside busyness and to cast off the utilitarian mind. It may require some effort to loosen up and be more spontaneous. But once you get into it, it just starts to flow.

Creating presence

This involves choosing to put our attention on present moment experience. It involves paying attention to, or being mindful of, the breath, the body, the emotions and the thoughts. Chapters 5–14 describe the way to create presence. These chapters describe a series of techniques that are actually more than techniques—they are ways of being. Mindfulness is not just a technique to reach a certain goal; it is a way of being present. Mindfulness is a way of relating to life with more presence, more connection and more gratitude for each moment of this precious life.

One of our meditation students recently asked, "Do you go through the steps of paying attention to breath, body, emotions and thoughts each time you meditate?" The reply was, "Yes, but they are not just steps, they are not just a means to get somewhere else. They are the reality of my present moment experience. And this moment, now, is the only reality there is . . . and has ever been. By paying attention to breath, body, emotions and thoughts, I turn away from fantasy and toward reality. So cherish these steps and surrender to them—don't hold back waiting for something that might happen. This is it!"

Being present

Having chosen to create presence, the next phase of mindfulness is simply *being* present. Being present is when our attention flows more effortlessly with ever-changing, present moment experience. Being present is when we recognize thoughts as just thoughts, without getting so caught up in them. When we learn to do this, thoughts lose much of their power to narrow our focus of attention and to distract us. We simply allow thoughts to come and go; they are neither important nor a problem. Being present is when we become more established in the "compassionate observer" or the "silent presence" that just notices breath, body, emotions and thoughts without judgment. Moving from creating presence to being present is a shift from "doing" meditation, to effortlessly allowing the meditation to unfold.

It may take some practice and patience to understand experientially this distinction between creating presence and being present; it is mentioned here as we are discussing effort and effortlessness in meditation. We will continue this discussion on presence in chapter 11, "Mindfulness of Thoughts and Stillness."

A light touch and a soft heart
Here are some tips for bringing a light touch and a soft heart to the practice of mindfulness, and meditation in general:

- Meditation is profound but should not be too serious. Be passionate but do not push too hard.
- Choose to enjoy each meditation rather than making it a rigid discipline. Choose to see the benefit in each meditation even if it is uncomfortable or you are feeling restless, impatient or bored.
- "Forget yourself!" Relax the doer and the doing. Meditation is about letting go of yourself and just being. It reveals the truth of who we truly are.
- Every step is an end in itself; the journey is the destination.
- Adopt a subtle, Buddha-like smile.
- Meditation is not about having blissful, peak experiences. It is about changing our relationship with our experiences and becoming less reactive, less goal-oriented, more present.
- Meditation is not about moving away from life to some other

reality. Meditation brings us back to our life so we can embrace it more fully and live it more compassionately.

- Keep it simple, follow the steps.
- Remember the Zen poem:

Sitting silently, doing nothing,
Spring comes,
And the grass grows by itself.

COMMITTING YOURSELF TO DOING NOTHING

Making time to sit and meditate, to do what in one sense appears to be doing nothing, is a challenge for many people. How do you justify it to yourself? Is it productive time? Is it wasted time? Is it certain to work and achieve the desired results? What is the minimum amount of time to commit to get the results? The utilitarian mind often struggles to accept and trust such a seemingly simple and effortless endeavor as meditation. The thinking mind likes to struggle; no pain, no gain.

Fortunately there is a vast amount of scientific evidence that confirms the benefits of meditation on the body, the emotions and the mind. Is the rational scientific evidence enough to persuade people to commit to doing nothing? In many cases, no, it is not enough. Even some of the people dealing with cancer who attend our healing and lifestyle programs find it difficult to make time to meditate. They have heard the scientific evidence, read the literature, listened to personal testimonies of long-term survivors who used meditation, yet still they struggle to commit and persevere—even with the strong motivation of dealing with cancer!

As you are no doubt aware if you have tried to practice meditation, there seems to be an in-built resistance to sitting and doing nothing. We can sit and watch TV, sit and read the newspaper, sit and listen to a sports broadcast, no problem, but sit and just be still—not so easy to prioritize, not so easy to commit to. Yet the inescapable fact remains: if you want to get the numerous benefits of meditation, you have to do it. These inspirational words about commitment are particularly relevant to the meditation journey:

Until one is committed, there is hesitancy, the chance to draw back. Concerning all acts of initiative (and creation), there is one elementary truth—the ignorance of which kills countless ideas and splendid plans: that the moment one definitely commits oneself, then Providence moves too. All sorts of things occur to help one that would never otherwise have occurred. A whole stream of events issues from the decision, raising in one's favor all manner of unforeseen incidents and meetings and material assistance, which no man could have dreamed would have come his way. Whatever you can do, or dream you can do, begin it. Boldness has genius, power, and magic in it. Begin it now.[3]

A regular meditation practice requires personal discipline and a strong, healthy commitment to yourself. We recommend that you see this discipline and commitment as a personal kindness, not as a restriction or an imposition. This is a commitment to a goal that is in your own best interests.

Meditation requires a strong commitment to:

- working on yourself
- breaking old unhealthy habits of thinking
- dealing with in-built resistance
- regular practice
- patiently persevering through uncomfortable times

It is not as though commitment and discipline are completely foreign to us: we all practice some forms of self-discipline, for example by getting out of bed, washing ourselves, working, preparing meals, servicing our car or bicycle, meeting with our friends and so on. Meditation can become as important, as regular, as natural, as daily showering. Paul says, "I personally start to feel slightly uncomfortable, as though something is missing, if I do not make time to meditate every day."

To make this commitment to sit and be still, we need a personal vision for ourselves, a vision of kindness and self-respect. Our personal vision can provide a healthy source of motivation to overcome laziness or busyness. Here are some of the personal motivations some people have nominated that help them to sustain their commitment to meditation:

- to enjoy more peace of mind
- to perform better at work or in sports
- to become a more loving person
- to know oneself more deeply
- to be less fearful and defensive
- for health and healing
- to know one's own mind better
- to follow a spiritual reawakening or calling
- to lighten up and drop some seriousness
- to release old resentments
- to become a better person
- to stop struggling with self, others and life

These personal motivations are important and useful to keep in mind. Can you relate to any of the above sources of motivation? What is your vision for yourself and how can meditation enhance it? Like many people, perhaps you need to remind yourself that it is okay, even essential, to make time for yourself. Time to be yourself, time to free yourself.

We will talk more in the chapters on mindfulness about dealing with resistance and obstacles to meditation. But for now, aim to continue on this meditation journey as a personal kindness. "Whatever you can do, or dream you can do, begin it . . . begin it now."

STEP 1

PREPARATION

CHAPTER 2

ESTABLISHING COMFORT AND EASE

*When the conditions are conducive
meditation occurs spontaneously.*
—Ancient Zen saying

How we set up the conditions for our meditation will greatly affect our practice. If, as beginners, we were to attempt to meditate in the center of a busy shopping mall, for instance, we might well find the distractions overwhelming. In this chapter we will clarify what supports meditation most effectively; what is recommended for beginners; and how to develop your practice as you become more experienced. In the long run, meditating in a shopping mall is eminently possible, but to begin with it may make good sense to start somewhere easier!

Let us begin with this mental fantasy. As you read the following, allow the words to create images in your mind and aim to go into the inner experience it leads you to.

A PLACE OF COMFORT AND EASE

Imagine a place where you feel particularly comfortable, particularly peaceful and particularly safe. . . . A place where you are surrounded by the loving presence of those who are closest and dearest to you. . . . Imagine a place where you feel physically at ease, where your body is deeply relaxed and free to rest in a contented stillness, while you feel your breath rising and falling in the natural rhythm of comfort and ease.

Imagine this place where you are so comfortable, so peaceful, so safe, that you are content to leave any thoughts of the past behind you . . . where you let go of any thoughts of the future . . . and simply rest in the awareness of the present moment.

In this place of natural simplicity and ease there is nothing to do. . . . There is nothing to make happen. . . . Meditation occurs spontaneously.

In the relaxed immediacy of this deeply contented environment and atmosphere, let go of the busyness of life, all the trials and tribulations, all the hopes and fears. . . . Simply let go. . . . Simply be.

This exercise may well have provided you with a taste of what a conducive meditative environment is like. As we prepare to meditate, the aim is to create a physical space that lends itself to feelings of relaxation, peace and calm. To achieve this end in our own daily lives, there are a number of details to attend to.

LOCATION AND ATMOSPHERE

The aim is to create a "meditative space" in your own home. This is most likely to be the quietest place; a place that you can go to and feel removed from the outside world, safe and comfortable. A place in which to relax.

Some people are fortunate and motivated enough to have a whole room that they put aside as their meditation space. More commonly, people use part of a spare bedroom or study, or just a corner of their living space. Ideally it works best to designate one area where you meditate regularly. You may mark it by keeping a particular chair, rug or cushion in that place.

Meditate in this same place frequently, so that it comes to represent meditation to you. After a while, simply by going to that place and entering into your meditative space once again, you immediately relax and quite effortlessly meditate. This space will become a friend and a support for your meditation.

Historically, people from many traditions would set up a home shrine to meditate in front of. This is an optional extra. Perhaps you prefer uncomplicated simplicity. Perhaps you will draw extra support from gathering together things that have meaning and spiritual value for you. A home shrine can be simple or complex. A simple shrine could be made up of a cross, a photograph of a spiritual teacher or master, or a candle or incense. Complex shrines might include a series of photographs, statues, special objects, flowers, offering bowls, candles and so on. Gather items that inspire you or that have pleasant associations and engender feelings of peace, or whatever helps to remind you of your spiritual roots and connections. In modern times it is easy to create your own version of a shrine if a traditional one is not relevant or appealing.

Sogyal Rinpoche has a wonderful way of expressing the value of a conducive environment:

> There are many ways of making the approach to meditation as joyful as possible. You can transform the most ordinary of rooms into an intimate sacred space, an environment where every day you go to meet with your true self with all the joy and happy ceremony of one old friend greeting another.

Taking tranquillity into daily life

Janet was new to meditation. She had a busy working life and was experiencing some mild anxiety with related high blood pressure and skin irritation. She set up her meditation space in a corner of her fourth-floor apartment that overlooked a local park. Being just above the tree line, the view was quite spacious and inspiring.

Janet began learning meditation sitting in a simple upright chair that she bought at modest cost specifically for that purpose. She then placed a low-level table she already owned in front of that window and covered it in a special old tablecloth her grandmother had made and passed down to her. Then she added a simple crystal candleholder in the center of the table, with a beeswax candle she lights every time before she meditates. To complete her "shrine" Janet arranges fresh flowers, which she replenishes regularly.

Some time later, Janet reported that just going to this particular space of hers, sitting in her special chair, pausing a moment to look out at the inspiring view, taking in the flowers that further remind her of nature, feeling the presence of her grandmother via the cloth, and then lighting a candle, gave her a reliable ritual that helped transport her from the busyness of the day into the simplicity of her meditation practice. Just knowing that this meditation space was there in her apartment had come to have the significance for Janet of a safe haven.

> . . . no matter how busy or frantic things get at work, I have this
> direct connection with peace and clarity. It comforts me. It is as
> if this space I have created at home has come to symbolize the
> inner peace I have been craving and needing so much. The feel-
> ing of it stays with me through the day, and each evening, when
> I go home, I renew, restore and strengthen the connection. The
> balance in my life is so much the better for it.

Here Janet provides a really useful tip: create a ritual that helps to make a special occasion of your meditation, an occasion that you feel good about, look forward to and get into the habit of doing.

Creating a ritual

Jeff was an overweight, somewhat unhappy builder. With two small children and a big mortgage, life was not so easy. Encouraged by his wife to attend a course, Jeff was still somewhat reluctant to try this thing called meditation. However, he surprised himself by really enjoying the practice sessions. While he was used to going to the pub after work and unwinding with his mates over a few beers, instead he started to add a regular few minutes each evening to sit quietly at home in his meditation space.

Jeff needed his wife's support to manage the children while he shut himself in the bedroom. He had only a blank wall to sit in front of, so he added a poster of a beautiful landscape with snow-covered mountains and a tranquil lake in the foreground. Jeff heard of using a blanket or shawl to put over your shoulders or knees to mark the meditation, and something in this resonated with him. He had an old shawl that he never wore, and he could not even remember who gave it to him.

> When I go and sit in my chair, I put the shawl over my knees and it feels comfortable. There is something in this that makes me feel peaceful. Maybe it doesn't make any sense—I haven't told my mates about it—but this little ritual really works for me.

As an important aside to Jeff's story, about a year after he began meditating, and without actually trying to change his diet, almost all his excess weight had gone.

> I think what happened was that before the meditation, I was stressed out at work and at home. My way of handling the pressure was to eat and drink too much. Once the meditation kicked in, I felt more relaxed and I just seemed to be okay with eating less. I still have a drink, but I don't rely on it anymore, and don't use it as a way to unwind. It's amazing. Even my wife is amazed.

So think about the best place for you to start your practice. How can you give this place a meditative atmosphere? How can you make it special? And is there some simple ritual you can use to set the tone for your meditation practice?

Once we have settled on the location, let us look at how to arrange the body.

POSTURE

Almost all of the great meditation traditions recommend that the best posture is some variation of sitting cross-legged on the floor. But that is for spiritually focused meditation and it does not suit many untrained modern Western bodies. We simply do not bend that way so easily, and unless we want to go through some severe readjustment getting used to such a posture, we can in fact benefit from doing something simpler—at least to begin with. Here are a few simple principles concerning posture that you can readily adapt to your own situation—and flexibility!

External balance leads to inner balance

The first principle is to take up a balanced position. Meditation has the intention of bringing balance into our lives and helping us to maintain that balance. Therefore, whether you sit up or lie down, aim to have symmetry in your posture so that your body is balanced on both sides. However, if for some reason, such as pain, injury or disability, you cannot sit in a balanced, symmetrical position, that is fine. It is possible to meditate in any posture, any position.

Meditation is a very practical thing. There are ideals that can be recommended and which will serve us well if we can follow them, but it is always possible to adjust these ideals to suit our needs.

To sit up or lie down?

Again, this is a practical matter. If it is possible to sit up, so much the better. You are more likely to stay awake in this position, and the sitting posture does support meditation practice best. However, if you have a bad back or for some other health-related reason are unable to sit comfortably for any length of time, you can manage quite well lying down, as long as you stay awake!

If you do lie down it is best to lie on your back, legs a little apart, feet falling naturally outward. Keep your arms straight by your sides and, if possible, the palms of the hands turned upward. Many people seem to find this awkward, though, in which case palms down is a reasonable option. It is also best to lie in a place where you do not usually sleep.

For sitting, the choices are a chair, a stool or the floor. A chair suits many who are unable to manage cross-legged on the floor. A simple, upright chair with a back for support, with or without armrests, works well. Ideally, your spine will be upright and your hips and knees positioned at right angles. Your hands can rest comfortably on your thighs, or on the arms of the chair if preferred.

If you do sit on the floor, either sit flat on the floor or on a cushion. Using a cushion raises the backside off the floor a little and so supports the natural bend in the lower spine. In the authors' experience, many people find using a cushion preferable. Some find it useful to sit astride the cushion, shins against the floor. Another option is to use a meditation stool: kneel on the floor and place the low stool over the backs of your calves and then sit back onto the stool.

However you sit, the main thing is to sit in an upright, inspiring and open posture. Imagine a mountain: tall, still, majestic. You are doing something important, something significant. Sit like a mountain.

The traditional approach
If you want to take up a classical meditation posture you could use the following, based on seven key elements.

1. Sitting
Sit cross-legged on the floor with your backside on a cushion. For the lotus position, cross your legs and then pull each foot up onto the opposite thigh. If you can sit in full lotus, then do so; if not, half lotus (with only one foot up on its opposite thigh, the other foot on the floor). If both lotus positions are difficult, simply cross your legs.

2. Hands
Place your hands in a relaxed fashion on your knees or thighs, palms facing down. This is a very relaxed way of sitting and is sometimes called the "mind in comfort and ease posture."

3. Back
The back needs to be straight "like a pile of coins balanced one atop the other."

4. Arms
The arms and elbows are just out from the body, like a great bird spreading its wings a little.

5. Head
The head is tilted forward just a little, the chin slightly tucked in.

6. Eyes
The gaze is directed downward, along the line toward the tip of the nose.

7. Mouth
The mouth is slightly open as if you are about to say a gentle "aahh." The tip of the tongue can be touching the hard palate behind the teeth, but if this is difficult to maintain or feels uncomfortable, simply leave it where it is.

What about the eyes?
For beginners, learning to meditate with the eyes closed is generally easier and more effective. As you progress, often the eyes will simply open a little as you relax more; or you can choose to adopt an open-eye method.

With eyes open there are two choices. First, you can gently focus your gaze upon a single point. This is effective if you plan to use concentration to sharpen your meditation. Alternatively, you can adopt a broader focus, a bit like looking at the forest in the landscape rather than a particular tree. This broad focus is helpful if you aim to relax or simply be more open in your approach to meditation. The broad focus is what we would recommend in general.

The hands
The word *mudra* is used to describe the way we position our hands and fingers. There are a great many mudras, but again we recommend

a simple approach. Simply rest your hands on your knees or thighs, or as a second option you can cup them in your lap.

The paradox of discomfort

The final thing to say about the recommended posture requires some explanation. Ideally, your posture will support your practice better if it is a little uncomfortable. Yes, uncomfortable. This was one of the things Dr. Meares explained:

> If we get into a comfortable position, say by lying in or on the bed, then it is easy to relax. We relax our body, and the relaxation comes from our body. On the other hand, if we were to relax in a position that is slightly uncomfortable to begin with, we need to use our mind to relax through the discomfort. In this way, the relaxation comes from our mind. Therefore it is actually quite helpful to make sure that we use a position that is just slightly uncomfortable for us.

For most, this will be sitting upright in a chair. If you plan to meditate long-term, as we hope you would, then it may be advantageous to gradually become used to sitting cross-legged on the floor. When you do, you will find that this posture really does support your meditation and that it is actually easier to stay in this posture for extended periods of meditation—once you are used to it.

GETTING STARTED

How long do we meditate?

Begin by establishing a regular daily practice. While it is true that any meditation, even once a week, has benefit, it is ideal to do it daily. Aim to spend even a few minutes each day taking up your posture and practicing your meditation.

Most of the benefits of meditation established by research into preventing or treating ailments of the body or the mind have been based on meditation practice of ten to twenty minutes, once or twice daily. For most people, this is a practical and effective level to aim for.

In our experience helping people with major illness, more intensive levels of practice appear beneficial. Dr. Meares reported this same observation. Most people who have used meditation to foster the healing of a major illness like cancer report that three daily sessions each of forty minutes to an hour may well be more effective.

Establishing and maintaining our meditation

Many people find that the hardest thing is to actually stop doing whatever else is going on in the day and actually sit down to meditate. Once they do start, a few minutes often flows into a few more minutes, and fairly soon they have a good practice going.

The best solution for our inherent inertia and laziness is inspiration and enjoyment. Inspiration comes from reminding ourselves of our motivation, our reasons for meditating. Inspiration also comes from having teachers you can admire, respect and even have devotion for, establishing a personally relevant shrine, attending a group, reading books or listening to CDs. Make a conscious effort to be inspired, and at the same time seek enjoyment in your meditation. This enjoyment comes when you have reliable teachers and teachings, are using a good method, and when you encourage and support yourself with healthy acknowledgment and reinforcement of your practice.

The challenge is to use the right sort of self-discipline so that you do practice regularly. When we talk of self-discipline we mean a particular way of understanding discipline. This way is to realize that self-discipline is a personal kindness. That's right, to be disciplined is to be kind to ourselves. Now, to be kind to ourselves, we need to know what we want and how we can get it. And then we need to do it. That is what being kind to ourselves is: doing what we need to do, doing what is in our personal best interests.

When it comes to meditation, the intention is to be relaxed, calm, mindful and at peace. Perhaps you aim to prevent illness, to heal, to be well. *Really well*. Maybe you want to follow the spiritual path. Meditation is integral to all these things. You just need to do it. So be kind to yourself and do it!

Supporting our good intentions!

As well as applying self-discipline, you can support your good intentions with a routine, meditating in the same place at the same time each day. You can anchor your meditation into the day by linking it to already established routines: get up in the morning, shower, meditate and have breakfast. That way, the meditation becomes a part of your morning routine.

Perhaps you could meditate with others in the household, or just know that your friends meditate in their homes at the same time as you do each day, in this way supporting one another. The aim is to consider what will inspire you, what will give meaning to you, what will bring you the joy and enthusiasm to meditate regularly. The aim is to establish and maintain a regular practice.

ATTITUDE AND THE THREE NOBLE PRINCIPLES

These three principles come from the Tibetan knowledge of meditation. They are recommended as a way of enlivening our meditation practice, of transforming our meditation from being something that is useful and somewhat mundane into something quite extraordinary and transformative. In fact, these principles can be adopted and used in a fairly pragmatic, ordinary way and they will still be useful, but if we go with this and use them more fully, they can be very potent and really add to our meditation.

The Three Noble Principles are: good in the beginning, good in the middle and good at the end.

1. Good in the beginning

This first principle refers to our motivation for doing meditation in the first place. We may have a very immediate, personal and obvious motivation: we want to relax, to be calm, to let go of stress, to be well, to heal. But what is suggested here is that the more we can expand our motivation, the more encompassing our motivation, the more meaningful our meditation becomes, the more we will value it, the more likely we are to do it and the more benefit it will bring.

So if our motivation is to be well and to be happy, that will be nice;

but what if we were then to go on to consider others? If our motivation is to get well so that we can be of greater use to others, then that adds purpose to our practice. The Tibetans recommend that at the start of our meditation we bring to mind a strong wish that everyone, every living being, comes to be free of suffering and to experience true happiness. In the Tibetans' understanding, true happiness comes with realizing our own true nature, the truth of who we really are. So we wish this for everyone. More specifically we wish that we will become enlightened so that we can then use our enlightenment to bring enlightenment to all beings. This is good in the beginning.

2. Good in the middle

The second principle concerns our attitude, the attitude we have in our mind as we do the practice. The intention here is to let go of judgment, to let go of any sense of struggle or striving during the practice. We aim to remain unattached to any thoughts or any emotions that arise, to let go of the past and the present, and to simply be in this very moment. This is the state of mind that is good in the middle.

3. Good at the end

The third and final principle is an interesting and new notion for most Westerners. It speaks of dedicating the merit. This means we recognize that taking time to meditate is an action that has merit. As an analogy, if we work at a paying job for a while we will earn a certain amount of money. This asset, this money, has possibilities—it has potential. If we leave the money lying around, who knows what will happen to it? However, if we put it toward a useful project, or give it to someone in need, it could be of immediate benefit. If we invest it wisely, it may grow and become even more useful and help even more people.

In recognition of this, at the end of our meditation we can take a few moments to not only dedicate the merit of our own small session of practice, but we can combine this with all the merit we can imagine, merit from everyone who has ever done, or will ever do, anything useful, including meditating, so that this huge amount of merit can be dedicated directly to something beneficial. We could dedicate the merit to our own immediate and obvious needs, but the larger and more comprehensive our dedication, the more value the meditation will hold, and we just may make a difference.

So we could dedicate the merit to someone we know who is in need, to someone who is ill, or even to someone who has died. We could dedicate the merit to a cause or to world peace. We could expand and dedicate the merit with the wish that everyone, every living being, is freed from suffering and comes to experience true happiness. We could dedicate merit to the enlightenment of all beings. This then is good at the end.

So to apply the Three Noble Principles, each time you meditate begin by reminding yourself of what you are doing and why, and then be conscious of the frame of mind you are in while you are meditating, and finally dedicate the merit at the end; to do these three things gives structure, meaning and purpose to your meditation. You are more likely to enjoy doing it and your meditation is more likely to be useful. Useful to you, to those around you and perhaps even—who knows?—beneficial to everyone.

DEEPENING THE BENEFITS

Developing muscles

Muscles? Yes, meditation muscles. When we first go to the gym to develop physical fitness, we start with light weights and gradually increase these weights over time as our muscles develop. It is the same with meditation. We begin in a conducive, easy environment and adopt a posture that is just slightly uncomfortable. As we continue to practice, it is wise to challenge ourselves a little so that we develop our capacity and our meditation "muscles." To do so, experiment by meditating in gradually more challenging environments and postures. The aim is to be able to be still, calm, relaxed and mindfully at ease in these more difficult circumstances. This helps us to develop a greater capacity to meditate when life becomes more demanding, and it deepens our experience of meditation as we learn to cope with the challenges.

Establishing comfort and ease

A reliable way to develop and deepen your meditation, therefore, is to begin by practicing regularly in a conducive, ideal place. Once things feel as if they are going well, meditate in new and different circumstances. For example, your routine may be to shut the door of the room that you usually meditate in, so now try leaving it open. Once this is manageable, perhaps leave the TV or radio on so that you have that distraction to cope with. Perhaps meditate in different rooms; try going outside to a balcony, the backyard or a park.

Keep coming back to the peace and stability of your usual place, especially if you find it takes awhile to be able to meditate in these more challenging circumstances. But do try to extend yourself regularly, to train your mind and develop your meditation.

You can also experiment with more challenging postures. If you normally sit in a chair with a back support, try sitting forward a little so that you need to concentrate and pay attention that little bit more to maintain your posture. Have a go at sitting on the floor. Or sit on a hard bench or in a place where there is a breeze blowing that could distract you.

The intention is to challenge yourself, little by little, gradually getting used to meditating in more and more difficult postures and environments. Eventually you will be able to meditate in any situation, in a way that is independent of your environment. In this way your meditation will become very stable and reliable.

At the beginning, make your environment and posture as conducive as possible. We know that it is possible to simply relax into the environment, relax into the posture, to feel the calm and the ease of it all, to be content to let go of thoughts of past and future, and to simply rest in the now of this present moment. To simply be.

However, if the only time, the only way that we could meditate was when it was perfectly quiet and our body was perfectly comfortable to begin with, we would rarely manage to meditate. And what use would it be to us anyway?

So do what you can. Choose a conducive environment and adopt a conducive posture. But then accept what you are unable to change or alter, and transform any challenges into something that actually supports you as you train your mind to be at peace with what is.

Now that we are prepared and have created a conducive environment, let us move on to learn how to relax.

STEP 2

RELAXATION

CHAPTER 3

LEARNING TO RELAX

*In these days of tension, human beings can learn a
great deal about relaxation from watching a cat,
who doesn't just lie down when it is time to rest,
but pours his body on the floor
and rests in every nerve and muscle.*
—JULIETTE CLARKE, *A Cat Lover's Notebook*

Having established a conducive environment and adopted a supportive
posture along with a curious, nonjudgmental state of mind, we are now
ready to begin to learn how to master the process of relaxing the body
and calming the mind.

This type of relaxation—relaxation of body and mind—is the ideal
prelude to all forms of meditation. In our method of Mindfulness-Based
Stillness Meditation, relaxation flows quite naturally from good preparations. In a conducive environment it is easy to relax our bodies, and
as we do this our minds tend to find their own inner calm. However,
we can learn and develop the techniques of relaxation of body and mind
in ways that will bring great benefits to our lives. This is another life
skill worth taking the time to master.

The word *master* is used deliberately, as the techniques of relaxation are skills that warrant learning, studying and practicing until we become so adept at using them that we can do so free of effort. As discussed, from being the awkward beginner we become the tentative learner, and then advance through the early stages of accomplishment until finally we master what we have set out to learn. This process of learning is worth mentioning repeatedly and reflecting upon until we really get it. What we need to "get" in this context is being comfortable with where we are at. As a beginner, we have beginner's experiences. It is natural as a beginner to have some uncertainty, even awkwardness or critical appraisal going on inside.

Remember, though, particularly as you learn to relax, to do so in a relaxed fashion! Avoid the temptation to turn relaxation into a stressful business. Take your time. Be realistic. Once you learn these techniques and practice them a little, you will find they lead to deep and satisfying relaxation.

GETTING READY FOR PROGRESSIVE MUSCLE RELAXATION (PMR)

We are aiming to master the process of relaxing the body and calming the mind. It is really very simple. We start with an age-old method that reliably and deeply relaxes the body, and then we learn how to bring that experience of relaxation into our minds and our daily life.

The Progressive Muscle Relaxation (PMR) exercise probably has its origins in the ancient traditions of yoga. It is simple to learn, reliably relaxes the body, frees us of any tension we may be carrying in the body and leaves us feeling really comfortable and at ease. The technique involves learning to focus our attention on the feeling of each part or segment of the body as we contract and then release the muscles in that area, starting with the feet and moving progressively up through each muscle group until we reach the head.

There are four things to be aware of as we bring our attention to each part of the body. So first we will take the time to learn and practice these four things; then we can put them all together and practice the PMR exercise effectively.

1. Bringing awareness to the body

To begin with, we take a real interest in noticing, or being aware of, how each part of our body is feeling when we first give our attention to it. The key thing is to be just a bit curious. So start with the feet and take a real interest in what they feel like today. Then take your attention to your calves: How do they feel? And what about your thighs?

During this simple exercise, aim to let go of expectations. Let go of thoughts such as "It should be like this or that" and "Why is it like this or that?" And we aim to let go of judgment, of "This is good, am I doing this right?" or "This is bad, there must be something wrong with me." Relax into relaxation itself by simply being content to notice how your body is feeling today.

Even if you do have some discomfort or pain, aim to let go of wishing it away. Almost paradoxically, yet in a way you will come to really understand, the more we can suspend our hopes and fears, the more we can simply take a nonjudgmental interest in how it really is right now; the more we relax, the more comfortable we become; and the more at ease we are, the more likely it is that this simple method of relaxation will flow on into meditation. This is a crucial point. While the majority of people who use this approach will already be basically physically comfortable and so will find that bringing awareness to their body is straightforward, if you have pain or some physical disability, these techniques can transform your experience of and relationship to your body. The key is to adopt an open curiosity as to how your body feels today, right now as you do this exercise, to accept that this is the truth of the matter, this is how it is, and then to use these techniques to lead your body into a deeper, more peaceful relaxed state.

The joy of all this is that it does work, and it works in quite a direct and simple way. We spend a few moments, perhaps fifteen to thirty seconds, exploring how a particular part of our body is feeling, and then we go on to the next step, and explore a different sensation.

2. Contracting the muscles

Next, just briefly, we contract the muscles in the particular area we are giving our attention to. The aim is to notice the difference in the feeling that is created in each part of the body by tensing up the muscles. We only hold the tension for perhaps five or ten seconds—just long enough to appreciate the feeling of tension that is created. Tight, tense, contracted. What does it feel like? Again that gentle curiosity. Free of expectations, just interested to notice, to be aware of the feeling of tension in this particular part of your body.

3. Feeling the muscles letting go

Then we relax the muscles. We do this in a measured, gradual way. It takes a few seconds. This is not like releasing a rubber band that we have stretched and let go with a sudden ping. What we do here is gentle. Simply relaxing and releasing. Notice the muscles softening and loosening, the tightness and tension draining away.

As we do this, not only do we release the tension we artificially created by contracting the muscles, but we release any residual tension that may have been stored in the body as part of a chronic pattern of tension.

Also, as another great benefit of this exercise, as we experience letting go of the muscle tension we become increasingly familiar with the feeling of letting go—in other words, we come to recognize the feeling of relaxation. We recognize and know what it feels like to relax the body, and as we continue to practice this exercise we begin to be able to relax anytime, anywhere, just by paying attention. This is a wonderful life skill to have. And anyone can learn it.

4. Familiarity with the feeling of relaxation

Finally, we give our attention to noticing what each part of the body feels like once it is deeply relaxed, and we develop a familiarity with the feeling of relaxation itself. Once we are able to know what it feels like to be deeply relaxed, we have a benchmark. We know what it is to be relaxed.

Now, many might say that this is a little absurd; of course I know what it feels like to be relaxed. Well, in fairness, our observation over several decades is that many people constantly carry significant levels of tension in their bodies and have simply become used to the feeling of it.

For example, way back in his early days of teaching, Ian remembers a man named Brian who thought he knew how to feel relaxed. Ian recalls: Usually I close my eyes with beginners groups and meditate with them. Fairly invariably, at some stage in the meditation, beginners tend to open their eyes to check out what is going on. Seeing my eyes closed seems to give the sense that I am confident that they will be okay, and they soon close their eyes again and relax into it.

This day I happened to open my eyes, and Brian was sitting there, deep furrows across his brow, shoulders hunched and hands tightly squeezed in two fists. Once we had finished, I asked Brian how he had felt during the exercise, and he replied through clenched teeth, "Oh, fine, really relaxed."

I was a bit taken aback. What Brian had demonstrated and helped me to learn—his particular gift, if you like—was that many people have this muscular tension in their body and that they have become so used to the feeling of that tension that they do not even consciously register it anymore. Their bodies and their minds have adapted to this unnatural and quite uncomfortable state. What Brian was saying when he said he felt fine was that he was used to how he felt. For him, to be tense was his common experience; it was the norm. What Brian was not saying, and what he helped me to realize, is that he, like many other beginners we have helped over the years, did not know what being deeply relaxed felt like.

This then is a wonderful benefit, almost a side effect of learning to relax. As we practice these techniques, we come to learn how to relax at will and to know what it feels like when we are relaxed.

Once Brian got into the habit of practicing relaxation as a lead-in to his meditation, he began to pay attention to the feeling in his body. As he did so, he began to notice something quite new. After a few weeks he reported, "I feel a lightness in my body. The backaches and shoulder pain have gone and I seem to have more energy." This all occurred courtesy of a simple technique for releasing tension and letting go into relaxation.

RELAXING EACH PART OF THE BODY

Let us now return to contracting and relaxing the muscles. These days many people have done the PMR exercise before, but if it is new to you what follows describes how to contract and relax the muscles in each of the main areas of your body. In the next chapter, we will use this knowledge as the basis for practicing the PMR exercise.

Learning how to contract and relax the muscles at will only takes a few minutes and is best done in the posture you intend to use to meditate. The descriptions that follow are based on a sitting position in a chair, but are easily adapted if you need to lie down or use some other posture.

After doing this exercise your muscles should feel all loose and floppy like a rag doll. Most people find it fairly easy to work out how to contract the muscles in each given area of their body, but some need a little more help. We offer some suggestions in the text below.

The feet

Start with the feet. The aim here is to contract all the muscles in the feet, making them stiff and tight. Hold your attention on the feeling this tightness produces in your feet for just a few seconds, and then relax the muscles again, allowing them to go soft and loose.

You can imagine your feet are in sand and you are trying to curl your toes down into the sand. At the same time, brace the muscles along the tops of your feet to resist that movement. This will make the muscles in the tops and the bottoms of your feet rigid. It will create tension in your feet, and you will notice the feeling that it creates. The feeling of tension is quite different from the feeling in your feet when you first pay attention to them.

The calves

As you contract the muscles in the calves, some muscles in the feet or the thighs might also contract a little too. Just ignore this if it happens and concentrate on the feeling in the calves.

If you find it difficult to contract your calf muscles on command, keep your feet flat on the floor and press the balls of your feet down on the floor. This will contract the muscles at the back of the calves. In a similar way, you can tighten the muscles in your shins by resisting this attempted motion, or if it helps, imagine pulling your toes up off the floor while resisting raising them.

The thighs

This is the biggest muscle group in the body, so we can get a good sense of the technique here. It is best to be sitting in a chair for this and to place your hands on your knees. Attempt to lift your feet off the floor as you hold your knees down. This contracts the big muscles on top of the thighs. Without actually moving your feet, feel your calves and heels pulling back toward your chair again. This contracts the muscles at the back of the thighs.

The buttocks

Lift yourself up off the chair a little by tightening the big muscles of the backside. Then relax again.

Once we get into the larger areas of the backside, torso, tummy and chest, there is another technique that is very helpful in bringing the feeling of relaxation into every part of the body, not just the muscles. The muscles of the backside cover a significant portion of our hips, pelvis and genital area. We can take the feeling of relaxing the buttocks and aim to convey that feeling throughout the hips, pelvis and genital area.

We use the muscles of the body to get the feeling of relaxation, and then we extend that feeling throughout the areas of the body that are not made up of muscles—areas like the pelvis, internal parts of our tummy and the inside of the chest, for instance.

The benefit of all this is that the relaxation begins to flow into every part of the body. As well as the internal parts of the torso, the bones, joints and head all relax, and as we come to feel this relaxation all through the body, it flows into the mind. We relax the body and the mind goes with it. We feel deeply relaxed. It is very simple—no effort required. We just do it, and it flows.

The tummy

Imagine you are lying on your back and someone is about to drop something heavy onto your tummy. You brace the muscles at the front of the tummy, along with those of the lower back.

The chest

This is easy. Contract the muscles tight like a barrel. The image of Tarzan is good for men. And Jane for the women! While that may be a joke, the idea is simple. Hold the rib cage tight for a moment, and then let the muscles go.

The arms

Next, brace the arms in whatever position they are in. Do this as if you are trying to hold your arms still while someone attempts to move them. Some people find it helpful to clench their fists, but it may be easier just to make your hands and fingers rigid in whatever position they are in.

The shoulders

Lift the shoulders up and the chin down a little, and then feel the relaxation through the neck and the throat as well as the shoulders.

The jaw

Bite down gently on your teeth, closing your mouth firmly. Then relax and feel the jaw drop open a little. Feel the mouth and tongue becoming soft and loose.

The eyes and the forehead

Close the eyelids tightly and then release them. Finally, for the forehead, furrow your brow (frown), and then lift the eyebrows a little.

RELAXATION: IN SUMMARY

As you learn how to relax your muscles in order to practice the PMR, pay attention to four things:

1. Notice how the area feels in the particular moment that you first pay attention to it.
2. Contract the muscles in that area and hold the contraction long enough to notice the feeling that the tightening of the muscles creates.
3. Slowly and smoothly relax the muscles, noticing the feeling of tension releasing and the feeling of relaxation that follows.
4. Give attention to what that area feels like now that you have relaxed it. Notice the feeling of relaxation in the muscles and extend that feeling throughout every part of the body—that is, all through the feet, all through the tummy, all through the head.

MINDFULNESS AND THE PMR

Now that we have worked out how to contract and relax the different muscle groups throughout the body, we are nearly ready to begin the practice of the PMR. However, before we begin there are two more useful pieces of advice to consider that are of value to the experienced meditator and to the beginner alike.

There are two ways to do an exercise like the PMR. One way is to do it mindfully, the other is mindlessly. While mindfulness is a major contributing element to our meditation practice and later chapters will delve more deeply into the subject, for now suffice it to say that mindfulness quite simply is paying attention to what we are doing. It is concentrating on what we are doing in a way that is free of judgment.

Mindlessness, on the other hand, is when we do not pay attention, when we do not concentrate, and when our mind wanders off and thinks about all sorts of other things. Virtually everyone has periods of mindlessness, but you will find it very beneficial to learn to be more mindful, to keep your focus on what you are doing, to be less judgmental and to notice what will work for you.

As we practice the PMR exercise, we do need to concentrate, but it will work best if that concentration is light rather than too intense. Consider a stringed instrument such as a violin or a guitar: if the strings are either too tight or too loose it will sound bad. The strings need just the right amount of tension for them to be in tune and for the instrument to sound its best. So it is with the mind. If we are too relaxed, too "loose," it will not work so well. Too intense, too serious, too much effort, and again it will not be so useful.

Sogyal Rinpoche has a terrific way of explaining how to balance this need for being alert, being able to concentrate and to relax. He recommends that for meditation we should employ about 25 percent of our maximum effort in concentration. What is 25 percent exactly? Well, that is something that we do not need to dwell on too much. The important bit is that we do aim to concentrate, but in a light, relaxed sort of way.

Almost everyone will find that, as they do these exercises, the mind will wander, there will be times when they will become distracted, and for most this will happen fairly regularly. So another 25 percent of our attention needs to go toward noticing what our mind is up to. We need to notice whether it is on track and actually doing the exercises, or whether it has wandered off, become spaced out, got lost in some other thoughts and become generally mindless. Again, we are all highly likely to experience our mind wandering off, so we need to use the vigilant part of our mind to notice when we do become distracted and, once we recognize this, to bring the mind gently back to the exercise again.

The key here is to avoid beating yourself up in the process. Be reassured that this is the normal experience. Especially for beginners, the mind does tend to wander and become distracted. You just need to notice this when it happens and bring your attention back to the PMR again. This is a normal part of learning any meditation method. It is a normal part of training the mind and, as you do so, you will find that you develop the capacity to concentrate better, and to hold your attention more consistently and for longer periods of time, not only in your meditation but in anything else you do during the day. This is another of the really useful life skills you develop as you learn and practice meditation—the ability to concentrate.

Now, if you have been doing the rather simple math, you will have noticed we have 25 percent of our focus given to concentration and 25 percent to noticing when our concentration wanders and to keeping it on track. What of the other 50 percent? Well, we aim to just leave that spacious. The whole exercise is intended to help us to relax. To feel more comfortable, more at ease. It will not help us to attempt to force our mind to relax; to attempt to confine it, to suppress it. This would be like trying to tame a wild horse by confining it in a tight space. A wild horse faced with that restriction gets more restless, more agitated, more wild. Let such an animal loose in a big paddock, let it have space, and it may well run around for a few minutes. Perhaps it will even kick up its heels, but then, in a relatively short period of time, it will settle and become calm and relaxed. It will find its own natural peace and ease. So give your mind space. Avoid the temptation to attempt to squeeze your mind into submission, to confine and restrict it—that will just make it wilder! Use light concentration, gently correct it when it wanders, and patiently give it time and space. Remember, 25 percent concentration, 25 percent vigilance, 50 percent spaciousness.

So now, knowing how to contract and relax your muscles, and being prepared to use concentration and mindfulness, we are ready to begin the actual practice of the Progressive Muscle Relaxation exercise.

CHAPTER 4

PROGRESSIVE MUSCLE RELAXATION

The way you use your body determines how well it works,
how clearly you think, and how good you feel.
—F. M. ALEXANDER

We now come to the actual technique of Progressive Muscle Relaxation (PMR). Also included in this chapter are three variations on this technique that will help you to learn how to relax deeply, quickly and effortlessly. We recommend you take about two weeks to learn and practice each one of these techniques in turn. Each builds naturally on the previous one, and by taking your time you will soon master the art of relaxation.

Each exercise has what we call a "script." These are the words we would use if we were leading you personally through the exercise. These words are specifically designed to instruct you in what you need to do, while at the same time conveying the atmosphere of relaxation, calm and ease.

We recommend that as a beginner you either learn the script well enough so that you can lead yourself through the exercise or use a recorded script on CD or an mp3. You do not necessarily need to learn the scripts word for word, although you can if you prefer. For example, in the first exercise, the PMR follows a simple pattern of contracting the muscles and relaxing them, starting with the feet and then moving progressively up through each significant muscle group of the body. Hence the name, Progressive Muscle Relaxation. The phrases we recommend you use between each set of muscles are intended to keep the mind focused and to build a feeling of relaxation all through the body. The fewer phrases you need to use to stay focused and the longer the gaps between the words before you become distracted, the simpler the whole exercise is and the better it works.

The best way to lead yourself through the PMR is to start by taking your attention down to your feet. Notice how they feel for a few moments, and then say to yourself silently words like "contract the muscles . . . and let them go." The short gap between these two phrases allows you to give attention to the differences in feeling created by contracting the muscles and then letting them go. These silent gaps are indicated by using ellipsis points (. . .) in the script.

Once you have contracted and relaxed the muscles in your feet, take a few moments, perhaps while you breathe in and out once or twice, and then say the next phrase.

Of course, initially it can be helpful to be led by an experienced teacher through exercises like these, and many people find listening to CDs very useful, especially as beginners. But either way, the intention is to learn to do these exercises for yourself, and to repeat them until you master them in the way described.

Here, then, is the Progressive Muscle Relaxation script to lead you through this simple yet highly effective technique.

1. PROGRESSIVE MUSCLE RELAXATION

The following exercise should take fifteen to twenty minutes to complete.

PROGRESSIVE MUSCLE RELAXATION

Begin by taking a moment to settle into your position. . . . Adjust your posture if you need to . . . get your body settled . . . and when you are ready, let your eyes gently close.

Take a moment to remind yourself of your motivation . . . and remember that this is an opportunity to consciously relax your body . . . and to allow your mind to go with it.

So begin by taking your attention down to the feet . . . perhaps moving them a little . . . really feel what they are like at the moment. . . . Contract the muscles of the feet . . . feeling the difference that makes . . . and then let them go. . . . Feel the muscles softening . . . loosening . . . relaxing . . . releasing . . . just simply letting go.

Now take your attention up into the calves. . . . In your mind, move your attention through the calves, noticing any sensations that come to your awareness. . . . Notice if they are warm, or cool, or neutral . . . whether there are any sensations on the skin, like the touch of clothing or a gentle flow of air . . . perhaps sensations deeper into the calves. . . . Just noticing . . . like a gentle curiosity . . . free of judgment . . . free of reaction or analysis . . . just noticing. . . . Now, contract the muscles, feeling the difference that makes . . . and let them go. . . . Feel the muscles softening . . . loosening . . . relaxing . . . releasing . . . just simply letting go.

Now the thighs . . . notice how they are feeling. . . . Contract the muscles . . . and let them go. . . . Feel it all through the thighs . . . and down the calves . . . and into the feet . . . feeling it deeply . . . completely.

Contract the muscles in the buttocks, lifting up off the

---

chair or the floor . . . and then let them go. . . . Feel the weight settling down once again . . . feel it all around the hips and through the pelvis. . . . Sometimes it helps to imagine there is a belt or a band around the hips that is being loosened a little . . . just going with it . . . going with it . . . letting go.

Now the tummy. . . . Contract the muscles in the front of the tummy and the lower back . . . and then let them go. . . . Feel it deeply all through the tummy . . . calm and relaxed . . . just going with it . . . calm and relaxed . . . just simply letting go.

Notice where your attention is . . . and if, at any stage, you do find your mind wandering or becoming distracted, gently bring your attention back to your body once again.

Take your attention to the chest. . . . Contract the muscles, tight like a barrel . . . and then let them go. . . . Just allow the breath to take up whatever rhythm feels comfortable for you at the moment . . . quite effortlessly . . . effortlessly . . . letting go.

Now the arms. . . . Contract the muscles . . . and let them go . . . feeling a wave of relaxation flowing down through the arms. . . . First the upper arms, softening . . . loosening . . . down around the elbows and into the forearms . . . relaxing . . . releasing . . . and then the wrists, hands, fingers. . . . Sometimes you might notice what feels like a warmth or a tingling flowing down into the hands and the fingers . . . a feeling of lightness . . . go with it . . . go with it . . . just simply letting go.

Now the shoulders. . . . Contract the muscles by pulling the shoulders up and the chin down . . . and then let them go. . . . Feel the shoulders drop a little . . . feel it deeply . . . completely . . . and feel it up through the neck and the throat . . . more and more . . . deeper and deeper . . . just simply letting go.

Take your attention to the jaw. . . . Contract the muscles by closing the jaw firmly . . . and then let them go. . . . Feel the jaw drop a little . . . the tongue soft and loose . . . and feel it all through the jaw and all around the mouth . . . going with it. . . . And feel it up over the nose and through the cheeks.

. Now the eyes. . . . Contract the muscles, closing the eyes firmly . . . and then let them go. . . . Feel the eyelids smoothing out . . . feel it deeply . . . all through the eyes . . . almost like the eyes could be floating in their sockets . . . just going with it . . . and the temples soft and loose. . . . And feel it around the ears . . . the back of the head . . . up over the top of the head . . . calm and relaxed . . . just going with it . . . calm and relaxed.

Now contract the muscles in your forehead by furrowing your brow a little . . . and then let them go. . . . Feel the forehead smoothing out . . . feel it deeply . . . completely . . . feel it through the body and the mind . . . going with it . . . going with it . . . more and more . . . deeper and deeper . . . just simply letting go . . . letting go . . . quite effortlessly . . . effortlessly . . . letting go . . . letting go.

Now sit quietly for as long as you want to. Then when you are ready, gently open your eyes again.

Practice the PMR for a few weeks in order to master the exercise. You will probably find within a week or two of beginning this practice that you can do the PMR without having to think about it too much. Be warned that as you become more familiar with any exercise there is a tendency to lapse into doing it on automatic, in that way we describe as being mindless. So as you become more familiar and proficient with this and all the other exercises, remember to do them mindfully. The key principle is to pay attention and be interested in what you are doing; interested in that open, curious and nonjudgmental way.

Once you have become familiar with the PMR exercise we recommend that you develop your relaxation skills in two ways. One is to learn how to speed up the process so that you can relax more *quickly*. The other is to spend more time on the exercise, doing it in even greater detail so that you can learn to relax more *thoroughly*. First we will look at two techniques for relaxing more quickly.

2. THE RELAXING BODY SCAN

The Relaxing Body Scan is a modified version of the PMR—a simpler, quicker version without muscle contractions.

As with the PMR, we take our attention to each part of the body, starting with the feet and moving progressively up to the head. However, for this exercise, instead of contracting and relaxing each muscle group, we simply "overlay" the feeling of relaxation on each area. We take our attention to the feet, notice how they are feeling, and then we feel the feet relaxing. We leave out the contraction of the muscles, but we aim to relax the muscles thoroughly and to end up with the same feeling of relaxation in the feet. Then we do the same with the calves, the thighs and so on. Effectively, what we are doing in this exercise is combining relaxation and mindfulness.

This exercise takes around fifteen to twenty minutes to complete.

THE RELAXING BODY SCAN

Take a few moments to adjust your position . . . get your body settled . . . and when you are ready, let your eyes close gently.

Begin by taking your attention down to the feet . . . really concentrating on the feet . . . perhaps moving them a little . . . really feeling what sensations there are in the feet right now. . . . Remember that for this exercise there is no right or wrong . . . the exercise is simply one of noticing and working with whatever sensations there might be in the feet and the rest of the body right now. . . . As you notice and hold your attention on the feet . . . feel the muscles softening a little . . . relaxing and releasing . . . softening . . . loosening . . . just simply letting go.

Remember there is nothing else you need to be doing right now. . . . Having given yourself the time and space for this

---

exercise, there is nothing else you need to be doing . . . nowhere else you need to be . . . no one else you need to be pleasing or satisfying. . . . It is just a time for relaxing . . . releasing . . . letting go.

So now, move your attention up to the calves . . . it is almost like you are moving your attention up *through* the calves. . . . Feel what sensations might be there at the moment . . . perhaps some parts feel different from others . . . And again, even if some areas feel tight or tense or uncomfortable, just be interested to notice how they feel at this particular time . . . almost like an impartial observer . . . just noticing . . . being interested. . . . It is a gentle curiosity . . . just notice how your calves are feeling at this particular time. . . . And as you hold your awareness on the calves, feel the muscles softening and loosening . . . relaxing and releasing . . . just simply letting go.

Take your attention up to the thighs . . . and feel them relaxing and releasing . . . feel it deeply, completely . . . all down through the thighs and the calves and the feet. . . . Sometimes it might feel almost like the muscles are melting down into the chair or the floor a little . . . just relaxing and releasing . . . perhaps feeling a little heavier . . . like they could be melting or merging . . . just feeling them letting go . . . deeply . . . completely . . . letting go.

And now feel it all through the buttocks, the hips and the pelvis. . . . Sometimes it helps to imagine there is a belt or band around the hips that has just been loosened a little . . . the big muscles around the hips, softening and loosening . . . relaxing . . . releasing . . . quite effortlessly . . . effortlessly . . . just going with it.

Bring your attention up to the tummy . . . you will probably notice it rising and falling a little with the breath . . . and then that feeling of letting go again . . . all through the tummy . . . calm and relaxed . . . just going with it . . . calm and relaxed.

Move your attention up to the chest . . . again, just being aware of the chest rising and falling with the breath . . . and feeling the ease of it all . . . just allowing the breath to take up whatever rhythm feels comfortable for you at the moment . . . quite effortlessly . . . effortlessly . . . just going with it . . . more and more . . . deeper and deeper . . . letting go.

Now feel a wave of relaxation flowing down through the arms. . . . First the upper arms, softening and loosening . . . and down around through the elbows and into the forearms . . . relaxing . . . releasing . . . letting go . . . and then down through the wrists . . . the hands and the fingers. . . . Sometimes you might notice almost what feels like a tingling flowing into the hands and the fingers . . . a feeling of lightness . . . almost like they could be floating . . . just going with it . . . effortlessly . . . effortlessly . . . just going with it.

Now feel it all through the shoulders . . . perhaps just raising and lowering the shoulders a little. . . . Feel the head moving from side to side . . . and the muscles up either side of the neck . . . softening and loosening . . . just feeling it all through the shoulders . . . the neck and the throat . . . feeling the ease of it all . . . just going with it.

Bring your attention to your face. . . . With your lips just lightly touching, feel the jaw drop a little . . . the tongue, soft and loose. . . . Feel it all through the mouth . . . and feel it up over the nose and through the cheeks. . . . Feel the eyelids smoothing out . . . feeling it deeply . . . all through the eyes . . . and the temples . . . soft and loose. . . . And feel it around the ears . . . the back of the head . . . up over the top of the head.

And now feel the forehead smoothing out . . . feel it deeply . . . completely . . . feel it all through the body . . . more and more . . . deeper and deeper . . . just letting go . . . going with it . . . feel it through the body, and the mind . . . going with it . . . going with it . . . more and more . . . deeper and deeper . . . just simply letting go . . . letting go.

Take as long as you choose to sit quietly. . . . Then, when you are ready, you might like to take a deeper breath or two . . . perhaps move your feet a little . . . feel your hands move a little. . . . And then, when you are ready, let your eyes gently open again.

This exercise, like the PMR, is best done for a few weeks until you feel you have mastered it reasonably well. The aim with this second exercise is to physically relax to the same degree as you did using the full PMR, but now you are learning to use a somewhat simpler, more direct technique.

As you are learning the Relaxing Body Scan it may be helpful to alternate between it and the full PMR for a while. When you feel confident with these first two exercises, move on to the Rapid Relaxation exercise. This is an even quicker and more direct way of relaxing the body.

3. RAPID RELAXATION

This exercise draws on one of the body's natural ways of relaxing: the sigh. Test this for yourself: take a fairly deep breath in, and then gently sigh out the breath. You will notice what feels like a gentle wave of relaxation simply flowing down through the body as you sigh out the breath.

In the Rapid Relaxation exercise we utilize this by consciously breathing in more deeply, sighing out the breath and feeling the natural wave of relaxation that comes with the exhalation. Let go of any awkwardness you might feel and actually make the sound. Take a deeper breath in, and then breathe out, making a gentle sighing sound like "ahhhhh."

What we also put to good use in the Rapid Relaxation exercise are subtle movements of the body itself. We sway the body a little from side to side and come to feel where the point of balance is for our body. To appreciate the benefit of this part of the exercise, sit up straight and take a moment now to sway or bend your back a little to the left. You will soon feel as if you are tipping over; you are off-balance to the left. Then, if you lean over to the right, you will soon feel that you are tipping over to the right. You only need very small movements for this, and will find it easier to notice the subtleties when you do it with your eyes closed. Move slowly, swaying your spine a little from left to right, and you will soon get a good sense of where the center of balance is for your spine; then you come to rest in that point of balance.

Do the same with your head. Small, gentle swaying movements from left to right help to get a good sense of where the point of balance is. Then simply rest, relaxed and still, in that point of balance.

The following exercise should take three to five minutes.

RAPID RELAXATION

This Rapid Relaxation exercise is best done with your body fairly upright, so take a moment to adjust your position, ensuring your back is as upright as is comfortable.

Place your feet flat on the floor, a little apart, and then find where your hands are most comfortable—probably just resting on your thighs or cupped in your lap. Just notice what works best for you, and then, when you are ready, let your eyes gently close.

Now, take a deep breath in . . . and gently sigh the breath out . . . ahhhhh. . . . You will probably notice a wave of relaxation flowing down through the body . . . the muscles softening . . . loosening . . . relaxing . . . releasing . . . just simply letting go.

Do that once again . . . another, deeper breath in . . . gently sighing the breath out . . . ahhhhhhh . . . and then just allowing the breath to take up whatever rhythm feels comfortable for you at the moment . . . quite effortlessly . . . effortlessly . . . just feeling the ease of it all. . . . Now notice the feeling of letting go a little more with each out breath . . . just simply letting go.

And now, move your back a little from side to side in a gentle swaying motion . . . just enough to feel your spine moving across its point of balance. . . . And as you do that, feel the muscles along either side of the spine softening and loosening . . . relaxing . . . releasing . . . and then the spine coming to rest in its point of balance.

Another deeper breath in . . . gently sighing the breath out . . . ahhhhhhh . . . just simply letting go.

Then move the head a little from side to side . . . again just a gentle swaying motion . . . just enough to feel the head moving across its point of balance. . . . And as you do that, feel the muscles along either side of the neck softening and loosening . . . relaxing . . . releasing.

And the head coming to rest in its point of balance . . . Another deeper breath in . . . gently sighing the breath out . . . ahhhhhhh.

And now moving the head a little from front to back . . . and then tilting it a little from side to side. . . . Feel the ease of the movement . . . almost like the head is a helium balloon just floating there . . . and the neck, like a string, gently holding it in place. . . . And then the head coming to rest in its point of balance. . . . Simply resting now in that point of balance . . . quite effortlessly . . . effortlessly . . . just feeling the ease of it all . . . the ease of it all . . . just going with it . . . going with it . . . simply letting go.

Again, sit quietly for as long as you choose. . . . Then, when you are ready, just let your eyes gently open.

Practice this particular exercise until you feel confident with it and by then the relaxation will come fairly easily and directly. The aim is to get to the point where you are able to sit down and, almost like flicking a switch, rapidly relax your body. This is a wonderful skill to learn.

4. Relaxing Deeply

While you are learning to relax quickly, use some of your other practice sessions to learn to relax more deeply. This is another important step in learning the art of relaxing the body.

To learn to relax more deeply, we focus our attention on small areas of the body and take the time to relax them very thoroughly. It is more useful to describe this technique rather than provide a specific script.

A good place to start is with one big toe—either one is fine. As you sit in your meditation place, take up your usual posture, focus your attention on that one toe, and imagine going into every part of the toe and relaxing it in great detail.

This exercise is helped by having already become familiar with the feeling of relaxing the muscles, and also the experience of extending that relaxation into other areas of the body beyond the muscle groups, such as we did with the inner areas of the abdomen. We are now aiming to generate a deep sense of relaxation through every part of the body, not just the muscles.

Begin this process of deep relaxation by taking your attention into each muscle, each part of the toe, and then feel it relax. Feel the skin relaxing, and then the area under the skin. The area under the nail, and through the joints. Feel the relaxation through the relatively tiny bones of the toe. Do not dwell on the literal anatomy of the toe—although if you happen to know anatomy well, it can be fun. Just have the feeling of relaxing each part of the toe.

Spend quite a deal of time on this one toe. It is like you are right inside the toe, sensing and feeling and relaxing each part of it. Quite deeply. Completely. Even imagine the relaxation at the cellular level. Each cell is deeply relaxed. The components of each cell are relaxed. Maybe even the molecules that make up each cell. All deeply relaxed. Profoundly relaxed. And feel the ease of it all. The natural ease of it all. Feel what it is like to profoundly let go of any tension. The natural simplicity of letting go.

It is possible to spend many minutes, maybe many sessions, on just one toe, deeply relaxing it in this detailed way. The key point is to remember the feeling of profound relaxation in that part of the body. Then move on to another part. Perhaps the next toe. And the next. Then the whole foot, the calf, the thigh and so on, until you have taken the time and made the effort to thoroughly relax each part of the body.

And remember the feeling. By remembering the feeling, you can go back to that feeling more directly and more rapidly. Now you know what deeply relaxed is. Your body remembers what it feels like, and you can go back to it more easily.

RELAXATION AND MEDITATION

Take your time to practice these relaxation methods that involve learning to relax the body first more quickly and then more deeply. The next step is to put the two together so that in one simple process we can relax both quickly and deeply. For many people this does become almost like flicking a switch, as described. We sit down to meditate and simply let go, returning to that deeply relaxed state.

For others, however, it may continue to be helpful (even necessary) to use a slower and more methodical technique like the PMR, the Relaxing Body Scan or Rapid Relaxation. Experience tells us that most people derive great benefit from taking the time to learn and experiment with a number of relaxation options. At different times in your life, even just from one day to the next, different techniques may be more or less helpful, and you will benefit from developing a range of relaxation techniques that can be used as the situation requires. Learning and practicing the relaxation techniques described above is probably all you need to do to cater to your differing needs.

What our experience tells us is that each time you meditate, you will derive great benefit by consciously relaxing your body first. What this means is that on a day when you are already fairly relaxed and calm, maybe you will just sit and relax without employing a particular technique. Just like throwing the switch, remember how your body feels when it is deeply relaxed, and simply let go. There is very little you need to do in such circumstances. Just let go and be still. On another day—perhaps you have been working hard in the garden, or feeling pressured at work—you sit to meditate, your body is restless and your mind is all over the place. In this situation it may work best to do the whole PMR again. Do it quite formally, concentrate on the words you say to yourself, perhaps use a guided CD, focus on the feeling in your body, and as you contract and relax the muscles, steadily let go of the tension and anxiety of the day, relaxing your body and settling your mind.

With a little practice and experience you will know what is needed. Just as you automatically adjust your driving to suit a four-lane highway or a narrow, windy dirt road, you will know on a given day whether to relax quickly or more thoroughly. Again, the aim is to consciously relax your body so that your body supports your meditation and also contributes to relaxing your mind.

RELAXATION IN DAILY LIFE

Now we need to learn how to take this feeling of deep relaxation into our daily life. In addition to learning to relax as a lead-in to meditation, it is also of great value to be relaxed throughout each day, and throughout the ups and downs of life.

The starting point is recognizing the value of being calm and relaxed, realizing what this actually means and that it is actually possible. Some people think being "relaxed" is the same as being slack—lying about, lazy, indifferent, unmotivated, dull, uninvolved. This is a real misunderstanding. The best practical definition of relaxation is using the minimum amount of energy possible for whatever you are doing. So someone on holiday may relax by lying under a coconut palm, while a hundred-meter sprinter may relax while expending a tremendous amount of energy while running. Businesspersons may be relaxed while remaining passionate about what they are doing, and while being efficient and having a high output.

Relaxation is also a key element of mindfulness. For some people it may seem to be a paradox, but a little reflection reveals the truth of this: to be mindful is to be relaxed and alert. A practical example of this is the ideal state of mind in which to drive a car. To be physically relaxed while driving, with no excess muscular tension, while at the same time being mentally alert, aware and mindful, is to drive very safely. There is nothing slack, dangerous or dull about it. This is the key to safe and skillful driving.

The automatic benefits of regular practice

The fact is that regular sessions of meditation reliably and automatically lead to relaxation and mindfulness. Particularly when you use our preferred method of Mindfulness-Based Stillness Meditation, you are actually training yourself very specifically to develop these qualities. You are learning to relax physically and you are learning to develop mindfulness. So naturally the benefits of your learning and practice flow on automatically into your daily life. This is why regular practice is recommended—you might like to think of your time in formal meditation practice as creating a positive "hangover." After your meditation you feel more relaxed, and you are more calm and mindful. These qualities stay with you for a while as you go about your day, and then you meditate again, and soon you have a positive snowballing effect as the benefits steadily accumulate.

For many, this automatic flow-on effect is enough, but for some, a more structured approach to integration may also be useful.

Training in relaxation and mindfulness

Throughout the day, remember to relax and be mindful. Many find it useful to use "triggers" to prompt them. Red traffic lights are excellent for this. Many people with an untrained mind stop at red lights and practice getting stressed! Instead, learn to stop, consciously feel the body relax and consciously practice mindfulness by bringing your attention into the present moment. Remember to be relaxed and mindful: to be alert, calm and engaged. Another great opportunity is before each meal. Sit, be grateful for the meal, say grace if you choose, and then check in with your body and mind. Feel the relaxation, be present.

These simple reminders throughout the day are very easy but profoundly effective. With just a little regular practice you will soon establish a habit that can have extraordinary benefit. Once relaxation and mindfulness become a part of your day, good health, healing and well-being are highly likely to follow.

Before we move on to explore mindfulness in greater detail, we will look at more ways to calm and relax the mind.

RELAXING THE MIND

So far we have given most of our attention to relaxing the body. This is the logical place to start, but now we need to consider how we then relax the mind. By relaxing the mind we mean letting go of stress and anxiety, and developing inner peace and calm. This relaxation of the mind is a simple, natural state. It has nothing to do with some profound mystical experience or altered state of consciousness. Just a simple, relaxed mind. A mind at rest, a mind in a state of natural ease.

There are three ways that reliably lead to a calm mind.

1. Simply letting go

This is the direct approach, where we just relax the mind and allow it to find its own natural ease. We let go of thinking, reacting, judging. We just allow our mind to be.

When the mind is busy and full of thoughts it can be likened to a glass full of muddy water. If we continue to think, to agitate, to cogitate, it is like swirling your finger around in that glass of muddy water: you just get more muddy water. However, if you put down a glass of muddy water and leave it undisturbed, the mud settles to the bottom and the water clears. Just as the water left undisturbed becomes clear, so too does the mind. Now, while this is true, for many beginners it is really difficult to simply leave the mind undisturbed and allow it to settle naturally. Many of us benefit from the extra help that comes from using one or more of the following reliable methods.

2. Concentration

Concentration involves focusing our attention on just one thing. The more completely we are able to do this, the less room there is for other thoughts and distractions. Particularly if you have been stressed or anxious, or if your head is full of a jumble of thoughts and emotions, concentration is a really useful way of focusing the mind, effectively cutting through any distractions and bringing it to a point of peace and calm.

3. Mindfulness

While mindfulness is covered in more detail in the later chapters, it warrants another mention in this context. By paying attention to our present moment experience, deliberately and nonjudgmentally, we take the reaction out of our thoughts. This defuses worries, fears and anxiety, and leads directly to a calm mind.

Concentration, mindfulness and relaxation

There is a beautiful synergy between relaxing the body and calming the mind. The more we relax the body, the more that relaxation flows on to calm the mind. The more we calm the mind, the more the mind sends out messages that relax the body. Therefore, when we bring concentration and mindfulness to the process of relaxing the body, this synergy leads to profound relaxation of both the body and the mind.

By concentrating on the feeling of relaxation in the body, it is as if we become absorbed in the feeling of relaxation itself. As we feel the body relax, the mind goes with it. The relaxation of the body flows into the mind. Our body is relaxed. Our mind is relaxed. And we simply rest in that feeling of relaxation.

Relaxing mindfully, we simply take an open, curious interest in the feeling of relaxation. We let go of any judgment or reaction and the mind is at ease. No stress. No anxiety. Just natural ease. So you see, this is how we can use a simple exercise like the PMR or the Relaxing Body Scan to go beyond basic relaxation into meditation. We do the exercises with concentration and mindfulness.

In our experience this approach works well for many people. In fact, when Ian first started to teach meditation, this was all he taught.

Many people reported developing a deep awareness of relaxation in both the body and the mind, and were satisfied with this as a reliable technique for meditation. However, our more recent experience highlights the benefit of developing the next two steps of Mindfulness-Based Stillness Meditation. There is real value in learning more about mindfulness and stillness.

STEP 3

MINDFULNESS

CHAPTER 5

MINDFULNESS OF BREATH

Why not wake up this morning?
—RUMI

The first two steps of Mindfulness-Based Stillness Meditation (MBSM), preparation and relaxation, can take as long as fifteen to twenty minutes if the Progressive Muscle Relaxation (PMR) is done completely, or as short as three to five minutes if the Rapid Relaxation exercise is used. In either case, preparation and relaxation lead naturally to the practice of mindfulness.

WAKING UP TO LIFE

Mindfulness is the ability to notice and pay attention to what is actually happening around and inside of us at each moment. Mindfulness is like waking up to life. Have you ever felt that you are moving through your life almost like a sleepwalker? When we fall into mindlessness our days can become a blur. Instead of noticing the rich variety of colors in life, a mindless life becomes beige. In a mindless state we notice less and take so much for granted. Do you ever take time to enjoy the simple pleasures of everyday life? The warmth of the sun, a child's laughter, a friendly smile, a small act of kindness, a refreshing shower, a soft breeze, a delicate flower? With the practice of mindfulness, we come to our senses and start to actually show up in our own life. Mindfulness meditation is the practice of waking up to the present moment by paying attention to the here and now.

The meditative paths of the various traditions of Buddhism, the yogic traditions and several others have established the practice of mindfulness meditation over many centuries. Mindfulness develops attention, concentration and the ability to simply be present with little or no future orientation, past orientation or goal orientation—choosing to be a human *being* rather than a human *doing*.

Mindfulness meditation cultivates a state of awareness that is less dominated by thinking, less stimulated by imagination and memory, less active, and more open, receptive and in touch with the aspects of one's experience that are here and now. Mindfulness practice slows down the forward projection of the thinking mind, which is overly committed to achieving, getting, having, holding and protecting. Mindfulness practice slows down the momentum of the ego or the personality, and allows contact with a deeper, stiller, quieter part of one's true nature.

Through this practice, the meditator steps off the treadmill of chasing dreams and running from nightmares. They put down the masks and roles in the drama of life. Rather than going somewhere to be someone and attain something, the meditator just listens, watches, feels and pays attention to present moment experience. Effortlessly, the dreams and dramas become less important and less addictive.

These simple words by Michael Leunig beautifully describe a mindful life:

God help us to live slowly
To move simply
To look softly
To allow emptiness
To let the Heart create for us
Amen.

We will begin the practice of mindfulness in this chapter with a narrow focus of attention through the technique of Mindfulness of Breath. In chapters 7–13 we develop a more open, inclusive practice of mindfulness, which leads into stillness. This open, inclusive practice, which includes mindfulness of the breath, body, emotions and thoughts, is a complete approach that has many benefits. We will describe those benefits in some detail in later chapters, yet the simple, narrow focus of Mindfulness of Breath in itself can take you directly into stillness.

MINDFULNESS OF BREATH

The most basic, yet possibly the most profound, mindfulness technique for meditation is paying attention to the experience of breathing. Across the various meditation traditions, this may well be the most widely practiced of all meditation techniques.

Mindfulness of Breath is practiced by continually focusing our attention on the breath and simply bringing our attention back to the breath each and every time it wanders. There is no need to change, deepen or improve the breathing pattern; simply pay attention to the breathing as it is. This is a mindfulness practice, not a breathing exercise. The aim is to be aware of the feeling of the breath rather than controlling it in some way or trying to achieve a particular outcome with the breath.

We start by noticing any aspect of the breath. For example, we may notice the air as it moves through the nostrils and over the area above the upper lip, or we may be aware of the feeling of the breath in the chest and abdomen. Perhaps, if we listen closely, we can even hear the subtle sound of our breathing. Attention can be directed to the sensations of warmth or coolness, or movement as the air touches the nostrils, or we could direct the attention toward the movements of the chest and tummy. Or our attention can be inclusive of both areas. We can notice the beginning of the inhalation, then the middle and finally the end of the inhalation. We can notice a gradual feeling of filling and rising as we inhale. As we hold our attention more particularly on the breath we may notice a slight, effortless pause between the end of the inhalation and the beginning of the exhalation. Then we notice the beginning, the middle and the end of the exhalation. We can notice a gradual feeling of sinking or emptying as we exhale. We may notice another effortless pause at the end of the exhalation prior to the next inhalation.

One-pointedness

By continuing to bring our attention back to the feeling of the breath and then learning to hold our attention on the breath, we are developing *samadhi*, a Sanskrit word meaning "one-pointedness." Samadhi is produced by concentration, and when applied to the breath, it creates presence—the ability to dwell more in the experience of the present moment and be less distracted by thoughts.

Remember, we do not try to change the breath. It may change naturally, commonly becoming softer, slower or deeper, but we just pay attention to the breath without judging it, without controlling it and without expecting any particular outcome other than a fuller experience of each breath. Give up the struggle to achieve anything or get anywhere, and just be with the breath. Observe what becomes obvious, that we cannot breathe in the future, nor can we breathe in the past. Try it and see! The breath is always flowing *now*, and by being mindful of the breath our attention gradually rests more and more in the present moment.

Mindfulness of Breath can be a stand-alone practice or it can be integrated into the complete practice of Mindfulness-Based Stillness Meditation. For beginners on the path of meditation, Mindfulness of Breath is a wonderful introduction to the profound benefits of mindfulness.

Here, then, is the formal exercise with which you can practice and develop Mindfulness of Breath as the focus of attention. When beginning, practice for five to fifteen minutes to establish familiarity and ease with the technique.

Take a moment to adjust your position . . . gently close your eyes and settle into your body. . . . If you are sitting, ensure your body is as upright and open as is comfortable for you. . . . If you are lying down, lie in a balanced and symmetrical way.

Now, in your own way, take a few moments to relax your body. . . . Perhaps feel the muscles softening and loosening . . . relaxing and releasing . . . just simply letting go. . . . Perhaps taking a deeper breath or two helps . . . and as you breathe out, notice that natural feeling of relaxing and releasing a little more with each out breath . . . just simply letting go.

With your eyes gently closed, become aware of the space before your eyes . . . like a field of darkness . . . perhaps there are some muted shapes or colors . . . just simply rest your attention there.

Now pay attention to any sounds outside the room . . . just listening . . . with a gentle curiosity. . . . Let the sounds come and go . . . no need to judge. . . . Now notice any sounds that may be coming from inside the room. . . . Now the sound of your own breathing . . . even if very soft . . . just listening.

As you bring your awareness to your breath, notice what sensations there are as you breathe in . . . and as you breathe out. . . . Feel the air touch your nostrils. . . . Feel the slight movement of your chest and your tummy. . . . Listen to the gentle sound of your own breathing. . . . Allow your breath to take up whatever rhythm feels natural for you at the moment . . . quite effortlessly.

If you notice your attention wandering or becoming distracted . . . simply bring your attention back to the next breath . . . being aware of this breath . . . and this breath . . . being aware of what it is to be breathing in . . . and breathing out . . . simply being with the breath . . . aware of the breath.

Boredom, restlessness and impatience

These are the three most common forms of resistance to the practice of mindfulness. They are natural withdrawal symptoms from stimulation-addiction and excess thinking. In a way, they represent the thinking mind's attempts to hold on, to create a problem and thereby to generate more drama and stimulation even while meditating. Slowing down and just being present gives the thinking mind little to do, and initially this can be an unfamiliar and uncomfortable experience. The withdrawal symptoms from being busy, being stimulated, planning and worrying are similar to the withdrawal symptoms when giving up coffee or sugar. But with patience and by persevering with the mindfulness practice, boredom, restlessness and impatience are gradually transformed into feelings of peace and spaciousness.

John, an avid sportsman and gym fanatic, came to an eight-week MBSM course with high expectations of "mastering" meditation and attaining instant success. However, he found it very difficult to even sit still; he had a nervous habit of constantly jiggling his legs up and down, a common form of restlessness. The movement of his thoughts matched his restless legs.

After two sessions John came to Paul and told him he wanted to drop out of the class, saying, "I just can't do it—it's impossible for me to sit still!" Paul reassured him that his restlessness was very common and not a problem. He told John about another young man who came to the eight-week course suffering from Tourette's syndrome, which caused him to twitch and convulse wildly many times during a meditation session. The young man with Tourette's was so used to his twitching it did not bother him and he was able to meditate deeply even in the midst of a spasm. John's competitive nature clicked in and he decided to continue with the course, but he was encouraged to be more kind and patient with himself.

John was advised to meditate on the restless feelings, to notice them "with a gentle curiosity" and not to fight or suppress them but just to watch. He began to watch himself without self-criticism. This was quite an amazing breakthrough for John! In just a few more weeks he was sitting comfortably. His restlessness had reduced substantially and, more important, he was now at ease with himself. John was beginning to experience the peace he was seeking.

If any of these uncomfortable feelings arise, just accept the boredom and restlessness; accept them as physical and emotional withdrawal symptoms. Be careful not to buy into thoughts such as "I can't do this, it's too hard!" and "This is stupid and I'm not getting anywhere!" and "If only these thoughts and feelings would go away, then I could meditate!" If this type of thinking arises, do not take the thoughts too seriously, accept any uncomfortable feelings and, whenever possible, simply shift as much attention as you can back to your breathing. Notice the next breath. The old habits of being judgmental (of yourself, the technique or your teacher) and of being goal-oriented are attempting to dominate your attention. Notice the next breath.

We will go further into dealing with feelings of boredom and restlessness in chapter 9, which describes the practice of Mindfulness of Emotions.

Sleepiness and mindfulness

If you find yourself frequently becoming sleepy when you meditate, this may well be another form of resistance to simply being in the present moment. It is almost as if we have an on/off switch in our brain and nervous system: when we are busy worrying, judging and planning, the switch is in the on position; when there is nothing to plan, judge or worry about, the switch goes to off and we fall asleep. Through the practice of mindfulness, we are training the mind to be awake and alert when there are no problems to solve or goals to achieve—so we can just *be* and enjoy peace, quiet and simple, present moment pleasures. We are replacing the on/off switch with a dimmer switch, so we can dim the lights but someone is still at home. We lower the level of stimulation but we are still awake.

Here are a few tips to help move through sleepiness while meditating:

1. Do not be too hard on yourself. If you are really tired, stop meditating and have a rest.
2. Adjust your posture. If, as a result of sleepiness, your posture has collapsed, then gently make your posture more upright along the spine and more open across your chest.
3. Make your breathing a little stronger. In particular, slightly emphasize the in breath.
4. Open your eyes and, with a soft gaze, look directly ahead of you without focusing on anything in particular, and continue with the meditation.
5. Make your posture a little more challenging, a little more uncomfortable, as we discussed in chapter 2.

Lightening up

Possibly the most common obstacles to mindfulness practice are trying too hard and being too serious. Often underlying these habits is the agenda of practicing Mindfulness of Breath in order to achieve an imagined outcome such as bliss, no-thought, deep relaxation and so on. This agenda generates expectations of where you would like to be and judgments of where you are.

Anne, a university student, came to a residential meditation retreat hoping that meditation would help her with anxiety. For her, learning to meditate was really important as her anxiety was affecting her university results. She took the meditation practice very seriously, just as she did her studies. With this attitude of urgency she tried too hard to meditate, and as a result she actually noticed herself becoming more anxious when she started meditating. When she came to ask what she was doing wrong she was encouraged to have a subtle smile on her lips when meditating, to notice any feelings of anxiety but to continue with the subtle smile and to lighten up, to enjoy the feeling of each breath. With some practice Anne learned how to be more accepting of her feelings and more gentle with herself. With more lightness, her anxiety decreased to a level at which she could function well in her university studies, and her results steadily improved.

Remember, with mindfulness, you are not trying to change the contents of your awareness—your thoughts, feelings and sensations. Rather you are simply and profoundly changing your attitude to the contents of your awareness. You are cultivating an attitude of acceptance by "just watching" what comes into your awareness. So nothing has to change. There is nowhere to go, nothing to do; just the choice to be present and, wherever possible, to return your attention to the next breath.

As an antidote to seriousness while meditating, we often suggest adopting a gentle smile by very subtly lifting the corners of the mouth and eyes—an imperceptible smile. Such a smile will instantly release seriousness and bring a degree of effortlessness and lightness to the practice. Expectations bring judgment, frustration and heaviness in their wake. Lighten up and pay attention to the simplicity of the breath, without trying to get somewhere else.

Surrendering to the breath

Mindfulness of Breath is much more than a mechanistic concentration exercise. The breath is simple, the breath is present and the breath is true. The breath is very real and something we can easily focus on in this present moment. After all, everything other than this present moment is just memory or imagination. The breath has existential truth (no imagination), and by "surrendering" to the breath we are aligning ourselves with this existential truth, and letting go of subjective hopes, wishes, dreams, expectations and judgments while we practice. The grandiosity of the goal-oriented thinking mind may seek to attain "great heights of spiritual attainment," but simple breath awareness can cultivate humility, patience and presence. "Surrendering" to each breath is like savoring each breath, giving it full attention or, as Sogyal Rinpoche describes the intention of Mindfulness of Breath, becoming the breath.

The Three Goodwills

Perhaps the deepest resistance to Mindfulness of Breath is the effort to control the meditation, or trying to "do" meditation. This common attitude of beginners often results in attempts to change or improve the meditation with "add-ons" or adjustments to make it more effective or productive. The antidote to this form of resistance is simple humility: notice the thinking mind judging, planning and controlling, and then simply bring as much attention as possible back to the next breath. The practice of this kind of humility in mindfulness meditation is supported by learning the following skillful choice, the Three Goodwills. Paul was taught the Three Goodwills by Lama Thubten Yeshe. They are:

1. Bring goodwill to your meditation teachers.
2. Bring goodwill to the meditation practice—do not try to change, improve or adjust it; keep it simple and "surrender" to its simplicity.
3. Bring goodwill to yourself—do not judge yourself or create high expectations and goals. Be patient and kind and gently persevere.

When the Three Goodwills are practiced with your meditation, meditation becomes just like a dear friend:

- You love spending time with it.
- You give it your full, loving attention.
- You cherish every meeting.
- You treat it with respect and reverence.

In this way, meditation ceases to be a chore or a discipline and becomes, instead, a blessed and special time.

A focus on simplicity

In our own practice, we have both encountered all of these obstacles and forms of resistance to meditation, and still do at times. Nowadays we can recognize when we are hoping for something to happen, or when we are taking ourselves too seriously or judging our experience. We can feel when we are beginning to struggle to achieve something, and then we simply smile and notice the next breath. By simply choosing to come back to the breath, effort and struggle subside. Awareness becomes more expansive and light. There is a moment of peace.

Whenever the thinking mind creates problems and complexity, just choose to keep it simple.

Creating spaciousness

Boredom, restlessness and impatience can actually be signs that the mindfulness meditation is working and doing its job. Instead of keeping ourselves busy and stimulated, mindfulness reveals any underlying restlessness so that it can be accepted, acknowledged and healed.

Other emotions like sadness, grief, fear or anger may also arise spontaneously as you meditate. One of Paul's teachers used to refer to meditation as "creating a space for grace"; it could equally be called "creating a space for healing." When we do less, interfering less with our natural processes, whatever needs to be healed can gradually emerge.

As you practice mindfulness, sometimes old memories may arise or emotions may come forward that have been held back for a long time. Some meditation students have reported tears rolling down their cheeks for no apparent reason. Others have reported memories arising during meditation that "come from nowhere."

Just allow emotions or memories to come and go naturally, if and when they arise. A gradual and natural unwinding happens from the inside once we get out of our own way. The aim is to accept any memories that arise and any emotions that may happen to emerge; just let them be present. There is no need to analyze what is happening, just let it come and be welcomed into the present moment. When you can, return your attention to the next breath, without denying or indulging any feelings.

TIME FOR PRACTICE

We are often asked, how long should a session last? This is a good time to expand on what has already been said, for two reasons:

1. The quality and consistency of the meditation is more important than quantity of time in any one session.
2. Everyone is different: some people need more structure and discipline in their lives, where others need more gentleness and kindness.

As part of the complete MBSM, the narrow focus of Mindfulness of Breath is practiced for a few minutes at the beginning of the meditation, and then the attention is opened to include breath, body, emotions and thoughts. We will explore this in later chapters.

To develop Mindfulness of Breath by itself, start with sessions of five to fifteen minutes and grow your practice from there. Once you become reasonably comfortable with a short session of five to fifteen minutes, then you can increase the length of the session to twenty to thirty minutes, or even longer. Short sessions have great benefits; longer sessions allow you to sink more deeply into the mindfulness practice. Longer sessions will gradually give you a fuller experience of letting go of doing, of controlling, of hoping, of expecting and of judging and, therefore, a deeper experience of stillness. When you have gained the experience of longer sessions, your shorter sessions will also benefit.

Mindfulness of Breath should not be a rigid discipline; one definition of "discipline" describes it as "the undesirable imposed on the unwilling." A much better definition of discipline is the one we have given already—that of a personal kindness. We know what we want and out of kindness to ourselves, we do what is in our own best interests. Meditation needs to be seen more as a delight than an imposition.

For the therapeutic and healing benefits of meditation, particularly when dealing with a major illness, we recommend consistent practice of longer sessions of forty minutes, even sixty minutes, two or three times each day.

VARIATIONS ON MINDFULNESS OF BREATH

The three most common variations on Mindfulness of Breath are:

1. counting the breath;
2. naming the breath; and
3. naming the thoughts.

1. Counting the breath

For some meditation beginners, the feeling of the unforced breathing may be either too subtle or too simple to hold their attention. Using numbers and counting creates a stronger focus for their attention. Men in particular seem to find counting the breath easier to practice as it is more active, meaning that instead of simply noticing the feeling of the breath, counting the breath assigns each breath a number. As you breathe in, say the number "one" in your mind; as you breathe out, mentally repeat the number "one." On the next inhalation, say the number "two" in your mind; on the exhalation, repeat the number "two." Or you may choose to count the breath just one way, as it comes in or goes out. Continue the counting until you reach ten, and then start again from one.

One downside to this practice is that it tends to localize the attention in the head rather than following the breath down into the body. The benefit of Mindfulness of Breath is that attention moves down into the core of your being—your chest and tummy. Counting the breath also tends to focus attention on words and concepts, which is similar to the habit of excessive thinking. In addition, because numbers are linear and sequential, counting can stimulate goal orientation, causing you to try too hard. If counting the breath is used, we suggest that it is best at the beginning of the meditation—perhaps for five minutes—to settle and focus the mind. After this initial phase, the counting can cease and attention move to Mindfulness of Breath.

If you get caught up in thinking, either notice and let go of the thoughts, or return to the counting again.

2. Naming the breath

In this variation, the mind assigns words to the process of breathing. On the inhalation, you might say in your mind, "Breathing in" or "Rising"; and on the exhalation, "Breathing out" or "Falling." This technique has the same benefit as counting the breath in that it creates a stronger mental focus for attention. However, words are slightly more descriptive and less abstract than numbers, so they can bring the meditator closer to the actual experience of the breath. Also, the words describe a more circular and repetitive process, as opposed to the linear and sequential process of counting. Therefore, we have found them less likely to stimulate goal orientation and excessive effort. Nonetheless, the words are still active and tend to trigger the thinking mind, whereas simple mindfulness is a more passive process of pure observation. Again, we suggest that naming the breath be used in the first five minutes of meditation and then ceased so that attention can be moved directly to the breath.

3. Naming the thoughts

This is a technique that helps meditators to detach themselves from a particular distracting stream of thought by naming it. For example, while practicing Mindfulness of Breath, you may notice that your thinking mind has drifted into thoughts about preparing the evening meal. As you become aware of the thoughts, you can name them by simply saying in the mind, "Planning, planning" or "Worrying, worrying," and then open your awareness to include the Mindfulness of Breath again. Or, if you noticed thoughts of self-criticism, simply name them by saying in your mind, "Judging, judging" or "Criticizing, criticizing," and then open your awareness to include Mindfulness of Breath again.

With this technique, once the thoughts are named, then no further analysis or judgment is entered into; just return your attention to the breath. Naming the thought can be an extremely useful way to understand the incessant and addictive nature of excessive thinking. It also enables the meditator to identify repetitive patterns of thinking and, therefore, to not take them too seriously. The "monkey mind" is clearly identified in all its seductive guises. As such, naming the thought is a very valuable variation on Mindfulness of Breath. It does have some negative potential to stimulate thought and self-analysis, but if that trap is avoided it can be a useful tool for detachment from compelling thoughts.

Again, we would recommend that it be used in the first five minutes of meditation and then ceased as attention is returned to simple Mindfulness of Breath. If, at any time during meditation, thoughts become strong and compelling, making it difficult to return to the breath, naming the thought can be reintroduced.

CHAPTER 6

HABITS OF THINKING
AND AWARENESS

As you become more mindful of your breathing, you will find
you become more present, gather all your scattered aspects
back into yourself and become whole.
—SOGYAL RINPOCHE

Mindfulness is a simple technique for changing unhelpful habits of thinking and attention. As we have been discussing already, the problem is that these old habits of thinking can be unnecessarily reactive, defensive and judgmental on the one hand, and are a distraction from facing present moment reality on the other.

Do you ever find yourself being too quick to judge without really knowing the whole story of what has happened? Reverting to a knee-jerk reaction instead of a more patient and compassionate approach? Buddhist philosophy would explain these habits of thinking as being driven by craving and aversion, desire and fear, or running toward some imagined future happiness and success, and away from perceived suffering and failure. In either case, craving and aversion keep us running. Through the practice of mindfulness, we choose to stop "running," anticipating and planning, and instead pay attention to what is around us and inside us right here and now. In this way, mindfulness creates a deepening self-acceptance, self-esteem and self-love, and with these qualities comes more inner peace.

To further appreciate the impact of mindfulness, it is helpful to understand the nature of the stress response and the relaxation response.

STRESS AND THE "EMERGENCY MODE"

The stress response is triggered when we perceive or interpret a situation as being a threat or a challenge. The threat may be real or imagined. The challenge may be paying off a big mortgage, or wanting to be liked and accepted by your work colleagues, or trying to change your partner's behavior, or working a sixty-hour week. Many challenges are created by excessive craving and aversion; many are the result of old emotional wounds and self-doubt.

Whatever the cause, once we have interpreted it as a threat, the part of the brain called the hypothalamus sends signals to the master gland, the pituitary, to stimulate biochemicals that are then released into the bloodstream and travel to where they stimulate the adrenal glands. These glands in turn release stress hormones into the bloodstream. In this process, the sympathetic nervous system is activated, which assists stress hormones to raise the metabolic rate, thus elevating blood sugar levels, increasing the heart rate and mobilizing energy to deal with the perceived challenge. When the sympathetic nervous system dominates, thinking becomes fear-based and/or goal-oriented; craving and aversion are activated and the "running" begins.

Gearing up for a challenge and tightening up to face a threat are normal and healthy functions of the survival instinct. However, these stress mechanisms are designed to be used in the short term and then switched off, allowing the relaxation response to take over and balance to be restored. Prolonged activation of the stress response, out of habit or lack of awareness, makes us sick and unhappy: we suffer. Chronic tension without sufficient rest gradually breaks down our mind, our emotions and our body.

In contemporary society, for many the stress response has become both an addiction and a way of life. An addiction to stimulation, control, struggle and "drama." Instead of switching off the stress response, it is indulged to the extent that it becomes a source of energy and hyped-up motivation as well as becoming tied into our sense of personal identity. We overuse it.

Steven, a psychiatric nurse with prostate cancer, told an all-male support group that he would find it very difficult to change his sixty-hour work week to make time for self-healing. He revealed to the group that he experienced such a "buzz" from dealing with very difficult psychiatric emergency cases, and he was so good at it, that he could only imagine life without work as boring. Even though Steven was dealing with a quite advanced cancer that required his full commitment, he still found it hard to contemplate life with less work. His work was his life but he realized it could have been his death had he not relented.

The stress response is also often deployed as a defense mechanism aimed at protecting old wounds and insecurities. For others, stress is a form of social conditioning—the drive to achieve, attain, possess and succeed. Apart from acute bouts of stress often triggered by the demands of external circumstances, many people suffer from chronic, low-grade stress that is often self-created and self-perpetuating. In many ways, being "hyped up" and constantly busy are glorified attributes in our society, reinforced by packaged and fast foods, sensationalist media and materialistic priorities. If we are not busy and driven, we are bored and listless. We avoid downtime, free time and alone time, and time to chill out, unwind and enjoy moments of peace. Chronically operating in the stress response has been described as being stuck in "emergency mode" whether the emergency is warranted or not.

The impact of stress

As we look at the specific aspects of "emergency mode," the link with chronic disease and poor physical, emotional and mental health should become obvious. Prolonged emergency mode is associated with the following effects on mind, body and spirit:

- a contracted and tense body—as adrenaline flows into the muscles they contract in readiness for action;

- shallow, faster breathing patterns—more costal (rib cage) breathing, less slow and deep diaphragmatic (abdominal) breathing;
- more anaerobic metabolism—cells and tissues are less oxygenated, resulting in more acidic waste products of metabolism;
- a more acidic internal environment for cells and tissues;
- elevated cholesterol and sugar levels in the blood;
- elevated heart rate and blood pressure;
- an imbalanced immune system—either hyperactive (more prone to inflammation, allergies and autoimmune diseases) or hypoactive (more prone to infections and tumor growth);
- suppressed digestion and elimination—digestive enzymes and acids are released inappropriately, causing nutrient deficiencies, digestive upsets and ulcers. Decrease in peristalsis and sluggish movement through the bowel causing constipation and increased absorption of toxins into the bloodstream; and
- poor lymphatic drainage.

The psychological changes associated with stress include the following:

- hyperactive and excessive thinking, which is fear-based and "problem-saturated" or excessively goal-oriented, as opposed to creative and holistic thinking, which takes in the big picture;
- anxiety—caused by a hyperactive "threat detector";
- aggression and excessive competitiveness;
- social isolation and loneliness—excessive internalization or suppression of emotions coupled with poor communication;
- disconnection and desensitization—getting out of touch with one's needs, feelings and instincts. Also getting out of touch with other people and nature;
- lack of empathy and compassion for self, others and the natural world; and
- rigidity/inflexibility of body, emotions and mind (fight response), or collapse and despair (flight response).

In prolonged emergency mode, the body–mind shuts down or slows down the following essential life-promoting functions:

- nourishment—from food and relationships (that is, we are not open to receive);
- healing—physical and emotional healing are put on hold as we move into a coping pattern;
- digestion—we do not fully absorb nutrients from our food, nor do we take the time to digest and integrate the lessons of everyday life; and
- detoxification and letting go of the past—we contract, hold on, control, defend, push forward and lose the ability to release and let go.

The benefits of the relaxation response

Our health and well-being depend on the flexibility to use the stress response when needed, but also to be able to switch it off when it is not. Think for a moment about what most drives and motivates you in your life. Survival? Happiness? Possessions? Status? Love? As human beings, there are two significant drives or instincts: the need for safety/protection and the need for growth. The stress response fulfills the need to protect ourselves and to fight for survival. The relaxation response allows us to put down our defenses, to slow down and to open up. It enables us to heal and grow and be happy.

Regular access to the relaxation response is associated with many positive effects. The physical benefits of the relaxation response include:

- a more relaxed body
- a slower, deeper breathing pattern
- more aerobic metabolism, and therefore, more oxygenated cells and tissues and more energy
- a more alkaline internal environment for all cells and tissues
- lower cholesterol and sugar levels in the blood
- lower heart rate and blood pressure

- a balanced and responsive immune system that detects and responds to foreign, unwanted and toxic pathogens
- improved digestion, absorption of nutrients and elimination of wastes and toxins
- improved lymphatic drainage

The psychological benefits of the relaxation response include:

- a balance between thinking and feeling
- more creative and intuitive thinking, and a generally more holistic approach to life
- less anxiety as the "threat detector" relaxes
- less panic, more confidence and ease in a wide range of situations
- less aggression, less defensiveness and fewer controlling behaviors
- more empathy and compassion for self and others
- better connection with our needs and feelings
- the ability to connect more with others and the natural world
- more flexibility and resilience, and the ability to trust and "go with the flow" when appropriate

The relaxation response facilitates growth by enabling us to open up emotionally, to interact, to give and receive, to listen, to be present and available, to heal, to let go of what is not needed, to be more spontaneous and less serious, and to have fun. Mindfulness meditation is a powerful tool for breaking the habit and addiction to the stress response, and accessing the benefits of the relaxation response.

It is understandable then that as the demands and pressures of our contemporary world are "hooking" more people more deeply into the stress response, many are looking to meditation as a healing antidote.

MINDFULNESS AND THE THINKING MIND

We will describe the method for Mindfulness of Breath in some detail as this understanding will become the basis for all the mindfulness practices.

Mindfulness of Breath is simple but not easy. It challenges the old habits of the "monkey mind." Monkeys tend to nibble on something, get distracted, drop what they are nibbling on, grab something else and then nibble on that. The monkey mind is the type of thinking that is hyperactive and distracted; it wanders and jumps from one thought to another and follows any old thought that pops up. Monkey mind is not the kind of creative thinking that leads to decision-making and appropriate action—it is filled with what-ifs ("What will I do if that happens?") and if-onlys ("If only that would happen, then I would be happy"). Monkey mind is excessive rumination on hopes, wishes, dreams, concerns and worries that habitually recycle through the mind. Or monkey mind can wander to recalling fragments of an old song, rehashing past conversations, replaying scenes from a TV show . . . anything to keep the brain active, stimulated and distracted from the present moment experience.

In his book *Quantum Healing*, Dr. Deepak Chopra quotes a study in which the researchers concluded that the average person thinks approximately 65,000 thoughts per day. The researchers also concluded that about 95 percent of these thoughts are exactly the same thoughts that passed through the mind the day before. Through the practice of mindfulness meditation, the monkey mind is gradually tamed and thinking becomes less hyperactive and compulsive.

For many beginners it can come as a major breakthrough to realize that the monkey mind is not tamed by fighting thoughts or trying to eliminate them; that hope or expectation would only create struggle and, again, trigger the stress response. The old habit of excessive thinking is healed through the application of patience, acceptance and gentle perseverance with mindfulness practice. To understand how to "tame" the habit of excessive thinking it is extremely helpful for the meditator to understand the nature of thinking, and to appreciate the difference between thinking and awareness. Through the practice of mindfulness, the meditator is developing the ability to be more aware; or perhaps, more accurately, the meditator is developing a more open awareness that is less dominated by thinking.

The nature of thinking

Thoughts are ideas, images or concepts in the mind. Take a few moments to close your eyes and think about what you might be doing this weekend. In particular, notice what form the thoughts take. Perhaps you are planning to go to the beach, and in your mind find yourself saying, "I am going to the beach," while seeing images of towels, sand and waves breaking. You might have noticed that your thoughts take the form of words or pictures that may evoke certain feeling associations.

Thinking uses imagination and memory in the form of mental words and pictures. Using memory and imagination involves us in projecting our attention away from our present moment experience. Thinking gives us the ability to focus our attention and speculate on possibilities for the future, or to focus our attention on recalling experiences from the past. More than any other animal, as far as we know, human beings have the ability to abstract our attention from the flow of moment-to-moment felt experience and to entertain ideas about our experience. This ability enables us to shape, structure and in many ways control our experience. We are able to learn from past experience and plan a future.

Used creatively and appropriately, the thinking mind gives us huge potential for growth (a potential we will explore in more detail in chapter 17, "Meditation Using Intention"). However, used habitually and excessively, the thinking mind creates too much control and can act as a defense mechanism, a defense from feeling emotions directly. Some newcomers to meditation initially feel anxious when they start meditating because they find themselves gradually letting go of some of their control and defensiveness. Some even find it challenging just to close their eyes when meditating in a group. However, this unconscious control and defensiveness only serves to prolong the stress response and makes it difficult for us to relax, trust and let go.

Excessive use of memory and imagination also creates the contemporary obsession with time.

Come beloved, and sit at the gate of Nothingness,
God will bring you bread without the taste of bread,

Sweetness without the honey or the bee,
And when the future and past are dissolved
There will only be you, lying senseless like a lute
On the breast of God.

         —Rumi

As we continue to develop our understanding of the mind and the benefits of mindfulness, it is useful to remember that the thinking mind is utilitarian; it is a goal-oriented, problem-solving mechanism. The thinking mind sees everything as a means to an end. The thinking commentary of words and images in the mind is mostly trying to help us to stay alive and then to anticipate and avoid physical, emotional and psychological pain, while we maximize pleasure, comfort and ease. The tools used by the thinking mind to avoid pain and achieve safety and comfort are:

- planning
- judging
- evaluating
- comparing
- analyzing
- interpreting
- labeling/categorizing/naming
- speculating
- anticipating
- remembering

By judging, evaluating and comparing, the thinking mind places a value on our experience. This value falls somewhere along the spectrum of good to bad, right to wrong, like to dislike, agree to disagree, love to hate. "I like my brother," "I don't like my boss," "She's funny, I like her," "He's too serious, I don't like him," "My friend has a good work ethic but his son has a bad one," and so on. The thinking mind often reinforces old values and holds on to old ways of seeing things. Memory assists in holding on to old associations.

Paul will never forget a middle-aged schoolteacher, Anthony, who came for counseling to discuss his "failed marriage." He had only been married for two years but had realized that his wife was too vain, superficial and materialistic for him. His thinking mind had evaluated his wife and found her lacking. He was adamant about his assessment; in fact, he was very self-righteous in the way he criticized her. As he explored this complaint more deeply, it became obvious that Anthony was afraid of commitment and had never had a relationship that lasted longer than two years. His fear then fueled his thinking mind in making the evaluation that he was right, she was wrong; he was good, she was bad.

By analyzing and interpreting, the thinking mind also places a meaning or conclusion on our experience. This meaning comes from the desire to understand and categorize our experience so we can then react in accordance with our interpretation and judgment (for example, "My mother likes my sister more than me," "My boss always thinks he's right," "Football is violent and only for dummies," and so on).

Anthony would watch his wife looking in the mirror as she brushed her hair at night and say to himself, "She is so vain, she loves herself!" If he saw a new dress in the closet he would say to himself, "She's so materialistic, not spiritual like me!" He interpreted nearly everything she did in this judgmental way and always felt justified and righteous. Anthony had become stuck in this story of self-righteousness; mindfulness practice helped him to become unstuck and see himself more honestly. He realized that he was using these judgments of his wife to keep his attention away from his own fears. By acknowledging his fears, he was able to begin the process of healing them.

The thinking mind constantly weaves a story about our experience using interpretations and evaluations. Using memory we hold on to old stories. Then using imagination, we are able to project our attention in time and space away from our present moment experience to other times (remembered or imagined) and other places. We either reflect on the past or speculate on the future. Either way, we are "out of time," not paying attention to what is occurring in the "here and now."

Naming, labeling and categorizing help us to describe, to store and to recall information, and to manipulate ideas in order to form interpretations and judgments (for example, "He's a middle-aged factory worker," "She's a single mother," "He's a rebellious teenager," and so on). The thinking mind does its job by naming, interpreting and analyzing the people and events around us. It creates a commentary and weaves a story.

When we are calm, centered and grounded, and when our needs are met, the commentary is more likely to be accurate, appropriate, flexible, creative and open to growth and change. When we are under low-grade chronic stress, which is like being in "emergency mode," the commentary is more likely to be incessant, judgmental, critical, defensive, controlling, inflexible and reactive. We call this compulsive and reactive thinking "excessive thinking." Excessive thinking arises from stress; it creates and perpetuates stress. Excessive thinking prolongs the emergency mode and makes it a habit and a way of life.

The core components of emergency mode promote:

- *contraction*, physically, emotionally and mentally, for defensiveness and control;
- *projection of attention* away from present moment experience by a hyperactive and hypervigilant thinking mind. This creates excessive memory and a preoccupation with holding on to the past and/or excessive imagination and speculation about the future; and
- *disconnection* of attention from feeling experience; of mind from body; of mind from needs and feelings. This means we do not pay attention to what we are feeling or what we need. We are distracted by excessive mental activity—that is, excessive thinking. Disconnection results in a lack of honest self-reflection and a lack of compassionate self-monitoring. This means we lose the capacity to listen to our own real needs, instincts, intuition and impulses. Feelings become held in the unconscious mind and stored in the body in the form of contraction and defensiveness.

EXCESSIVE THINKING

Angelica, a woman in her mid-thirties, came for counseling because she was feeling "trapped" and frustrated with her life. She had given up work as an interior decorator eight years ago to embrace motherhood. She had become a chronic worrier and was tormented by her own "excessive thinking." She worried about being good enough as a mother, and she worried about her children's schooling and their future. She wanted to resume her career but worried about having the ability to return to the workforce. Her confidence was low or lacking. She worried about her husband's disapproval of her returning to work, so she never dared to discuss it with him. She also worried about the family finances, as her husband, Michael, had a fairly low-paying job, but she was also concerned that talking about their financial situation would upset him.

Angelica loved her husband and her children, but her anxiety and frustration were beginning to turn to resentment and despair. Her excessive thinking took the form of excess imagination and excess analysis, which led to passivity and procrastination. Too much analysis creates paralysis! It was commendable that she made the decision to seek some help.

In contrast, Angelica's husband was an easygoing man who rarely worried. He did not have to, she did enough worrying for both of them! Through the counseling process Angelica became aware of her habit of catastrophizing, so she decided to challenge her worries. First, she decided to talk to Michael about how she was feeling and her wish to return to work. After she spoke to Michael, he told her how relieved he was that she was seeing a counselor; he had been concerned about her obvious unhappiness. He was also supportive of her return to interior decorating and would do whatever he could to assist her.

Angelica began to realize that most of her stress was self-created. As she began to practice mindfulness meditation she became more aware of her excessive thinking habits and was able to free herself from them. As time went on, and she practiced more, she reported that she could see more possibilities and opportunities in her life rather than feeling like a victim of her circumstances. She reported that her confidence in herself had grown enormously, not just because she had returned to work, but because she felt able to listen to and respect herself.

Excessive thinking, as a component of the stress response, is rarely creative thinking. More commonly it is driven by craving (or desire) and aversion (or fear), and is often aggressive or defensive in nature. Excessive thinking loves to "attack" problems and anything or anyone that either creates problems or stands in the way of their resolution. This type of thinking is mostly "problem-saturated," critical of self, others or life in general, and judgmental. There are always problems. We can find them everywhere, and the thinking mind is busy trying to avoid, anticipate or fix them. However, this type of mind can turn every innocent little thing into a problem.

It is clear to see that in Angelica's case, for several years, she had been both problem-saturated and self-critical. In her own mind she would regularly attack and doubt herself.

Excessive thinking thrives on "should," "have to," "ought to," "can't" and "must" (for example, "I shouldn't be so stupid/fat/lazy," "He should be less selfish," "I have to go to work," "Everything is so boring," and so on). It holds on to old images of self, others or life in general, and forms a self-identity that is obsessed with I, me, my and mine. This is the root of the pandemic personality disorder called narcissism. Narcissus was a handsome youth in Greek mythology who was doomed to fall desperately in love with his own reflection in a pool of water. Getting lost in excessive thinking can lead to the narrow focus of self-obsession.

If the monkey mind is not judging or attacking ourselves or others, it can keep itself busy by creating all manner of distractions from whatever needs to be felt, faced, owned and dealt with. It can move toward denial, particularly of feelings.

Limiting core beliefs

Excessive thinking is a contracted, narrow-focus form of thinking that thrives on unconscious, limiting core beliefs about:

- safety—how much we can relax, trust and "let go," or how much we need to "hold on" tightly and be in control;

- capability—how much power or capacity we have to influence our life circumstances, whether we are a victim or a creator of them;
- worthiness—how much we deserve in life. These are core beliefs about whether we deserve abundance or scarcity of what really matters, and core beliefs about whether we deserve a life of struggle or support; and
- possibility—beliefs about what is possible, what is impossible and what we can dare to dream.

Limiting core beliefs are reinforced and re-created by old habits of excessive thinking. "Beliefs become biology," said Norman Cousins, acclaimed author of *Anatomy of an Illness*. Our beliefs become embodied in our breathing pattern, muscular tension, our posture, our behavioral habits and our thinking habits.

"Problem saturation," the "more syndrome" (always wanting more), stimulation addiction and compulsive busyness are all forms of excessive thinking. But do not despair! We are not suggesting that we all need a brain bypass operation. The thinking mind has amazing potential for manifestation through the power of imagination, planning and organization—it is only excessive thinking we must address: when we are just spinning our wheels, and in the process hurting ourselves and others. Mindfulness meditation helps to restore the balance between head and heart, between thinking and feeling, and between knowledge and knowing.

Catastrophizing

Excessive imagination can easily cause feelings of uncertainty (which are fairly normal and manageable) to escalate into "catastrophizing." Instead of accepting and handling feelings of uncertainty, excessive imagination can create an overwhelming range of worst-case scenarios. Feelings of uncertainty or vulnerability, which may naturally just come and go, can become entrenched as habits of worrying. Thinking too much can create never-ending worrying, or even panic and paranoia. The famous author Mark Twain was referring to catastrophizing when he said, "I am an old man and have known a great many troubles, but most of them never happened." Mindfulness methods of dealing with uncertainty, fear, anxiety and panic are described in chapter 9, "Mindfulness of Emotions."

Many cancer patients have allowed feelings of uncertainty about their future to escalate through unrestrained imagination into catastrophizing and, in the process, have unwittingly created a great deal of stress as well as feelings of hopelessness and despair.

Lisa was a young woman who was dealing with primary breast cancer at an early stage, and although her prognosis was quite good her mind was full of worry. She began by worrying about her husband remarrying after her death, then she worried about her children having to deal with a stepmother and, of course, about whether or not her children would remember her once she had gone. Lisa still had so much to live for, she was not in any physical pain, her surgery had been successful and she was learning about all the lifestyle changes that could radically improve her prognosis. Yet her mind, as a habit, filled with worst-case scenarios. In fact, she was grieving the change that had come into her life, but excessive thinking was escalating the grief and making it worse. Learning mindfulness meditation helped her to stand back from her worrying, and gave her a better perspective and the space to respond more constructively to the challenge of cancer. Lisa continues to improve her quality of life and to live well.

Habits of worrying can easily undermine our self-confidence and also become self-fulfilling prophecies, attracting the negative outcome they imagine. Worrying is a negative form of visualization or imagery. Mindful attention to present moment, felt experience (such as through Mindfulness of Breath) can curb habits of excessive worrying and provide great relief for worriers. The habit of dwelling in the future is replaced with the ability to be more present.

Excessive thinking can take the form of excessive analysis and interpretation, which can then lead to procrastination, despair, depression, self-pity, helplessness and hopelessness. These more passive forms of excessive thinking create "victim" states of mind that indulge habitual thoughts of "I can't," "Poor me," "Why me?" or "What if?" or "Why bother?" In terms of the fight-or-flight stress responses (which we'll discuss shortly), these are the flight responses. Overuse of the flight response can create a collapsed personality, whereas fight response habits can create a rigid personality.

Excessive judgment

Excessive thinking also leads to judgments of things or people as good/bad, right/wrong, like/dislike, agree/disagree rather than the more flexible approach to accept, forgive or cultivate understanding and compassion for ourselves and others. Excessive judgment creates unnecessary control, defensiveness and a reactive nature. With this habit, we become too ready to take a position and dig our heels in, insisting we are right. Being too quick to judge, we can become proud, self-righteous, stubborn, impatient and intolerant.

Do you ever find yourself taking a position like this and then wanting to win and be "right"? This habit creates all sorts of power struggles and dramas. When directed toward others, excessive judgment coupled with memory can lead to blame and resentment, which are ways of holding on to the past.

When directed toward ourselves, excessive judgment can produce guilt, self-criticism—even self-loathing. Through blame and guilt, we take a position, often unconsciously, and hold on to it, thereby keeping the past alive and draining our energy. These forms of excessive thinking turn defensive patterns, which are aimed at protecting old wounds, into habits of attack and aggression, even self-attack.

Fight or flight

Worry, blame and guilt are not really emotions: they are forms of excessive thinking that indulge and aggravate the emotions of fear, anger, remorse and sadness. Indulging these emotions by thinking too much can cause the emotions to get stuck instead of flowing, being experienced, expressed and completed. In terms of the fight-or-flight stress responses, these are the fight responses. Fighting and struggling can become a compulsive and habitual way of being, creating a rigid mind, body and personality. Struggling with life has become a source of identity for many people.

The other stress response possibility, flight, takes the form of withdrawal, internalizing feelings, keeping everything to yourself, avoidance of the problem at hand (for example through an addiction) and feeling like a victim of circumstances. Flight, which involves the urge to run away, can also become a habitual way of being, creating passivity and depression, and a collapsed mind, body and personality. Depression can result from excessive thinking and a lack of appropriate action. Both fight (rigidity) and flight (collapse) are created and maintained by habits of thinking and attention. They are defensive patterns that were perhaps originally necessary to cope with a particular situation. But in time these fight-or-flight responses can be recognized, healed and released. This will be discussed further in chapter 10.

Fight response habits (rigidity)

- blame
- pride
- stubbornness
- self-righteousness
- impatience
- intolerance
- perfectionism
- guilt

Flight response habits (collapse)

- despair
- depression
- helplessness
- hopelessness
- self-pity
- procrastination
- worry or catastrophizing

Can you see yourself anywhere in these habits of excessive thinking and overreaction?

Antidotes for excessive thinking

As we have seen, the thinking mind thrives on anticipating and planning, analyzing and judging. These are the strengths of the thinking mind, but it has its limitations. When we want to engage in anything that is simple, sensuous, emotional, fun and in the present moment, the thinking mind is not really needed. Remember, if you can, what it feels like when you are hugging your beloved, a friend or your child. Recall the warmth of the feeling and the whole-body experience of a loving hug. If you are hugging your beloved or your child and at the same time you are thinking about work, are you able to give yourself fully to the sensual and emotional delight of the hug?

There are myriad simple pleasures in which the thinking mind is not needed or is even a hindrance. Here are some examples:

- watching a sunset
- walking on the beach
- listening to birdsong
- playing with your children
- lying down with your lover
- communing with nature
- tasting good food
- enjoying a concert
- having fun with friends
- feeling sad
- resting for a while

Some of the pioneers in the study of the stress/relaxation responses, such as Hans Selye and Herbert Benson, suggested that we need to think, analyze and plan for about twenty minutes a day. The rest of the time we can just flow with our experiences, trust our inner knowing of how and when to respond, and enjoy the ride. Even at work, much of the time we can trust our experience, instinct and knowledge of what to do without getting lost in excessive thinking. But how frequently does excessive thinking intrude where it is not really needed, causing us to overreact or underreact and internalize our feelings? How often do you take things too seriously? And how do we go about changing all of this?

Here are some direct antidotes for excessive thinking:

- rest, relaxation and meditation;
- diaphragmatic breathing—the more deeply you breathe, the more you feel, and the more you can let go of excessive thinking;
- sensuality, awakening the senses—listening to music or really tasting your food;
- movement and exercise—when it is not too goal-oriented;
- contact with nature—gardening, hiking and so on;
- emotional intimacy—opening up to others;
- physical intimacy—allowing arousal, excitement and pleasure;
- trust—learning when to "wait and see";
- deeply listening with empathy to another person, nature or even yourself;
- fun and play—lightening up and being less serious; and
- constructive thinking—use your twenty minutes per day wisely!

Anything that involves connecting with yourself, others and nature usually requires little thinking. Anything that involves a "lightness of being," humor, spontaneity or creativity usually requires little thinking. Anything that requires presence is usually spoiled by excessive thinking.

Paul adds his personal experience: I know for a fact that my most profound, creative, deep and meaningful thoughts and insights come when I am not thinking. When I am in the shower, walking in through nature or just resting is when the creative flow opens up by itself.

Certainly we do need to think, analyze, reflect and plan . . . but how much? And what about the balance between thinking and feeling, doing and being? How can we change patterns of excessive thinking and develop presence?

Mindfulness develops presence. It can be developed as a regular meditation practice and then integrated into daily life. But first we need to understand what awareness really is and how it is different from thinking.

THE NATURE OF AWARENESS

Mindfulness of Breath simply involves developing more awareness of the natural flow of your breathing. As you practice, you become more aware and your mind gradually becomes less dominated by thinking. But what is awareness, and how is it different from thinking? To demonstrate the difference, try the following awareness experiment.

First, close your eyes for a moment and become aware of your body posture. Just become aware of the feeling of your body inside and the feeling of your body outside, the feeling you have of touching the chair, or the floor.

Now, there are the body sensations and there is the awareness of the body sensations. The awareness of the sensations is just like watching or noticing or paying attention to the sensations. You do not have to be constantly thinking in words, "I am sitting, my feet are on the floor, my tummy feels tight." Awareness is silent . . . a silent noticing.

As a further awareness experiment, close your eyes and become aware of all the sounds you can hear outside the room and inside the room. There are the sounds and there is your awareness of the sounds. The awareness of the sounds is just noticing, paying attention to the sounds. You do not have to be constantly thinking in words or pictures. Awareness does not use words or pictures; it is a silent noticing.

Extending the experiment a little further, become aware of any thoughts that are passing through your mind. Without judging or censoring any thought, just notice your thoughts.

Again, this is a silent noticing, almost as though you are curious as to what thought may come next. You will find that there are thoughts and there is the awareness of the thoughts. The awareness silently notices the thoughts.

With this experiment you have been paying attention to the contents of your awareness. The contents of your awareness include sensations, feelings, thoughts, impulses and instincts. The contents of your awareness are always changing, always moving, but the awareness is always still and constant. The contents of your awareness appear in the "field" of awareness. The contents appear, they change and they disappear.

Thinking is one of the contents of awareness, one of the components of our present moment experience. But when thinking dominates our attention, we lose awareness of sensations, feelings, impulses and instincts; in fact, we lose contact with our present moment experience. When thinking dominates our attention, we lose presence. The mind withdraws attention from the body and the senses, so excessive thinking is non-sense, i.e., nonsense! Mindfulness helps us to release the domination of the thinking mind so we can "come to our senses."

Contrasting thinking and awareness

Let us explore in more detail the difference between thinking and awareness:

- Awareness is silent, whereas thinking creates a commentary in words and pictures.
- Awareness is receptive and formless, whereas thinking is active, and has form in words and pictures.
- Awareness is always in the present. We can only imagine the future because it does not exist, it has not arrived yet. Thinking,

via the use of memory and imagination, projects into the future or the past. The bird sings a sweet note, and then the thinking mind says, "Sweet birdsong," but the note is already gone.

- Awareness is still and unchanging; it is the same now as it was five minutes ago and five years ago. Thinking, by contrast, is always changing (like all the contents of awareness).
- Awareness, being silent, is also by its nature accepting and nonjudgmental. Again, thinking labels, interprets and evaluates. Thinking is frequently judgmental: it struggles to understand, solve, improve or fix things. Awareness is the capacity to simply observe what is in this current moment.

Awareness is the still, silent background of our being; it is the alert presence that pays attention to everything we experience without judging. Awareness is sometimes described as the "witness," whereas the thinking mind is the "judge" or even the "critic." In spiritual philosophies awareness is often referred to as our "true self" or our "spirit." This will be discussed further in chapter 11, "Mindfulness of Thoughts and Stillness," and in chapter 19, "Meditation and the Spiritual Path."

Freedom comes with the breath

Through Mindfulness of Breath, simply by giving nonjudgmental attention to the breath, we practice freeing our awareness from the domination of the thinking mind. We do not judge the breath, we just watch it; we do not judge ourselves, we just patiently persevere—when distracted by thinking, we just watch the thoughts and then return to the breath. Just by noticing the thoughts we begin to "step outside" of the thought or detach ourselves from it, and then we can turn our attention more fully to the feeling of the next breath.

Both thinking and awareness have value. Both are natural aspects of the mind. The intelligent use of thinking helps us to plan and to get things done. Excessive thinking, however, reliably leads to suffering, stress, anxiety and unhappiness. Mindfulness practice helps us to learn how to use the mind in a balanced way as well as to be more present.

Dealing with thoughts

Reflecting more on the way our mind functions, many of us will realize that as a habit, thinking dominated our attention because we treasured and trusted our thinking mind more than our other ways of perceiving and knowing the world. In current society, it is common to have been conditioned to train and listen to our thinking mind more than the other, less conceptual forms of intelligence, like instinct, intuition, gut feelings and body wisdom. The seventeenth-century French philosopher René Descartes' famous assertion, "I think, therefore I am," drove a wedge between mind and body and created a separation between the two. The thinking mind was deemed superior, more objective and rational, whereas the body was inferior, mechanistic, subjective and prone to base emotion. Our culture, our science, our humanities, our schools and we ourselves still carry some of the deep, conditioned beliefs about the thinking mind being the "boss" and the body being the "servant." We identify with our thoughts and see ourselves as Thinkers living inside the shells of our bodies. Thinking, for many, has become the primary mode of perceiving the world, leading us to take our thoughts too seriously and, as a result, feeding them, indulging them and allowing them to dominate our attention. Too much thinking is non-sense!

The way to free our awareness from the domination of thinking and to break away from the identification of ourselves as Thinkers is not to fight thoughts, struggle with them or try to suppress them. Fighting our thoughts involves judgments like "thoughts are bad," as well as goal orientation to get free of thoughts. With judgment and goal orientation we are back into thinking: "I wish these thoughts would go away and then I could start meditating." Trying to get rid of thoughts is having thoughts about our thoughts, which is somewhat like a dog chasing its own tail.

The most effective way to free ourselves from the domination of thinking is to accept our thoughts and to take away the desire, hope and expectation to get rid of them. When our thoughts are not fueled by desire and expectation, they become just words and pictures in the mind, appearing against a silent background of awareness. Thoughts lose their power when not driven by desire.

The way to deal with thoughts when practicing Mindfulness of Breath is simply to notice the thoughts without making them a problem and without allowing them to be important. Upon noticing a thought, we do not fight it yet we do not continue to feed it or follow it. We simply open our awareness to include the feeling of our breathing—in other words, we turn our attention back to the breathing and allow the thought to run itself out, to move on through.

Narrow focus, open focus

Let us try a visual metaphor to demonstrate this way of dealing with thoughts. Raise your right hand, with your palm toward you and your fingers splayed open, and place it about eight inches from your face. Closely study the lines in your palm and across the joints in your fingers. Now, without moving your hand, soften the focus of your eyes and look through the spaces between your fingers, and around them, to see out into the room. As you do so you shift from narrow-focused attention on the lines on your hand to an open and inclusive attention that takes in the whole room. As you make this shift in attention, you do not have to do anything to your hand; you do not remove it, you simply make it unimportant. In this visual metaphor, focusing on the lines on your hand is like getting involved in a thought, and opening your attention to look out into the room is like returning your attention to the feeling of your breathing. Notice that you did not have to remove your hand or push it away. As you opened your attention, your hand practically became transparent as you looked through it into the room.

Form and formlessness

Here is another visual metaphor for dealing with thoughts while practicing Mindfulness of Breath—it is also a useful metaphor for the difference between thinking and awareness. First, look at the page of writing in front of you. You have been paying attention to the words and sentences on the page and from their meaning you have been constructing an understanding in your mind. Making a slight shift in perception now, begin to see the words as squiggles on the page—mere shapes and forms.

Now notice the white background on which these shapes and forms appear; let your attention rest on the white background and notice that it is between the words, around the words, inside the squiggles and even behind the squiggles. When you let your attention rest on the white background, the words become unimportant and the story they tell fades away. The attention shift is from an exclusive narrow-focused attention to a more open and inclusive attention—like opening up your peripheral vision. The words on the page are like thoughts; the white background is like awareness—that formless, silent presence. When you realize you are following a thought, then your awareness (the white background) allows you to return to your breathing. The thought holds less meaning and importance; it becomes a "squiggle" appearing on the background of awareness.

Letting go of judgment

As you practice Mindfulness of Breath, do not judge or struggle against your thoughts. Just treat them as though they were voices coming from a radio that someone has left on in another room. With the acceptance of thoughts, without taking them seriously, your practice will gradually become free of goals, expectations and judgments.

The choice to be present is not really a goal; it is simply choosing to pay attention to our present moment experience. Without this choice to be present, our attention will return to the default position of excessive thinking, daydreaming and problem saturation, with a past or future orientation.

The fact that thoughts continue to pop into your mind during meditation is not a problem. Each time you notice you have been following thoughts, return to the breathing and silently congratulate yourself for changing the old habit of attention by coming back to the present moment. If you notice yourself following a thought ten times in the space of a minute, then that is ten times you can congratulate yourself—not judge and criticize yourself. Gently persevere.

THE BREATH OF LIFE AND INTEGRATION

Mindfulness meditation, when practiced consistently, often begins to integrate itself into day-to-day life quite effortlessly and seamlessly. Louie, a feisty Italian man, attended one of the Gawler Foundation's ten-day residential programs. Louie, a father to four girls, was dealing with primary prostate cancer with secondaries throughout his body. Louie was deeply loved by his wife and four daughters, but they were constantly frustrated by his pride and stubbornness. Louie was a simple man who instinctively took to meditation and intuitively knew that it would improve his prognosis. His wife and daughters were astounded to see such a hyperactive man sitting in meditation for up to one and a half hours each day. After two months, Louie's wife called to express her deep appreciation. Not only had his PSA count decreased (a blood marker that can reflect prostate cancer activity) but Louie was a changed man. Louie's pride and stubbornness had softened remarkably and, to his family's delight, he rediscovered his rowdy humor and also began to express gratitude and love to his wife and daughters. Just two months of meditation and Louie was no longer such a grumpy old man. A month later, Louie returned to the Gawler Foundation. Tears welled up in his eyes as he humbly recounted the change that had come over him as a result of meditation practice. Louie had found his long-lost spirit and rekindled his faith in "the good in the world."

The virtues that are cultivated by such a simple practice as Mindfulness of Breath are many and varied. Mindfulness meditation has helped many practitioners to develop:

- patience—less hurrying and addiction to busyness
- empathy—letting others be themselves and listening deeply
- trust—less need to be always in control
- humility—realizing and accepting what we do not know
- self-discipline—training the monkey mind
- equanimity—less defensiveness, judgment and overreaction
- courage—accepting and exploring every aspect of ourselves
- gratitude—for the simple pleasures in everyday life

With consistent meditation, these virtues seem to grow organically from within. They develop naturally without our necessarily cultivating them. Of course, consciously recognizing and choosing these virtues as "skillful means" can enhance their integration; we will talk more on that later in the book.

The benefits of a teacher

While meditation may appear almost to be a panacea for all physical and psychological imbalances, quite often a meditator will need the help of a teacher, a counselor or a psychotherapist to navigate through difficult terrain. Practicing meditation gently invites past issues to come into awareness to be healed, and professional support may help in the healing. However, one's own daily practice is nonetheless an invaluable and irreplaceable tool for self-development and personal fulfillment.

A quick refresher

Such a simple and direct form of meditation, Mindfulness of Breath is also an immediately effective form of "mini-meditation" that can be practiced for a few minutes anywhere and at any time as a quick refresher. Just remember to breathe and let go of any excessive thinking. While standing in line riding on a bus, sitting on a park bench or driving along in your car, if you notice the momentum of the thinking mind taking you into the past or the future, through memory or imagination, you always have the choice to turn your attention to the soft caress of the breath. Rise and fall with the waves of your breathing and come back to simple presence. Breath awareness can simply and effortlessly bring you out of the realm of nonsense (non-sense) and place your feet back on the ground, here and now.

Breathing in and breathing out

In concluding, let us talk more specifically about the benefits of Mindfulness of Breath in developing a deep respect for the essential, life-giving resource of the breath. In English, we use the words *inspiration* for breathing in (and also for being inspired by something), *expiration* for breathing out (and also to mean dying) and *respiration* for the process of breathing. The Latin roots of these words are quite revealing: *inspirare* (inspiration) means "the spirit within"; *expirare* (expiration) means "the spirit leaves" and *repirare* (respiration) means "the spirit returns."

The breath is our connection with something wonderful and mysterious, our life force or spirit—those life-giving energies that are subtler than food and water. Through the breath we interact with the environment and gain sustenance from it. By watching the breath, we can become aware of the intimate connection between the inside of the body and the outside environment, and the constant interaction between the two. The breath is the life-sustaining rhythm that joins the inside with the outside, endlessly receiving new life and releasing what is not needed.

Ancient cultures used other words to point to this mysterious dance of life: *qi* (Chinese), *prana* (Sanskrit), *pneuma* (Greek) and *Great Spirit* (American Indian). Each of these terms refers to a union of breath, spirit, energy and awareness. These ancient philosophies understood and appreciated the importance of breath in the web of life. Just practicing Mindfulness of Breath can attune the meditator to this "knowing" without the need to consciously contemplate it. Attention to the breath can produce a deep respect and appreciation for the breath of life.

Remember to breathe

You may have seen the bumper sticker that extols the value of the breath— "Remember to Breathe!" Remembering to breathe can help to put a situation into perspective and it can tone down a knee-jerk overreaction.

Breath is the bridge between mind and body. Deliberate, mindful breathing helps to slow down a tendency toward excessive thinking and brings us back to our senses. The practice of Mindfulness of Breath is not only a profound meditation technique, it has the additional value of cultivating a deep respect for breath.

You can enjoy the practice of Mindfulness of Breath in its own right and also incorporate it into the complete practice of Mindfulness-Based Stillness Meditation. Chapters 7–14 will guide you.

CHAPTER 7

MINDFULNESS OF BODY

*Attention or conscious concentration on almost any part of the body
produces some direct physical effect on it.*
—CHARLES DARWIN

From the narrow focus of Mindfulness of Breath we now open the awareness to include Mindfulness of Body.

Our present moment experience consists of thoughts and feelings as well as the awareness of thoughts and feelings. As explained in the previous chapter, when our thoughts dominate our attention, our field of awareness narrows and we can lose contact with our feelings and our body. As a result, we pay less attention to our body's feedback—its signals and messages—which comes in the form of physical sensations. When the monkey mind dominates our attention, we are pushed and pulled by old habits of fear and desire (craving and aversion), and are less responsive to our needs, feelings, intuition and creative impulses. When the stress response becomes a way of life and we become stuck in the "emergency mode," we can easily lose touch with our real needs as well as our creative spark and our spirit. We also stop listening to our body.

Our body can tell us what and how much we need to eat, when we need to rest, when we need to play, when we need to move, when we need contact with others and with nature, and when we need alone time to connect with ourselves. Therefore it makes good sense to appreciate the importance of body awareness and to know how to listen, to feel and to get back in touch with our body. By contrast, living out of touch with the body is like only living from the neck up; research in the field of mind-body medicine tells us that this is at the core of many health problems and diseases.

We consciously and unconsciously turn our attention to that which we love. If we love possessions, pride, status and security, then our attention will gravitate toward those things. Mindfulness of Body brings our attention back to the present moment with love and respect for our body, our needs and our feelings. Mindfulness of Body is a simple but precious gift for becoming more aware and more present, and in the process, training our mind to pay more attention to our body. Through this simple sensuous process, we create a more intimate relationship with ourselves. In the words of Oscar Wilde, "To love oneself is the beginning of a lifelong romance."

FEELING INTO THE BODY

Mindfulness of Body involves resting your attention on and inside the body, and tuning in to the sensations you find there. You explore each body part with a gentle curiosity that is free of judgment, patiently connecting with the sensations you feel—whether they are subtle or strong, pleasant or unpleasant, comfortable or uncomfortable. When thoughts take your attention away, simply open your awareness to include the body sensations again and allow the thoughts to become less important. Paying attention to body sensations in this mindful way is similar to the manner in which the Progressive Muscle Relaxation (described in chapters 3 and 4) is practiced.

MINDFULNESS OF BODY: THE FOUR ACCESS POINTS

In the practice script that follows, your attention will be directed to what we call the Four Access Points to body awareness. These are the feet, the tummy, the shoulders and the face. By tuning in to the Four Access

Points, your awareness will open out to be more inclusive of the whole body from bottom to top without going into every body part individually. This is an abbreviated yet very effective form of whole-body awareness. To begin, practice for about five to fifteen minutes to establish familiarity and ease with this technique.

MINDFULNESS OF BODY: THE FOUR ACCESS POINTS

Take a moment to adjust your position. . . . Gently close your eyes and settle into your body. . . . If you are sitting, ensure your body is as upright and open as is comfortable. . . . If you are lying, lie in a balanced and symmetrical way.

Now, in your own way, take a few moments to consciously relax your body once again. . . . Perhaps that feeling of the muscles softening and loosening . . . relaxing and releasing . . . just simply letting go. . . . Perhaps a deeper breath or two helps. . . . And as you breathe out . . . notice that natural feeling of relaxing and releasing a little more with each out breath . . . just simply letting go . . . letting go.

With your eyes gently closed, become aware of the space before your eyes. . . . Relax your eyes . . . just simply resting your attention there. Now pay attention to any sounds outside the room . . . just listening with a gentle curiosity. . . . Let the sounds come and go . . . no need to judge. . . . Now notice any sounds inside the room. . . . And now the sound of your own breathing.

As you bring your awareness to your breath, notice what sensations there are as you breathe in . . . and as you breathe out. . . . Feel the air touch your nostrils. . . . Feel the slight movement of your chest and your tummy. . . . Listen to the gentle sound of your breathing. . . . Allow your breath to take up whatever rhythm feels natural for you at the moment . . . quite effortlessly.

Now, take your awareness down to your feet. . . . Feel into

your feet . . . feel the contact between your feet and the floor. . . . Move your awareness through your feet . . . noticing any sensations in them . . . again, just that simple curiosity. . . . Perhaps you notice feelings of pressure . . . tingling . . . softness or hardness . . . warmth or coolness. . . . Whatever sensations are there . . . comfortable or uncomfortable . . . that subtle sense of aliveness in your feet . . . this is how you know your feet are there . . . you feel them . . . just feel them . . . your toes . . . your heels . . . the surface of your feet . . . all through the feet. . . . And as you feel into your feet, feel the flow of your breath . . . just simply coming and going . . . the natural ease of it all.

Now bring your awareness up to your tummy. . . . Perhaps there is a tingling or a pressure . . . a softness or a hardness . . . a coldness or numbness here or there. . . . Feel any sensations . . . whether they are comfortable or uncomfortable . . . free of any judgment . . . let go of any reaction. . . . Then feel the slight movement of your tummy as you breathe in and out.

Take your awareness to your shoulders. . . . Notice the feeling in the muscles of your shoulders . . . the base of your neck . . . perhaps a softness or hardness here or there . . . a pressure or a tingling. . . . Just feel it, even if the feeling is very slight . . . stay with it . . . let go of any judgment . . . just simply noticing. . . . And as you feel into the muscles of your shoulders, feel the flow of your breath.

Be aware of the space before your eyes. . . . Become aware of any sensations in and around your eyes. . . . Move your attention through your eyebrows . . . and across your forehead. . . . Notice whatever sensations are there. . . . As you feel through the eyes . . . and across the forehead . . . feel the flow of your breath.

Now open your awareness to your whole body. . . . Notice

whatever sensations are coming to your awareness at this particular moment. . . . Perhaps the awareness of the space in front of your eyes . . . perhaps the feeling of your breath. . . . Notice the movement in the body as you breathe in . . . and as you breathe out. . . . Notice the slight pause between the in breath and the out breath. . . . If any thoughts do come to your awareness, just let them come when they do . . . and go when they are ready . . . and then gently come back to the feeling of the next breath . . . the feeling sensed through the body . . . and the awareness of the space before your eyes.

If at any time you notice your mind wandering or becoming distracted, just notice it . . . and gently return your awareness to your body once again. . . . Feel your feet on the floor . . . feel into your tummy . . . and the flow of your breath . . . as you are aware of the space in front of your eyes.

OBSTACLES TO MINDFULNESS AND THEIR ANTIDOTES

A common obstacle or resistance that newcomers have to the practice of Mindfulness of Body is a subtle form of impatience. This impatience comes from shame or a dislike of the body, or from an unconscious judgment of the body as more mundane and less important than the mind or the spirit. They want to get into the "spiritual stuff" and not waste too much time on the "physical stuff." Paul became aware of this judgment and impatience in his own practice and found it extremely liberating to let go of it. He came to realize the importance of body sensations and to respect the truth, wisdom and experiential reality of feelings throughout his body.

The true value of body sensations is that they involve no interpretation, no imagination, no judgment. They are our direct experience of now.

Feedback to and from our body

The totality of our being involves a multitude of communication processes and feedback loops, and the more we give attention to these processes the more sensitive and responsive we become. The stress response and the relaxation response are two major communication processes or feedback loops in the body, and there are hundreds of others that monitor our needs and the appropriateness of our reactions. We can block these communication processes through contraction and distraction of our attention and our sensitivity. In other words, we can stop feeling and responding to feelings. We can stop the flow.

Each of us is a network of resilient yet delicately balanced communication processes that are interconnected with networks in other people and in nature. These networks consist of signals, sensations, impulses and responses, from individual to environment, from inside to outside. Paying attention and being present are vital for staying connected and being responsive to all these messages. Through excessive thinking we tend to disconnect and stop listening, and our attention wanders away.

In Paul's words: In my practice, I found Mindfulness of Body tuned me in to and connected me with the experiential reality of impulses and sensations. I became aware that by paying attention to body sensations without judgment I was becoming more empathetic and compassionate to myself, and this naturally extended to others and to nature. Far from being mundane and purely physical, Mindfulness of Body sensations can attune us to a multilayered and interconnected experiential, feeling-based reality. Patience with this practice has profound benefits. The more I practice Mindfulness of Body sensations, the more the separation between mind and body dissolves. I find that when I bring non-judgmental awareness to the sensations, attention and sensations merge more closely. This closeness creates empathy, whereas judgment or expectation creates a distance between the watcher and the watched.

Feelings or images

Another common obstacle, most recently reported by an intellectual young man named Robert, who was determined to "master" mindfulness, is that it is often easier to visualize parts of the body, rather than actually pay attention to the physical sensations. For Robert, scanning the body was experienced like a sequence of movie images or pictures of body parts, but these images were located in his thinking mind.

Sometimes imagery can assist sensing. For example, as you take your attention inside your feet, an image of your feet may come into your head and the image may help you to locate and focus on the sensations in your feet. However, the imagery can dominate your attention and keep your attention in the head rather than on exploring a body part for physical sensations. Robert was trying too hard and the goal orientation was keeping his attention in his thinking mind. It was a small but important breakthrough for him when he was able to differentiate between imagery and actual physical sensations; he began to "arrive" in his body and connect with his feelings.

Overcoming dissociation

Yet another obstacle or challenge for some practitioners is that they find it difficult to find any sensations in their body. While not common, this does happen. The habit of excessive thinking can make us dissociate from the body, becoming unable to feel sensations. Metaphorically speaking, body parts can become cold, dark, hard, stagnant and forgotten when our attention has been withdrawn from them. Dissociation or withdrawal of attention can result from trauma or shame or occur through conditioning or modeling. Sensing is like bringing light and care into dark, cold, hard and forgotten places in the body.

If you are finding it difficult to connect with your body sensations, rather than making a problem out of this, just start with any sensation you can feel: your feet touching the floor, your bottom resting on the chair or cushion, the slight movement of your chest or tummy with your breathing, a slight ache or pain anywhere in the body. Rest your attention on the body part, allow your breathing to flow, and then be patient. If nothing happens, just move on to the next body part and feel into it. Patiently and gently persevere.

As you pay attention to the sensations in the body, you stop judging your body. Your relationship with your body changes: instead of creating an idealized or degraded body image, you connect with the actual feeling experience in your body in a nonjudgmental way. You become more familiar and intimate with your feeling body and stop struggling with it.

As you let go of a static body image, you connect with a more dynamic, ever-changing body experience. Sometimes this changing body experience can feel quite strange and a little disconcerting. Also, as you let go of judging and struggling with your body, your body–mind begins to relax.

As they do this, many people report subjective experiences such as feeling the body becoming very heavy or very light; feeling the body leaning or swaying when it is not actually doing this; feeling the body becoming hollow or even disappearing; or feeling the body becoming smaller or larger. As we discussed in chapter 5 on Mindfulness of Breath, if any of these subjective experiences appear during meditation, the most useful thing to do is to just accept the feeling without analyzing or judging it. Simply notice the feeling, then notice your breathing even if it has become very subtle, and continue the meditation. If the feeling becomes too disconcerting, stop meditating for a minute, open your eyes if you need to and, when you can, continue meditating.

These subjective sensations should be treated as neither a goal nor a problem. Some meditators become attached to these sensations and seek them. Then they can become an obstacle to meditation. Similarly, as you bring your attention into various body parts, memories or emotions may arise. Allow the memories and emotions to appear, neither fighting nor feeding them. They too are neither a goal nor a problem, although we will discuss them further in coming chapters. When you can, come back to your breathing, your body sensations, and continue meditating.

Transforming pain

Last, a common obstacle for some meditators while practicing mindfulness is encountering pain in the body. What to do? Should you avoid it? Should you try to meditate it away? Do not deny it or indulge it by judging or analyzing it; just pay close attention to the actual sensation of the pain. Notice your breathing and then move on to the next body part. It may be necessary to spend a little time with the painful sensations to let go of the judgment and reaction, and to explore the actual sensations of the pain. If the pain continues, allow it to continue in the background and move on to the next body part and the breath. Meditation for transforming pain will be described in detail in chapter 15.

VARIATIONS ON THE FOUR ACCESS POINTS

There are three main variations on the Four Access Points to body awareness. They are:

1. the Whole Body Scan
2. Breathing into Body Parts
3. Yoga Nidra

1. The Whole Body Scan

This is a mindfulness process of systematically moving your attention through the whole body, part by part. As you move your attention to each body part in turn, feel into it, noticing the physical sensations therein with a nonjudgmental awareness. You can start with the toes and work your way up to the top of the head, or start from the head and work your way down. This technique has much in common with the Relaxing Body Scan and in many ways is an extension of that method. The Whole Body Scan can be practiced slowly and thoroughly and, as such, can be a complete practice in itself. It is practiced with the same mindfulness as the Four Access Points.

The benefits of the Whole Body Scan are many and include:

- establishing a connection between mind and body
- effortless relaxation that comes without even trying to relax
- practicing patience and acceptance of both comfortable and uncomfortable sensations
- a willingness to explore the experiential reality within the body

The systematic thoroughness of the Whole Body Scan prevents the practitioner from avoiding or skimming over parts of the body that may be uncomfortable or less accessible. With practice, the body scan can be done in a few minutes without compromising the quality of mindful contact with the body, though initially it should take between ten and twenty minutes. It's worth noting that the length of the Whole Body Scan practice means it is quite easy to drift off or fall asleep—which certainly has relaxation benefits—so you may find the abbreviated Four Access Points practice can be more easily integrated into the complete Mindfulness-Based Stillness Meditation practice.

2. Breathing into Body Parts

This variation brings together mindfulness of sensations, conscious breathing, relaxation and imagery. This method is described by Jon Kabat-Zinn in his book *Full Catastrophe Living*. As you bring your attention to each body part, notice the sensations there, and then imagine that you are breathing into that part of the body and breathing out from it. With the out breath, there is an effortless sense of letting go of control and relaxing. This wonderful technique has benefited many people in Kabat-Zinn's Mindfulness-Based Stress Reduction program.

Although based on mindfulness meditation, this practice is more active and introduces the element of imagery. It is a stand-alone practice that is used widely in mind-body medicine. This is another technique that will be explained further in chapter 15, "Meditation for Transforming Pain," as it too is helpful in pain management.

3. Yoga Nidra

This is another variation on Mindfulness of Body sensations. Yoga Nidra is an ancient practice that starts with the Whole Body Scan, then a series of visualizations and, finally, the practitioner is guided to make a resolution to himself or herself. The body scan and the visualizations render the practitioner more receptive to the act of making the resolution, which is strengthened with each subsequent practice. Yoga Nidra is usually practiced by following the personal guidance of a yoga teacher or by using a recorded CD.

Mindfulness of Body and its variations bring nonjudgmental awareness to our often neglected bodies. In doing so we begin to listen and
respond to the body, and to know our embodied selves more intimately. We will explore the experience and the benefits of this in the
next chapter.

CHAPTER 8

KNOWING YOUR BODY

The body is your friend; it is not your enemy. Listen to its
language, decode its language, and by and by, as you enter
into the book of the body and you turn its pages, you will become
aware of the whole mystery of life.
—OSHO

YOUR BODY IS YOUR FRIEND

Do you feel at home in your body? Are you happy with your body the
way it is, or do you wish it were different? Do you take the time to listen to your body? Do you respect it and respond to its needs? Or do you
tend to neglect it until something goes wrong?

Too often we "human doings" treat our bodies as though they are
disposable. We treat them as though they were merely a means to an
end, a tool for getting things done. This is the utilitarian nature of the
thinking mind: it sees things in terms of productivity, output and working toward future goals. We push our bodies in order to realize our goals,
hopes and dreams; we push our bodies in order to get the most we can
out of them. It seems as though we do not have the time to really listen
to our bodies and care for them with respect and gratitude.

Perhaps an exception is when we worry about how we look, but the vanity industries only sell cover-ups for our lack of a deeper love and respect for our bodies. Advertising often sells body image and exploits body shame rather than promoting body connection and body respect. When we are not pushing our bodies, we often swing to the other extreme and reward ourselves through instant gratification with guilty pleasures and unhealthy treats. Fast minds seek fast foods.

How did we become so desensitized and disconnected from our precious bodies, the temple of the mind and spirit? Why is it that we can consistently deny, dislike, ignore and abuse our bodies? Is this neglect and abuse of the body at all related to the ways in which we neglect and abuse the body of the Earth?

DISCONNECTION AND ITS CONSEQUENCES

Through Paul's experience as a psychotherapist and counselor, and through his own life experience, he has seen four interrelated causes of this disconnection from our bodies.

1. Our culturally conditioned values and priorities

Values that emphasize individual success, competitiveness, productivity and hoarding of accumulated resources lead to disconnection. These values are also materialistic and create a world where success is defined by possessions and status. These external criteria of success dominate our attention and generate excessive thinking, overshadowing more internal criteria for well-being, such as acceptance, calmness, balance, kindness, presence, generosity and honesty.

2. Our culturally conditioned attitudes to the body

Popular culture and advertising create images of the attractive and acceptable body size and shape. Comparing ourselves to these ideals and falling short can create shame and guilt. This results in judgments of the body and a struggle with it.

3. Our culturally conditioned attitudes to pain

In our comfort-addicted society, we are taught to avoid or deny physical and emotional pain at all costs. Many of our medical paradigms focus on relieving symptoms rather than encouraging people to face pain, to deal with it, to talk about it, to learn from it and to give real support to those experiencing it. We opt for quick interventions and tranquilizers, which are often overprescribed, instead of giving empathy and interpersonal support. Otherwise we use a gamut of addictions to distract ourselves from our pain. These addictions create numbness and disconnection from body sensations.

4. Our religious and philosophical conditioning

The mind and the soul are considered superior while the body and the physical are mundane and inferior, often being regarded merely as a means to an end or, worse, a source of sin and temptation. Culturally, the mind is cultivated, stimulated, entertained and distracted as the body is disowned and neglected. In many religious doctrines, the "sins of the flesh" and sensual pleasures are frowned upon. Shame and guilt can drive us away from a closer connection with our bodily experience. Trying to avoid pain but feeling guilty about having too much pleasure can be a bit like being stuck between a rock and a hard place.

Monica, a single woman in her early thirties, came for counseling and meditation instruction. Monica had been dealing with bulimia for twenty years and was ready to heal the issues underlying her disorder and to change her behavior. As the counseling progressed she recalled overhearing a conversation between her mother and her grandmother when she was thirteen years old. Her mother was an airline hostess, a fashion model and a renowned beauty. Monica overheard her grandmother lamenting to her mother, "I always thought you would have a pretty daughter!" Poor Monica was shattered. She began to hate herself and her body. The onset of puberty only made things worse, and her self-loathing increased as she gained some weight. But now, after years of distress, she was ready to start to respect and take care of herself. Practicing Mindfulness of Breath and Body gradually enabled Monica to connect with her body and to inhabit it without shame and judgment. The process of releasing and healing the past began just by bringing more nonjudgmental awareness into her body on a daily basis.

As well as creating shame, the above four socially conditioned values and attitudes can cause us to "soldier on" and maintain a "stiff upper lip" rather than listen and respond to feedback from the body. For example, we may continue to work when our body is trying to tell us to rest. Not to "soldier on" is seen commonly as being weak, selfish, self-indulgent, even irresponsible. These socially conditioned values cause self-image problems and lead us to frequently say, "I should," "I have to," "I ought to" and "I must." These are all forms of excessive thinking, which can easily dominate our attention while body awareness fades into the background. We may listen to our wants but not our needs. Or we tend only to listen to our body signals when a physical or emotional crisis develops to get our attention, and then resort to quick, external interventions such as drugs to pull us through.

MINDFULNESS, THE BODY AND HEALING

Listen to these words from Eckhart Tolle's *The Power of Now*:

> The more consciousness you bring into the body the stronger the immune system becomes. It is as if every cell awakens and rejoices. The body loves your attention. It is also a potent form of self-healing. Most illnesses creep in when you are not present in the body. If the master is not present in the house, all kinds of shady characters will take up residence there. When you inhabit your body it will be hard for unwanted guests to enter.[1]

Through the practice of Mindfulness of Body, we can start to more fully inhabit our body. We can tune in to the nonverbal feelings, needs, instincts and impulses of our body. We turn the lights on so that "unwanted guests" know there is someone home. The more we inhabit our body the more our energy flows, the more responsive our body and mind become and the stronger the immune system.

We know that excessive thinking and a sedentary lifestyle are detrimental to our health. When we do not inhabit our body, when we do not listen to it and respect it, our "relationship" with our body breaks down. We may not know when we really need to rest, to exercise, to have some fun, to have some alone time, or when, what and how much to eat. When we disconnect from our body, our attention is dominated by thinking and we get stuck in our heads and our energy stagnates. We not only stop listening to our body, we stop trusting our body.

One significant consequence of this disconnection is that when we are sick we may overly trust external interventions, such as the specialist, the drug, the medical procedure, rather than trusting our body's healing resources and supporting it in the healing process. We have met many people who, when diagnosed with a serious illness, feel that their body has let them down. Perhaps the illness is a feedback mechanism aimed at getting our attention and informing us that we have not been listening to our body.

Healing and curing

Who would you be more inclined to trust with something of importance to you—a friend or a complete stranger? Have you become a stranger to your own body? Have you stopped listening to it? Are you out of touch with yourself? If we do not know our bodies and respect them, when it comes to the crunch—for example, when we experience an illness—we will not trust our body's resources for self-regulation and healing. We will be more inclined to trust and look for outside interventions and support.

Mindfulness meditation helps us to begin to trust and empower our body and our immune system by enabling us to:

- let go of some of the excessive thinking that creates catastrophizing and panic;
- allow and accept the healthy process of grieving, and to not struggle with our emotions; and
- spend some time connecting with our body by feeling into the body and giving it attention (nonjudgmental presence) through Mindfulness of Body sensations.

Disconnection of our mind and our attention from our body's sensations has allowed the curative and symptomatic approach to illness to dominate over more traditional and holistic approaches to healing and wellness. We have stopped trusting and supporting the body's own healing resources. Our society has a tendency, which is gradually changing, to trust external interventions more than the body itself.

This curative approach to disease focuses on the observable symptoms of an illness. Its treatments often take the form of a strong and short-term intervention in the form of drugs and/or surgery. The curative approach tends to treat the disease and not the patient. Practitioners of traditional Chinese medicine acknowledge the importance of the curative approach in dealing with the "branches" of an illness, but this holistic/healing approach also aims to treat the "roots" of an illness. Curative medicine works "from the outside in" through external intervention, whereas the holistic approach works "from the inside out" and looks at the whole person—body, emotions, mind and spirit. Often through lifestyle changes, the healing approach strengthens and mobilizes the body's own resources for repair and balance. This will be elaborated in chapter 14 on mind-body medicine.

Both approaches have their place in the management of illness and the maintenance of well-being, but when we are out of touch with our body, we tend to exclusively trust external interventions like drugs and technology.

Where is your focus? Where is your balance?

Healing	Curing
holistic	symptomatic
"root" of imbalance	"branches" of illness
works from the inside out	works from the outside in
lifestyle changes	external interventions
long-term/ongoing commitment	short-term

Mindfulness meditation has a key role to play in the field of mind-body medicine. Mindfulness is a healing resource that works from the "inside out." Mind-body medicine can restore trust in the body and empower the patient to make lifestyle changes while integrating the healing and the curative approaches to illness and well-being.

"SENSING" YOUR BODY MAKES SENSE

Mindfulness of bodily sensations involves bringing your attention to the physical sensations in various parts of the body. We call this skill "sensing." Let us do some specific sensing using our feet and hands to experience the value of this technique.

This exercise takes ten to fifteen minutes.

SENSING THE BODY

Either by closing your eyes or leaving your eyes open if you choose, take your attention right down to your feet. . . . Feel the slight sensations of pressure on the soles of your feet where they come in contact with the resistance of the floor. . . . Now feel the sensations around your feet, the warmth or coolness of the air . . . the touch of your socks on your feet . . . the gentle pressure of your shoes. . . . Just take a few moments to feel it.

Now take your attention inside your feet and begin to explore the subtle sensations there. . . . Feel inside your heels. . . . Perhaps you can feel that subtle sense of aliveness or energy in your heels. . . . It may feel like a subtle tingling or slight pressure. . . . Notice any physical sensations inside your heels . . . free of judgment . . . no need to label or understand the sensations . . . just feel it.

Move your attention through the arches of your feet . . . paying close attention to any sensation . . . subtle or strong . . . comfortable or uncomfortable . . . inside the arches and tops of your feet. . . . Now move your attention inside the balls of your feet, with a gentle curiosity, noticing any sensations there. . . . Then take your attention through your toes.

Now allow your attention to spread through the whole of both feet. . . . Noticing the subtle tingling . . . pressure . . . the energy inside your feet. . . . Rest your attention on these sensations, letting them come more and more into your awareness. . . . Free of any judgment . . . no need to label or understand the sensations . . . just feel it. This is the way you know your feet are there—you can feel them.

Now go through the same sensing process with your hands and fingers.

Paying attention to feelings

Sensing is turning our attention away from words, pictures, images, ideas and concepts and toward nonverbal physical sensations. In this way, sensing is a wonderful antidote for excessive thinking. We do not often pay attention to nonverbal sensations unless they are strong, such as when we have a problem or a pain, or when an urgency or emergency develops. With the practice of sensing, we are paying attention to the feelings in the body without the agenda of needing to understand, label, change, resist or fix anything. No thinking agenda, no problem, no goal orientation, just a gentle curiosity.

With a nonjudgmental attitude we are able to more fully connect with and give our full attention to the body sensations. When we label or judge, then much of our attention is caught up in the cognitive process, in which case our attention stands outside of the actual sensations. A gentle curiosity allows us to enter more fully into our body, to feel more and think less. The goal-oriented thinking mind likes to label, analyze, interpret and then react. Often this process is too quick and leads to reactive states of mind based on fight or flight, reaction or distraction. By sensing more we take the time to listen to our body, to feel more deeply and to connect more fully with the actual sensations—the direct experience.

Sensing enables a more intimate contact with the body. Our body is constantly speaking to us in the language of sensation, and this nonverbal language is a vital source of information for us.

Connecting with body and breath

Some body parts may be easier to feel than others. Some areas of the body require a little more patience in order to tune in to the physical sensations. Some areas may be like foreign countries that we have not visited for a long time: the terrain may be unfamiliar and require some time for orientation. Connect with whatever sensations you can find, and explore them without worrying about what you cannot feel. It is best not to make a problem or a goal out of sensing; keep it simple and direct.

You will notice in the practice script for Mindfulness of Body on page 154 that after you connect with each of the Four Access Points you are encouraged to feel the natural flow of your breathing. As you are bringing your attention to body sensations, the invitation is to open your awareness to include your breathing. Awareness of your breath will help you to feel more and think less. Remember the equation from chapter 6: *The more you breathe, the less you think and the more you feel.* You will, no doubt, notice that when you get caught up in a commentary or thought-stream, your breath flows less freely.

As you practice Mindfulness of Body, at times your attention will be distracted by a commentary or a stream of thoughts. When you realize your mind has wandered away, simply return your attention to the access point and the flow of your breathing. No need to analyze why you were distracted or to criticize yourself; simply open your awareness, let the thought be and come back to your body sensations.

If thoughts about your meditation practice intrude, including concerns about whether or not you are "doing it correctly," or wanting to get somewhere, just notice the thoughts—not feeding them and not fighting them—and see them as words or pictures in the mind. Then simply return your attention to the access point and the flow of your breathing. By not reacting to these thoughts, they will lose their power and simply become words and pictures moving through the mind.

EMBODIMENT AND "OUT-OF-BODY" EXPERIENCES

In her inspiring book *Passionate Presence*, Catherine Ingram writes: "We fail to see that fundamentally we are embodied expressions of an animating force, not disembodied spirits trapped in flesh, awaiting final release." As we begin to "come to our senses" and spend more time in our sensitive, feeling body and in the present moment, we gradually start to experience the joys and, inevitably, the pain of embodied life. We learn to accept and deal with pain, not run away from it.

Traditionally, many religions conceived of God and spirit as transcendent or outside existence, in a distant realm that we could reach only after our "final release." The body, in this view, had to be renounced, disciplined and purified so that we could enter the spiritual realm or the kingdom of heaven. Embodiment often carried with it the concept of original sin, and spirituality took the form of some kind of lofty detachment from a sensual and passionate life.

Rebellion against this stern view often swings in the other direction toward overindulging sense gratification: trying to be good, kind, sensitive, disciplined and selfless until you cannot stand it any longer, at which time you break out into being undisciplined, selfish and indulgent. Then guilt kicks in and you swing back the other way.

Another view of God and religion understands the spirit as immanent or inside existence, expressed through existence, and manifested in the world and in our body. In this view the body is seen as a temple to be honored, nourished and respected. The world of the senses is celebrated rather than renounced, and is seen as an access point to the sacred and the holy. This is the middle path the Buddha walked between renunciation and indulgence, and perhaps, in Christian beliefs, this is what Jesus represented: "God made man" or "God in the flesh"—an integration of the material and the spiritual. We will discuss this further in chapter 19, "Meditation and the Spiritual Path."

The sixties generation of spiritual seekers often looked for "out-of-body" experiences through drugs and psychic states as a way of bringing them closer to God, Truth and Spirit. The irony is that most people are having out-of-body experiences most of the time: excessive thinking is an out-of-body experience. But through mindfulness meditation, we have no need to leave the body to find God, Truth and Spirit. On the contrary, by going into the body with nonjudgmental awareness, we can simply and directly access acceptance, peace and truth. The Mindfulness of Body technique described on pages 154–56 is a key access point to this peace and truth, founded on paying attention to here-and-now experience.

Integration

Why this body? Why did God or Life create embodied human beings? Why do we incarnate? Why is it so precious and unique to be able to think, feel, sense, communicate, respond and choose? Why would God or Life bother to become man and woman? Just look at the human potential for creativity, destruction, love, war, kindness and cruelty. Just look at the human potential for growth and transformation, even in the face of tremendous adversity. Look at the potential our bodies give us to think, feel, act, respond, communicate, touch and be touched, see and be seen, love and be loved . . . all through thought, word and deed.

We live in, through and between our bodies and the body of the Earth. Our life is experienced in this wondrous body and expressed through it. Mindfulness of Body can develop our relationship with our body; it can deepen our respect for it and connect us more intimately with it simply by paying attention. What we give our attention to, we love or become attached to. Again, such a simple practice, such profound benefits.

Developing trust in the body

Mindfulness of Body cultivates more trust in the body. You will begin to trust its ability to heal itself physically, emotionally, mentally and spiritually. You will begin to trust its ability to handle more intensity of feeling experience without distraction or contraction, without flight or fight, without running away. For example, with ongoing practice, you will find that you can handle change, loss and disappointment without so much anger or fear. This will enable you to respond more appropriately and responsibly to the apparent difficulties of life. At the same time, Mindfulness of Body will also lead you to being more at ease within yourself and, as a natural consequence, more at ease with others, both in interpersonal and social situations. An ideal made tangible by paying attention to the ever-changing nature of the feeling-based reality in our body. This is the daily practice of letting go of control and facing the direct experience of uncertainty and vulnerability as it is felt in our sensitive bodies.

Mindfulness of Body is also the practice of "coming to our senses." As awareness is less distracted by excessive thinking, we find ourselves, thankfully, becoming more sensitive to colors, sounds, tastes and textures. There comes a personal awakening to the small joys and simple pleasures of everyday life. Through mindfulness meditation, we are able to stop and smell the roses . . . and find them to be deliciously intoxicating! We are more able to embrace what is good in life; to accept love, to celebrate, to be grateful, to be happy. Of course, the other side of the coin is also true—we become more sensitive to cruelty and suffering, and it moves us deeply, often to tears. Such is embodied life on the Earth—an ever-changing palette of experience. Life continually goes up and down, fluctuates and changes. Joy and suffering can be acknowledged as parts of our ordinary human experience and, as such, we can give up the struggle with them, and accept and delight in them as feeling experiences in the body.

Having made a mindful connection with the body, we can extend our awareness further by opening to Mindfulness of Emotions as the next inclusive step in Mindfulness-Based Stillness Meditation.

CHAPTER 9

MINDFULNESS OF EMOTIONS

As a species we should never underestimate our low tolerance for
discomfort. To be encouraged to stay with our vulnerability
is news that we can use.
—PEMA CHÖDRÖN

We began the mindfulness process of creating presence or choosing to be more fully present by bringing our attention to the breath and then to the body. To be more inclusive of all the components of our present moment experience, we now need to bring attention to our emotions.

A popular misconception about meditation is that it is used to "transcend," rise above or to negate emotions. However, mindfulness meditation can be used to accept and integrate difficult emotions, thereby transforming them into personal strengths and spiritual values. On the other hand, pleasant and uplifting emotions can be relished and more deeply felt through mindfulness. Turning our nonjudgmental attention to our emotions allows the energy of emotions to be experienced, to flow and to be integrated.

HOW AM I FEELING?

If you were asked, "How are you feeling right now?" where, in yourself, would you look to find a true response to this question?

When we ask this question to groups of participants in our meditation retreats, some people point to their head, some people point to their tummy, and some to their chest and heart area. To those who point to their head, we respond, "Yes, that is where you would find the words to describe your feelings, but where is the actual experience of your feelings?" Gradually, as people investigate more closely, the consensus of opinion agrees that our feeling experience is most intense in the center of our being: our throat, the center of our chest, our solar plexus or upper tummy, and our lower tummy. Try it now; see how you are feeling inside!

HOW AM I FEELING?

Softly close your eyes and become aware of the field of darkness in front of your closed eyes. . . . Notice the feeling of your breathing, rising with the in breath, sinking with the out breath. . . . Feel into your feet and notice the subtle sensations there.

Now, with the question "How am I feeling?" in mind, pay close attention to the sensations in your throat . . . then the center of your chest . . . then your upper tummy . . . and then your lower tummy.

Now just sit with your attention covering that whole feeling centerline of your body from your throat right down into your tummy. . . . Free of judgment or even labels, just feel into your center and let your breath flow. . . . Some areas may feel soft and comfortable . . . some may feel tight and uncomfortable . . . or shaky and vulnerable. . . . Some areas may have very little feeling and seem almost numb or empty. . . . No need to analyze . . . just feel into your sensitive center.

Certainly, our brain perceives and quickly interprets what is happening in the field of our experience. But then the feeling experience is carried in our center, our soft underbelly. This center of our being is where our sensitivity and vulnerability reside. The outside of our body is the precinct of the thinking and doing parts; the inside is the domain of the feeling and being parts. Our back provides support and protection. Our legs provide mobility to take us toward what we want and away from what we do not want. Our arms enable us to reach out, to embrace and to hold on; or they enable us to push away. Together, our head and our brain are the processing unit of the body with the functions of perception, interpretation and decision-making. Our center is where our needs, feelings, instincts and intuition are experienced.

Responding to our feelings

Research in the field of mind-body medicine tells us that wellness and healing are optimized when our mind is attuned and responsive to the messages from our body, particularly our feeling centerline, which communicates through needs, feelings, instincts, impulses and intuition ("gut feelings"). If our mind is not attuned to our center, then its decision-making is shaped more by conditioning and past agendas than it is by listening to our real needs and feelings now. If our thinking mind does not listen to our feeling centerline then we do not take care of ourselves. The more the mind listens to our gut feelings, the more whole and integrated we become.

Remember from our discussion of the stress response in chapter 6 that in "emergency mode" our attention, our blood and our energy are mobilized toward the outside of our body and the outside world, preparing us for action and defensiveness. For many people, emergency mode has become a habit and a default position. The consequence of this is that we are literally "uptight," and attention rarely returns to our center. We stop listening to our own bodies, and we get out of tune and out of touch with our feelings. When we pay attention to our center, we move out of emergency mode and into healing, connection and intimacy mode; our attention comes down and in, as opposed to up and out.

Mindfulness of Emotions moves us toward stillness through the complete acceptance and integration of emotions. Instead of running away from our emotions and avoiding them, or indulging them and judging them, we turn and face our emotions without judgment. Mindfulness of Emotions can also be called "centering" because we bring our attention into our feeling centerline. A wonderful gift of healing is made available through this practice.

Give yourself fifteen to twenty minutes for this exercise.

CENTERING

Take a moment to adjust your position. . . . Gently close your eyes and settle into your body. . . . If you are sitting, ensure your body is as upright and open as is comfortable for you. . . . If you are lying, lie in a balanced and symmetrical way.

Now, in your own way, take a few more moments to consciously relax your body once again. . . . Perhaps that feeling of the muscles softening and loosening . . . relaxing and releasing . . . just simply letting go. . . . Perhaps a deeper breath or two helps. . . . And as you breathe out, notice that natural feeling of relaxing and releasing a little more with each out breath . . . just simply letting go . . . letting go.

With your eyes gently closed, become aware of the space before your eyes. . . . Relax your eyes . . . just simply resting your attention there. Now pay attention to any sounds outside the room . . . just listening . . . with a gentle curiosity. . . . Let the sounds come and go . . . no need to judge. . . . Now be aware of any sounds inside the room. . . . Now the sound of your own breathing.

As you bring your awareness to your breath, notice what sensations there are as you breathe in . . . and as you breathe out. . . . Feel the air touch your nostrils. . . . Feel the slight movement of your chest and your tummy. . . . Listen to the gentle sound of your breathing. . . . Allow your breath to take up whatever rhythm feels natural for you at the moment . . . quite effortlessly.

And now bring your awareness to your center . . . the feeling centerline of your body. . . . With the intention to check in with how you are feeling and with a willingness to include body sensations, gently ask yourself, "How am I feeling. . . ?" Bring your awareness to your throat . . . feel into it. . . . With a gentle curiosity, explore the sensations in your throat . . . subtle or strong . . . comfortable or uncomfortable . . . any sensations . . . and, as you feel into your throat, feel the flow of your breathing.

Bring your attention to the center of your chest, feeling for any sensations . . . a slight pressure, an ache, a tightness . . . a hardness or resistance to the breath . . . or perhaps it feels soft and comfortable. . . . Explore the body sensations free of any judgment. . . . And, as you feel into your chest, feel the flow of your breathing.

And now bring your awareness to your upper tummy, your solar plexus, and again ask yourself, "How am I feeling. . . ?" Notice any sensations in the upper tummy . . . a softness, a tightness . . . a shakiness, a numbness . . . whatever sensations you find there. . . . As you feel into your upper tummy, feel the flow of your breathing.

Now bring your awareness down to your lower tummy . . . around and behind the navel. . . . There's no need to analyze whether the sensations come from a physical cause or an emotional cause. . . . Explore all the sensations in the lower tummy . . . and feel the flow of your breathing.

Now open your awareness to include the whole feeling centerline of your being . . . your throat, chest, solar plexus and lower tummy. . . . Keep the feelings company . . . with curiosity and compassion . . . just sitting with whatever feelings are there. . . . And as you notice the feelings in your center, feel the flow of your breathing.

Obstacles to Mindfulness of Emotions, and their antidotes

Judging emotions

The first and most common obstacle to the practice of Mindfulness of Emotions is the desire to fix or "therapize" uncomfortable emotional feelings. This tendency, although understandable, brings evaluation and judgment into the practice.

If you feel a rocklike tightness in your solar plexus, just feel it, be with the feeling and keep it company even though it is uncomfortable. By judging the emotion as "bad, negative, unwanted," we struggle with it as we try to change it. When we struggle with an emotion, we can't meet the feeling with true, nonjudgmental compassion. When we judge, we stay on the outside of the emotion.

Nonjudgmental awareness, without any agenda, is subtle enough to gradually penetrate even the most rocklike feeling and open it up to more awareness and deeper compassion. So do not try to fix whatever feelings you find inside; do not make them a problem. Just explore the feelings with a caring curiosity and an intention to meet the feelings more fully and patiently.

Balancing observing and connecting

There is a delicate balance between observing an emotion and compassionately connecting with an emotion. The word *observing* is often associated with objectivity and coolly watching from the outside. Mindfulness of Emotions, on the other hand, is more like observing amid the feelings with deep empathy. The usefulness of words is limited here; you will need to find the balance through your own experience. There is a big difference between bringing the thinking mind, with its agendas, to meet an emotion and bringing awareness to meet it. Remember to keep your breath flowing. When you think about an emotion you will tend to hold or tighten the breath. Discovering true compassion for your own inner reality is an immensely healing and stabilizing experience. The following chapter provides more detail on this point.

Lack of feeling

The next obstacle to Mindfulness of Emotions is not being able to feel anything when you check in to the feeling centerline. The antidote is simply to keep trying each time you meditate. Spend a few minutes checking along the feeling centerline, and then continue with Mindfulness of Breath and Body.

When you first begin practicing Mindfulness of Emotions you may only be able to feel an emotion if it is accompanied by a very strong sensation, like a pounding heart, nausea in the tummy or a tightness across the chest. With patient practice, you will begin to feel less intense, moment-to-moment emotions.

There is always a feeling inside; many feelings are not particularly strong or dramatic. When people decide to give up seasoning their food with salt or sugar, at first they cannot taste anything. It takes a while before the taste buds in the mouth and tongue begin to recognize subtler tastes. Similarly with Mindfulness of Emotions, it takes a while before you notice emotions as they are forming; when you do, however, you will be able to respond to them earlier and more appropriately.

Emotions, stories and experiences

Another obstacle to Mindfulness of Emotions is finding your thinking mind getting busy with the "story" of the emotion. The next chapter provides more detail on how to distinguish the *story* of the emotion, which involves the thinking mind, from the *experience* of the emotion in your body. The antidote is to bring your attention back to your breath, and then check back along the feeling centerline for the felt experience of the emotion. Make the breath and the feeling experience more important than the story.

Another obstacle or difficulty with Mindfulness of Emotions is feeling overwhelmed by the intensity of the emotional experience along the feeling centerline of your body. There are two antidotes here: first, check to see if you are feeling overwhelmed by the actual sensation or experience of the emotion, or by the many stories and reactions your thinking mind may have to the emotion. Quite often the story is bigger and more dramatic than the actual feeling experience. Keep bringing your attention back to the breath and the feeling sensations in your throat, chest, solar plexus and tummy. Keep your breathing slow and deep. If you become caught up in the story about the emotion, your breathing is likely to become fast and shallow. Part of the story about the emotion may be thoughts like: "I can't handle this!" or "This is too much for me!" or "This is terrible!" Notice these thoughts, accept that this is difficult for you and, when you can, come back to mindfulness of the breath and the emotions along the feeling centerline. Be gentle with yourself. You may only be able to spend a few moments with some particularly intense emotions. You can always bring your awareness back to them again a little later.

Other antidotes for particularly intense emotions are to seek help from a counselor, or to do emotionally expressive writing about the issue and your feelings. Read over what you have written several times and then come back to Mindfulness of Emotions. Again, the next chapter has more detail on this.

CHAPTER 10

CONNECTING WITH FEELINGS

The heart heals itself when we know how to listen to it.
Befriending and mindfully surrendering to our most dreaded
emotions, we discover the heart's native intelligence.
—MIRIAM GREENSPAN

FEELING IS HEALING

Healing, or making whole, often involves consciously turning our attention toward those parts of ourselves that have been ignored or disowned. Frequently, this means listening and responding to our own needs and feelings instead of neglecting them. By avoiding our emotions we create an inner struggle—a struggle between the thinking mind and the feeling body. The ability to listen to our physical, emotional and spiritual needs, and the feelings that accompany them, can be severely restricted when our attention is dominated by habitual patterns of excessive thinking.

Psychoneuroimmunology (PNI) is the scientific study of the impact of thoughts, feelings and behavioral patterns of response on our immune system. In this field of study it has been found that the same biochemical messengers that communicate needs and feelings also regulate the functioning of our immune system. To the surprise of many immunologists, it turns out that needs, feelings, thoughts and instincts are mediated by chemicals called neuropeptides, which also regulate our body's defense and healing mechanisms. The more our emotions flow and are expressed appropriately, the better our health and wellness.

Research findings in the field of PNI shattered the simplistic myth that "negative emotions" cause immune dysfunction and "positive emotions" promote it. The critical issue is not the presence of "negative emotions" but whether they are experienced and expressed, or repressed and withheld.

Gary Schwartz, professor of psychology at the University of Arizona, conducted research in the field of PNI from 1980 to 2000. Schwartz found that healthy people with a strong immune system characteristically attend to feedback signals from their bodies, whether they come in the form of symptoms, sensations or emotions. For example, by paying attention to a headache, one might realize it reflects some tension at work; or by attending to tiredness and irritability, one might respond by making more time for rest and sleep; by paying attention to sadness or vulnerability in the feeling centerline, one might accept the need for alone time and personal kindness.

On the other hand, Schwartz found that those people who do not attend to symptoms and sensations, and who repress emotions, are much more likely to suffer ongoing imbalances in their mind-body systems and, consequently, dysregulation of the immune system. People who chronically repress emotions are more likely to develop an immune system that is either hypersensitive and overactive with a tendency to allergies, asthma and autoimmune diseases, or hyposensitive and underactive with a susceptibility to infectious diseases and cancer.

The ACE factor

Schwartz discovered that our capacity to *attend to*, *connect with* and *express* symptoms, sensations and emotions—he termed this the "ACE factor"—supports our well-being and ability to heal. The "attending" and "connecting" components of the ACE factor are actually Mindfulness of Emotions. In collaboration with Schwartz, Dr. Mogens R. Jensen followed the progress of a group of breast cancer patients for two years.[1] Women who suffered more rapid spread of cancer shared certain personality traits: repression as a way of coping, non-expression of emotions and feelings of helplessness. In other words, they avoided *attending to*, *connecting with* and *expressing* the difficult emotions associated with their illness and with their lives in general. By contrast, women who displayed or developed the ACE factor had a rate of remission 46 percent higher than those who repressed emotions.

Schwartz and Jensen showed that the ACE factor is important for people wishing to prevent or recover from many illnesses involving the immune system. Although this work is still considered radical in some quarters, it has been supported by extensive research in the field of mind-body medicine, including the work of: Dr. Lydia Temoshok and her work on the Type C personality; Dr. Jon Kabat-Zinn and his Mindfulness-Based Stress Reduction program; David Spiegel's Supportive–Expressive therapy; Dr. Joan Borysenko and her mind-body clinical program; Dr. Dean Ornish, founder of the Preventative Medicine Research Institute; Dr. Candace Pert and her work on molecules of emotion; Dr. James Pennebaker and his work on the healing power of expressing emotions. We will discuss this further in chapter 14, when we consider meditation and mind-body medicine.

Repression and emotional responsibility

Repression is a defense mechanism and a survival skill. It is useful as an immediate, short-term measure for coping with threatening or overwhelming situations. Repression as a way of managing difficulties usually begins in childhood and helps children to maintain a degree of emotional stability in painful circumstances. By using repression, we push away painful or unwanted thoughts, feelings, fantasies, memories and impulses, and store them in our subconscious body–mind.

Repression involves denial, distraction and projecting attention away from feelings and sensations. We do this by using excessive thinking, shallower breathing and muscular contraction. Through repression, we subconsciously judge our emotional energies as being negative and undesirable or scary and overwhelming, so we block and control them. But repression does not make the feelings, sensations and emotional energies go away; they are stored and accumulate in the body–mind, and become a potential cause of illness and disease.

Repression can become a habitual way of dealing with difficult emotions, and it can create emotion phobia—a default position of avoiding emotions—as well as all sorts of addictions and distractions. Here are some of the most common ways in which we use repression:

- We tell ourselves we have to be strong and responsible, and cannot give in to our emotions.
- We keep ourselves so busy we do not have time to explore our emotions.
- We tell ourselves we do not want to be a burden on anyone so we cannot dwell on, or explore, our feelings.
- We fill up with food so we do not feel our emotions.
- We chill out on alcohol, cigarettes or drugs so that we do not have to feel our emotions.
- We distract ourselves with television, movies, sports and other forms of entertainment so we do not have to feel our emotions.
- We tackle difficult situations with super-rationality and excessive thinking so we do not have to feel our emotions.
- We keep ourselves in our comfort zone and in control so we do not have to feel our emotions.
- We cry at movies or for others but are unwilling to feel empathy for ourselves.

Mindfulness of Emotions is the opposite of repression, and it can be used to release and heal repression, gently and compassionately, and thereby to release and heal the past. Through bringing mindfulness to our emotions, we turn and face them with a compassionate and courageous willingness to connect with difficult feelings. This creates emotional responsibility. Once they stop running away from their emotions, and learn how to be more mindful, many people find these feelings are not as bad, scary or overwhelming as they had imagined.

EMOTIONS—THE STORY OR THE EXPERIENCE?

If you look mindfully into your emotional reactions to any situation, you will find that emotions have two distinct components: a cognitive or thinking component and an affective or feeling component.

For example, imagine you are walking down a city street and you see someone you know. The thinking mind recognizes their face using perception and memory. You remember their name, and then a string of quick subconscious memories and associations flashes into your mind. Imagine that the associations and memories are pleasant—this is someone you like. These thoughts are called the cognitive component of the emotion. Then, in your body, particularly your center, you feel relaxed, warm, soft and comfortable. This is the affective component of the emotion. You smile and decide to greet them and chat.

Now, imagine you are walking down a city street and you see a different person. You recognize their face and remember their name, and a string of associations quickly flashes through your mind—but this time the memories are unpleasant. This is someone you dislike and distrust (the cognitive component). Then, in your center, you feel tight, hot, shaky and uncomfortable (the affective component). You decide to turn away and cross the street to avoid them.

The cognitive component of an emotion is comprised of a perception; an interpretation; an evaluation—such as good or bad, right or wrong, like or dislike, agree or disagree; an analysis; and perhaps a speculation such as, "This person will probably ask me for a loan." The cognitive component of an emotion is the *story* that the thinking mind constructs about the situation.

On the other hand, the affective component of an emotion is comprised of sensations in your center such as softness, hardness, tightness, shakiness, warmth, coolness, tingling, solidness, lightness, heaviness, constriction. This is the *experience* of the emotion; this is the actual energy of the emotion. The experience consists of nonverbal, nonconceptual feelings in the body. If the feeling is strong, it may spread out to other parts of the body.

Through defensive and protective patterns of repression, excessive thinking and emotion phobia, we tend to pay more attention to the cognitive component than the affective component of our emotions. We then become attached to and identify with our interpretation and judgment of the situation. This can create self-righteousness, pride, stubbornness and struggle as we adopt and believe in a particular position. In doing this we tend to make judgments to justify our position and defend it. As the story is embellished and solidified through excessive thinking, the experience in the body is overlooked, avoided and ignored. This is repression.

The trouble is that with repression, as attention is habitually withdrawn from the feeling centers, the energy of the emotion does not disappear but is stored and builds up in the body. Contraction of the body, distraction of the mind and shallowness of breathing can lead to stagnant emotions that are not attended to, not connected with and not expressed (the ACE factor). Mindfulness of Emotions brings our attention back to the experience of emotions.

The following chart summarizes the cognitive and affective aspects of emotion.

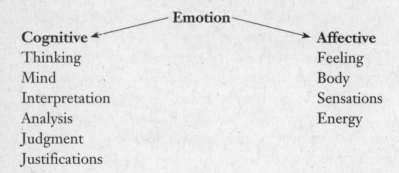

Emotion

Cognitive	**Affective**
Thinking	Feeling
Mind	Body
Interpretation	Sensations
Analysis	Energy
Judgment	
Justifications	
"The story"	**"The experience"**
Taking a position	Sensitivity
Holding on	Vulnerability
Wanting to win/be right	Compassion
Indulge/deny the feeling	
Creates moods/attitudes	

Body wisdom

Here is an example that demonstrates the difference between a story and an experience. During a residential program at the Gawler Foundation, as the group was moving out of the meeting room to take morning tea, a distraught woman, whom we can call Irene, rushed over to Paul. In an agitated and angry tone of voice she said, "See that young woman leaving the room? I think you, as a therapist, should go over and tell her how to behave properly in a group like this!"

Paul was slightly taken aback by this intensity of emotion in what was otherwise a very relaxed setting. "What has happened?" he asked.

Irene was forceful with her explanation. "This morning at breakfast, I was standing behind her in the food queue and I said good morning to her in a very friendly way, but she completely ignored me and went on talking with another woman! So I think it's your job to tell her to not be so rude. After all, we're all supposed to be here to support each other!"

Paul responded, "You are obviously quite upset about this." To which she immediately replied, "Of course I'm upset. Wouldn't you be if someone treated you like that?"

Paul said to the woman, "You may have a point, but just for now, as an experiment, take a deep breath and then tell me where in your body you experience this upset feeling." She looked at Paul suspiciously but took a breath. "Now, where do you feel that upset feeling?" he reiterated. A little reluctantly, Irene placed her hand on her throat. "Now take another breath," Paul encouraged her, and as she began to take the breath, a little tear came to the corner of her eye and her face began to lightly tremble. "Let that feeling come forward," he said, and the tear rolled down her cheek. She sobbed a little and, again, he encouraged her to stay with the feeling and breathe into it.

This upset woman had approached Paul with her story of blame. Irene clearly hoped that he would support her story and act on her recommendations. It seemed likely that she had used this story many times before. It was a story of self-righteousness. She had made a judgment, taken a position and dug her heels in. All of her attention went into the story and toward the young woman. This is called projection.

Her position was: "I'm right, she's wrong, she should change!" She was giving all her attention to the cognitive component of the story. Her body was tight with anger, her mind was full of judgment and justification, and her breathing was fast and shallow.

However, instead of supporting her story, Paul encouraged Irene to bring her attention back to the experience in her body, her center. To her credit, for a moment she did shift her attention back to her experience. In that moment, the energy of the emotion began to move and instead of being repressed was expressed: a tear appeared in the corner of her eye. It was when she touched her throat that Irene's attention moved from a verbal, conceptual argument to a feeling experience. A moment of Mindfulness of Emotion!

When this woman was caught up in her story of blame, the energy of the emotion in her body could not flow and be integrated. Body-oriented or somatic psychotherapies believe that the "healing is in the feeling." Paul spent another half an hour with Irene and supported her as she released some more of the emotion stored up inside her. After about ten minutes of lightly sobbing and crying, she looked up and said, "I know what it is now. It's my fear of rejection." Through the release of her emotion, her perspective changed as she let go of the blame story and connected with her feeling experience. Without looking for understanding, an insight arose once the energy of the emotion started to flow; Irene's mind and body were becoming integrated and were working together.

When our emotional energy is flowing, we are more open to our body wisdom, our intuition or inner knowing. When we are attached to the story, the cognitive component, we get stuck in our heads and our thinking can become predictably defensive.

Young children instinctively pay more attention to their emotional experience than to their stories. In fact, they have very few stories. Two children may be playing together happily until they fight over a toy. They scream, they shout, they cry, they may seek solace from a parent, and then after a few minutes all is forgotten and they play happily again. Their thinking minds have not become so strong and rigid. Their conditioning, roles and self-images have not become so tight. They do not hold on to a position of self-righteousness, pride, stubbornness and intolerance as adults often do. This enables children to feel their emotions, express them and move on to the next moment. Their emotional energy flows more freely and they are more open to passion, spontaneity and creativity. As their thinking mind develops, they may learn to manipulate, to sulk, to whine, to hold on to a position, to rationalize and to control their emotions. Of course, this is part of the journey of life; nonetheless, there is much that adults can learn from children about emotions. Remember, Jesus said: "Unless you are humbled and become as little children, you cannot enter the Kingdom of Heaven" (Matthew 18:3).

Focusing and the "felt sense"

One of the truly inspiring psychotherapists of the twentieth century is Eugene Gendlin, who created the therapeutic approach simply called "focusing." Gendlin and his colleagues from the University of Chicago began researching all the contemporary forms of counseling and psychotherapy, asking why therapy works for some patients but not for many others. In his small but very insightful book called *Focusing*, Gendlin concluded that, irrespective of the therapy and the therapist, successful patients were able to connect with their body awareness of emotions and their gut instinct or inner knowing. Gendlin called this fusion of body awareness and inner knowing the "felt sense." By focusing on their felt sense they connected with the issues in their lives and successful patients were able to make a "felt shift"—a movement toward healing and integration of mind and emotions. Patients who only talked about the story of the issues and problems in their lives usually failed to make a felt shift. They were primarily working on the cognitive level, not the feeling level of the problem.

In Irene's example given above, as a woman with a blame story, she was able to connect with the felt sense of her issue when she took a breath, touched her throat and, for a moment, took her attention into her emotional experience. Connecting with her felt sense enabled a felt shift, out of which came the insight, "It's my fear of rejection." Mindfulness of Emotions, or centering, will connect you with your felt sense.

As a practical exercise, allow yourself to be guided into an experience of your felt sense.

EXPERIENCING THE "FELT SENSE"

Close your eyes for a few minutes and bring to mind someone you love, trust and respect, someone you enjoy being around. . . . See the person's face in your mind's eye and mentally repeat the person's name a few times. . . . Perhaps some memories of the time you have spent with that person will come to mind.

Now, as you keep their image in mind, bring your attention to your center and feel into your throat . . . your chest . . . your solar plexus . . . and your tummy. . . . Notice the body sensations inside as you remember that person and repeat their name. . . . The sensations may be quite subtle or they may be strong. . . . You might feel a warmth or a tingling . . . a tightness or a softness . . . a spreading feeling or a contracting feeling. . . . There may be different feelings in different parts of your center. . . . The feelings may be described in individual words such as *love*, *sadness* or *grief*, or as a mixture of several feelings. . . . You may not be able to describe the sensations in terms of an emotion: that does not matter. What you are feeling inside is your felt sense about this loved person. . . . It is like a "body–feeling–knowing" of that person.

You could also do this same exercise for someone you find difficult or challenging, and notice the difference in the felt sense.

In fact, we have a felt sense all the time and it is constantly changing; but when thinking dominates our attention we give little attention to our felt sense until it becomes strong and dramatic. Then we are likely to use fight or flight, defensiveness, distraction or repression to deal with the strong emotions. Mindfulness of our felt sense enables us to listen to it, respond to it, express it and act from it more continuously—it is the ACE factor again (attend, connect and express).

The feeling centers in the throat, chest, solar plexus and tummy are referred to in some traditions as the *chakras*, a Sanskrit word meaning "wheel." The chakras have a range of functions, one of which is considered to be the processing units for emotional experience. When our emotions are flowing and being accepted, expressed and integrated, the chakras or wheels are turning. These energetic wheels turn when our breath is flowing freely and when we give attention and compassion to the sensations in our center. When thinking dominates our attention, we get caught up in stories and cognitive constructions, the wheels slow down or stop turning, and emotions are repressed and held on to. Mindfulness of Emotions enables the chakras to do their emotional processing; the energetic wheels can begin to move, and emotional energies of the recent or distant past can be accepted, experienced and then integrated.

Indulging or denying emotions

By creating justifications and arguments to prove a position—for example, the blame story of "I am right, you are wrong"—the thinking mind can make too much out of a situation and indulge an emotion, which causes the emotion to escalate. On the other hand, by creating excuses or rationalizations to minimize the impact of a situation, the thinking mind can deny emotions and not respond appropriately to them. A good example of this would be excusing a partner's abusive behavior by saying, "He doesn't mean it, that's just the way he is."

Unconsciously indulging an emotion through excessive thinking and self-justification can:

- turn anger into blame and resentment (escalating)
- turn hurt into blame and resentment
- turn anxiety or uncertainty into worry or panic (catastrophizing)
- turn sadness into hopelessness and depression

- turn repressed anger into depression
- turn grief into self-pity or despair
- turn pleasure into obsession and addiction (fantasizing)

Anger, fear, sadness, joy and grief are natural emotions that we all experience at times. Some emotions are comfortable and expansive, while others are less comfortable and their effect is contractive, even painful. Being natural and normal, emotions are neither negative nor positive. Calling some emotions negative only makes us struggle with them, and resist or repress them.

We will benefit greatly from accepting and normalizing all our emotions so that we can face them mindfully, take responsibility for them and express them appropriately. Otherwise we tend to deny certain emotions and indulge others. It is not the emotions themselves that are negative but the ways in which we deal with them. By indulging an emotion, it can be turned into a mood, an attitude or a way of being. Those who indulge their anger may even derive a sense of identity from being in conflict. While people who indulge their anger often deny their vulnerable feelings, those who indulge their vulnerable feelings often deny their anger. Some people unknowingly indulge their vulnerable emotions, like sadness, fear or grief, and turn them into timidity, self-pity or withdrawal.

Gina was a woman in her fifties who indulged her fear and denied her anger. She had been living with a verbally abusive man for fifteen years. Many times she had reached the point of leaving him, but each time she talked herself out of it. She justified her inability to leave him as being fear of financial independence, which, to a certain extent, was true. Underneath her fear was a deep, seething anger about his abusive behavior. But she never allowed herself to experience that anger; she was afraid of it.

Through counseling and by practicing Mindfulness of Emotions, Gina began to feel her anger. She was encouraged to express her anger in words and drawings, and then to feel it in her tummy. Experiencing and expressing her anger gave Gina the "fire" to leave her abusive partner. Her fear of financial independence lost some of its power as her self-respect returned.

Indulging or denying emotions—whether anger or vulnerability and fear—is not done consciously; it often results from our conditioning or modeling from our parents, or from being scared or ashamed of our emotions. The indulgence or the denial is achieved by shifting attention away from the experience of the emotion and toward the story or the distraction. If we have the courage to face our anger and to feel deeply into it, we will be able to contact the hurt or disappointment behind it. By experiencing the hurt or the disappointment, we can get a sense of the need or fear, the personal value or hope behind the emotion, and then we can deal with the need, value, fear or hope in a more responsible and creative way.

Mindfulness, caring and emotion

Projecting our expectations and demands toward others and the world in general is neither responsible nor creative—it only leads to judgments, criticism and power struggles. Introjecting (projecting inward) our expectations and demands toward ourselves leads to self-judgment, self-criticism and struggle within ourselves. Mindfulness of Emotions bypasses this struggle by cultivating a caring and compassionate connection with the actual experience of emotion in our sensitive center.

James, a single man in his mid-forties, came to see Paul for counseling and lifestyle coaching. His identified concern was his insomnia and, he also suspected, the onset of depression. It soon became obvious that James, although appearing confident, was very lonely. His manner of speaking and his body language demonstrated a sarcastic and deeply ingrained cynical way of relating to other people. James said that at work he was known for his abrasive humor and his way of teasing and "having a go" at his colleagues.

During his second session, James became aware of and explored some tightness and pain in his chest and solar plexus, which he said felt like a "metal plate." As he experienced these uncomfortable sensations, memories of two old relationship traumas came into his mind. The first was in his relationship with his mother, the second with a female lover who abruptly left him when he was in his late twenties. He and his lover had been together off and on for over ten years and James assumed that they would eventually marry. She left him and moved interstate with only a brief telephone farewell and no explanation. He was shocked, shattered and angry.

Through exploring and accepting the painful sensations in his chest and solar plexus, a series of memories and images came into his awareness. James felt the deep pain of abandonment and was able to talk about it. He also became aware of the way in which he pushed people away from him by using cynicism and sarcasm. He began to see the story that he told himself. It consisted of the following interpretations and judgments:

- "People can't be trusted, especially women."
- "People will let you down if you let them in."
- "I'll never let anyone hurt me again."
- "I have to be tough and in control."

This story kept James in a defensive and often passive-aggressive way of being, and it kept his attention out of the painful sensations in his chest and solar plexus. This was his holding pattern, but now it had affected his physical, emotional and mental well-being. As he continued with counseling, James experienced and expressed more of the pain in his center. Almost paradoxically, he began to know and like himself a lot more. His body relaxed—notably his face, his shoulders, his chest and tummy. His breathing pattern softened and deepened. His sarcastic and abrasive humor changed and he was able to joke about himself in a good-natured way.

His work colleagues noticed the change and began to feel safer around him. For the first time, James made some friends at work. He developed a deep interest in meditation and came to many of our meditation retreats. Whenever his sleep problems returned and he awakened in the night, he learned to simply sit in meditation and give gentle attention to his breathing and his feeling centerline; he practiced Mindfulness of Emotions. After fifteen to twenty minutes of centering, he could return to a restful sleep. James had learned how to shift his attention from a compulsive, cognitive focus (the story) to the emotional feelings in his center (the experience). Through this shift of attention, he developed more patience with himself and others, and more compassion for himself and others. By virtue of this mindful healing, James also became a safer person to be around, and his colleagues began to engage and trust him more.

Emotions and safety

The practice of Mindfulness of Emotions is a core relationship skill. Before learning to be a loving, committed, giving person, it is essential to become a safe person. Becoming safe is a discipline. The discipline is to widen our ways of dealing with change, loss and disappointment. Instead of the default position of fight or flight, freeze or please, safety involves learning how to take ownership of our feelings and to experience them directly. Unsafe people habitually and unconsciously project demands, expectations, hopes, dreams, judgments and criticism onto others and themselves. They project a story of should/shouldn't, good/bad, right/wrong, like/dislike, agree/disagree onto themselves and others. Compassionate attention to the feelings in your center curbs this projection. This is the practice of emotional responsibility that creates safety and allows others, and even yourself, to relax and be more at ease. Openness in relationships, and intimacy and growth need a safe environment.

Emotions and control strategies

When an intensity of feeling builds in our center, as a habit most of us shift our attention to a story that is a cognitive construction or a distraction. We live in a society that is so comfort-addicted that we immediately look for ways of moving away from intensity and discomfort. We do not trust intense feelings: we fear they may overwhelm us; we fear they may go on forever; we fear we may lose control of ourselves; we fear we may do something inappropriate, sinful, selfish or hurtful. Our thinking mind has become the boss, and the boss does not trust the workers, who are the body, the emotions, sexuality and instinct. They must be kept subordinate.

To our great loss, we have not been exposed to many courageous role models who trusted intense feelings, experienced them fully and expressed them responsibly and creatively. In our emotion-phobic society, our role models have shown us a range of control strategies to avoid inner experience and vulnerability. These control strategies provide a range of "masculine" ways of dealing with feelings, which include:

- The "contain and manage" model—"Don't be weak: keep a stiff upper lip and broad shoulders, and soldier on!"
- The "reason without emotion" model—"Be rational, be reasonable, argue your case, justify your position and win. Don't be childish, needy, silly, indulgent, selfish and emotional."
- The "endure, deny and escape feelings" model—"Be strong, be stoic, do your duty, have a stiff drink or two, keep yourself busy, go to a football game, unwind with the TV, and everything else will look after itself."
- The "transcend or bypass feelings" model—"Don't be so base, don't be so childish, don't be so animalistic; rise above your feelings, be more refined, sophisticated, intellectual and spiritual."

TRANSFORMING EMOTIONAL REPRESSION

The models listed above encourage repression as a way of life. The paradox is that our real strength is in the courage to face vulnerability and sensitivity. As the great psychoanalyst Carl Jung said: "One does not become enlightened by imagining figures of light but by making the dark more conscious." The imaginary "figures of light" are our images, our stories and all our cognitively constructed identities. "The dark" includes the feeling experiences that have been avoided through repression. Mindfulness of Emotions makes "the dark more conscious." As we turn and face "the dark" instead of avoiding or running away from it, we gain confidence and our emotional pain threshold grows. We gain confidence that we can handle emotional intensity; that our awareness is bigger than our emotions and can surround and explore them. Every time we habitually avoid emotions, we support the belief that they are bigger than us and that they will overwhelm us or undermine our control.

By facing the experience of emotional feelings in our center, we develop more resilience. Resilience is the ability to face challenges—and the intense emotions that often follow from them—without overreacting and without underreacting. Facing emotions is a very real and practical way of developing self-esteem and self-confidence. The cancer patients who come to the Gawler Foundation are often reminded that confidence in dealing with cancer does not come from knowing the outcome of the illness, because no one knows the outcome. Confidence comes from facing the uncertainty without denying it or indulging it, while at the same time acting in a way that is appropriate and empowering.

Facing the uncertainty as it is experienced in the feeling centers provides a gentle antidote to excessive thinking, panic and denial. The mind becomes clearer and more reliable. All too often we make decisions that are heavily influenced by fear, anger, grief or frustration. By facing the emotions first, they begin to unwind, to move and be integrated. Talking about the emotions helps. Facing emotions and being more spacious and less reactive around them allows more intuition to reach through to our thinking mind. When we struggle with emotions, they actually contaminate our thinking.

Thinking can be contaminated by unmet fear or by repressed anger. There is a wise old catchphrase that goes: "What we resist persists." By meeting our emotional energies in the center of the body, we stop them from creeping up and contaminating our thinking. This is true of sexual energy as well as emotional energy. Some people's thinking is contaminated by unacknowledged anger, which can lead to active or passive aggression in the form of abuse, violence, rage, pride, rebellion, stubbornness, self-righteousness, competitiveness and impatience. Others' thinking is contaminated by unacknowledged fear, which can lead to shyness, timidity, passivity, worry, compliance and isolation. Unacknowledged grief or sadness can lead to self-pity, helplessness, hopelessness, melancholy and despair.

Unacknowledged emotions are feelings in the center that have not been experienced mindfully. The feeling centers in the body are able to process intense emotional energies if we trust and enable them to do their work, but this, of course, takes courage and mindfulness. In this verse from the *Dhammapada*, the Buddha talks about the importance of facing emotional experience, not running away from it, and neither indulging nor denying emotions:

Praise and blame,
Fame and shame,
Gain and loss,
Pleasure and sorrow,
Come and go like the wind.
To be at peace,
rest like a great tree
in the midst of them all.

Buddha does not say to rise above emotions, or to have no emotions. He says, "rest like a great tree in the midst of them all." The trunk of the "great tree" is your throat, chest and abdomen; to "rest . . . in the midst of them all" means to pay attention to the sensations in your throat, chest and abdomen without avoidance or judgment. Mindfulness of Emotions enables us to "rest . . . in the midst of them all."

Beautiful intensity

As a natural therapist, the first treatment modality Paul practiced was called Rolfing. This is a form of deep bodywork that releases chronic muscular holding patterns, which are referred to as body armoring. Rolfing, like many forms of deep massage, is often painful—though many clients experience this pain as "good pain." What creates "bad pain" is when the therapist applies pressure and the client contracts and resists. When the client interprets the sensation of pressure and pain to be threatening and judges it to be negative and undesirable, they begin to contract to protect themselves. Paul had to develop the sensitivity to take the client to their pain threshold, to linger on that threshold and encourage them to breathe and relax as much as possible. Then the muscles would release and soften. If he pushed too hard, the client would tense up; if he did not push hard enough, the muscle would not release and soften.

Paul taught his clients to think of the pain as "beautiful intensity," to stay with the intense sensation without tensing up, and to continue to breathe deeply. The expression "beautiful intensity" became a catch-phrase and a source of comic relief. Being willing to just pay attention to the "beautiful intensity" of uncomfortable sensations can often have a transformative effect. Repressed feelings can be released and their energy can flow as a result of sitting with/being with/being mindful of intense energies in the body that have previously been resisted.

Gradually, the pain threshold of Paul's rolfing clients increased and they could tolerate more "beautiful intensity" sooner in the session. As they learned to trust Paul more and to trust their own ability to handle the pain, the sessions moved along more quickly and more release was achieved. In the process, not only did their bodies become softer but they grew in confidence and resilience. As they allowed their armoring to soften, they grew in "core strength."

Emotional alchemy and compassion
In ancient and medieval times alchemists attempted to transmute base metals into gold, to find the elixir of life and attain immortality. Alchemists placed lead and iron in a crucible, hoping through the application of intense concentration, heat and pressure to produce precious metals like gold and silver. The process was said to release the spirit of the base metals.

Mindfulness of Emotions is a bit like an alchemical process, only it works! The torso of the body, made up of the throat, chest and abdomen, is the "crucible." By bringing our attention to this crucible and by allowing intense feelings to be experienced, a process of emotional transformation is initiated. Out of vulnerability can grow courage and confidence. When we sit with uncomfortable emotions (lead), the emotions gradually unwind and are transformed; they become opportunities for developing spiritual virtues (gold).

The catalyst in this emotional transformation is compassion. *Com* means with, and *passion* means suffering. *Compassion* means "to be with our suffering" and not to avoid or run away from our vulnerable, soft center. We develop more compassion by patiently bringing our attention back to the feeling centerline, and by regularly checking in with ourselves with a gentle curiosity, asking, "How am I feeling inside? How am I doing?" Mindfulness of Emotions uses compassion as a catalyst for a process of emotional alchemy.

Take five or ten minutes now to practice compassion for yourself.

PRACTICING COMPASSION

Allow your breath to flow slowly and gently down your center-line. . . . Notice how the movement of your breathing brings a gentle massage to the feeling centers in your throat, chest and tummy. . . . Now ask, "How am I feeling inside?"

Gently bring your attention to your centerline. . . . Feel into your throat. . . . Explore any sensations there . . . subtle or strong. . . . Feel into your chest and allow the breath to flow into it. . . . How does your chest feel . . . ? A little tight and shaky . . . or soft and smooth . . . ? Free from any judgment, just notice the sensations in your chest.

Now feel into your tummy. . . . You may be able to feel the slight movement of your breathing. . . . Move your attention through your tummy and notice any sensations there . . . a softness . . . a tightness . . . a hardness . . . a hollowness. . . . Take a few more moments of patience and compassion to notice any sensations along your center and keep them company.

THE INNER CHILD AND MINDFULNESS

The feeling centerline of your torso is also where your Inner Child lives. The Inner Child is a metaphor for your vulnerability, your sensitivity, your fears and your needs. The Inner Child, which is experienced in your center, also carries the residual energies of your childhood wounds.

If as a child you were wounded by a deficiency of unconditional love, appreciation, support or acceptance, the wound will lie dormant in your center until current issues activate and reawaken it, for example when you believe you have been ignored or rejected. Or if you were wounded by abuse, the wound will lie dormant in your centerline until current issues trigger it. It may reawaken when you associate someone's current behavior with the original abusive behavior. In either case, a "beautiful intensity" of sensations will appear along the feeling centerline. Your Inner Child has awoken, presenting a healing opportunity for emotional alchemy.

As explained throughout this chapter, our normal habits of attention—contraction and distraction, fight or flight, please or freeze—turn our attention away from the "beautiful intensity" and away from our Inner Child. The particular situation is coped with, the feeling experience is repressed and the Inner Child is ignored. Whenever this happens, the Inner Child is abandoned by us and the original wound is compounded. As we turn away from our Inner Child, we project our attention toward others. We project hopes and dreams that others will behave in ways that will allow the Inner Child to go back to sleep and the wound to lie dormant. We project demands and judgments so that others will change their behavior, which will allow our Inner Child to go back to sleep and the wound to remain unhealed.

Mindfulness of Emotions is turning your attention toward your Inner Child—it is like taking your Inner Child's hand and keeping them company. It is like enfolding your Inner Child in a patient and compassionate presence. Your Inner Child has been waiting for some quality time with you; they have been waiting for your unconditional attention. When through loss, change or disappointment your wound is triggered and your Inner Child awakens, this is a healing opportunity. Allow the wound to be experienced, and let it be exposed to the light and fresh air instead of overprotecting it. Keep your Inner Child company so that they know you care. You will find your hopes, dreams, expectations and demands of others will lessen as you become a good parent to your own vulnerability and sensitivity. In this way, mindfulness becomes a form of self-soothing. It is all done by regularly checking in on your feeling centerline with a patient curiosity, asking, "How am I feeling inside? How am I doing?"

Through Mindfulness of Emotions, centering becomes a part of your regular meditation practice and you will develop an ongoing relationship with your feeling experience. To mix metaphors, holding your Inner Child's hand will enable you to "rest like a great tree in the midst of them all."

Growing with your Inner Child

Paul explains from his experience: When I first began teaching, facilitating workshops and giving public talks, my Inner Child would panic. It would feel like a hundred butterflies were flying around in my tummy; my solar plexus would tighten and tremble with fear. Initially I would try to talk myself into a more controlled state by offering myself assurances like "Everything will be all right. You can do it!" or "You are well prepared, you know your stuff, don't worry!" Reasoning and positive self-talk only produced marginal benefits. In time, I learned to accept the fear and to stop trying to control it. I learned to experience the feelings, to keep my Inner Child company with compassionate attention, and to breathe softly and deeply into the centerline of my body. As I gave attention to these vulnerable feelings, my self-talk changed to, "Yes, I know there is fear inside. I am willing to be with it," and I would say to my Inner Child, "I know you are scared. I am here for you, I care."

Instead of trying to push down my Inner Child so that I could be strong, in control and successful, I began to take my Inner Child with me into the lecture or workshop, and continue to give him some caring attention as I went about my business of teaching. Then I would check in with myself between lectures. I developed an ongoing relationship with my vulnerability and fear. Now it does not suddenly overwhelm me; I know it well, I visit it regularly and I actually cherish this sensitive part of my emotional nature. I have grown in confidence and self-esteem—not by controlling my fears but through acceptance of them. Through Mindfulness of Emotions, I have stopped struggling with my vulnerability, and consequently, it has become more integrated into my whole being. Nowadays, the vulnerability is still there to a certain degree, but I do not panic about it.

MINDING YOUR OWN BUSINESS

Mindfulness of Emotions is not only a wonderful and compassionate component of Mindfulness-Based Stillness Meditation, it is also a core life skill that has many benefits. It can be practiced as part of the MBSM or as a stand-alone meditative therapeutic practice.

We have already discussed the benefits of this practice, which include:

- developing compassion, patience and acceptance
- increasing self-esteem
- encouraging resilience
- developing the ability to self-soothe through emotional intensity
- reclaiming your Inner Child
- healing the habit of defensiveness

Another important benefit of this centering practice is that it helps you to MYOB, that is, mind your own business. It encourages emotional responsibility by helping you to accept and take ownership of what you are feeling inside, which is, after all, very much your own business. As described, by taking ownership of our emotional experience, we become a "safe" person. Safe people are those who do not project their hopes, wishes, demands and judgments on others. They take responsibility for their feelings, needs and concerns, and are willing to experience them directly.

Healthy boundaries and mindfulness

Becoming a safe person is important for healthy relationships; it is essential to become safe in order for trust and intimacy to grow. They can only grow and develop in a safe environment in which we are not dumping our needs, fears and feelings on others. This willingness to take responsibility for our emotional experience, and to connect with it, creates healthy boundaries. A healthy boundary is the space we need physically, mentally and emotionally to get in touch with ourselves without being too influenced by others. A healthy boundary helps us to develop a sense of self that is not too caught up in someone else's emotional reality, and does not expect others to be caught up in our emotional reality.

We can care for the emotional reality of others but we cannot take responsibility for it. We need to develop a clear sense of what we can control and what we cannot; what is our business and what is not. We can only deal with and integrate our own emotional feelings, not those of others. Of course, we can care for others and feel compassion toward them, but we cannot do their emotional work for them.

Mike was a young man who came for relationship counseling. He spoke of several times when he and his fiancée went out for dinner or to see a movie. If she did not like the food, he would get offended and an argument would follow or, if she did not enjoy the movie, he would try to convince her that it was a good movie. He couldn't just allow her to have her own feelings and opinions. In fact, he did not know how to handle his own discomfort when his fiancée did not behave how he hoped she would. Instead of connecting with his own "beautiful intensity" he projected his attention toward her and tried to change her reality by convincing her that she was wrong. He did not know how to mind his own business.

Mike had to learn how to take ownership of his own emotional reality. He was asked to close his eyes and to recall the many times his fiancée did not respond in the way he hoped. As he brought these memories to mind, he was reminded to allow his breathing to flow and to pay attention to the feeling along the centerline of his body. Mike became aware of heat in his face, a tightness in his chest and a sick feeling in his tummy. He was encouraged to stay with the feelings, to keep them company without judging or analyzing them.

After a few minutes, Mike reported that the tightness in his chest was softening but the sick feeling in his tummy was spreading and intensifying. Again he was encouraged to stay with the sick feeling and to explore it with a gentle curiosity. After another minute or so he said, "I think I'm scared." Mike was invited to feel back into the sick feeling in his tummy and check to see if the word *scared* was accurate in describing it. Another minute passed and then he replied, "Yes, I'm scared of losing her."

This insight arose because he stayed with his feeling experience. Now he was beginning to mind his own business instead of trying to change his fiancée. By the end of his counseling session, Mike said that he felt an immense relief now that he knew where the problem really existed. We then agreed that it was not so much a problem as a healing opportunity. He felt great appreciation for being introduced to his scared Inner Child and for learning the practice of Mindfulness of Emotions. As he was leaving, Mike was given the following excerpt from Khalil Gibran's *The Prophet*:

But let there be spaces in your togetherness,
And let the winds of the heavens dance between you.

Love one another, but make not a bond of love:
Let it rather be a moving sea between the shores of your souls.
Fill each other's cup but drink not from the same cup.
Give one another of your bread but eat not from the same loaf.
Sing and dance together and be joyous, but let each one of you
     be alone,
Even as the strings of a lute are alone
though they quiver with the same music.

Give your hearts, but not into each other's keeping.
For only the hand of Life can contain your hearts.
And stand together yet not too near together:

For the pillars of the temple stand apart,
And the oak tree and the cypress grow not in each other's shadow.

We all need more space. Space in which to listen to ourselves, connect with ourselves, know ourselves and heal ourselves. Space is a vastly undervalued commodity, and it is free! We need to begin to value space and give ourselves permission to nurture and protect spaciousness. Minding your own business and Mindfulness of Emotions give access to more precious space.

INTEGRATION

Mindfulness of Emotions is a component of the complete Mindfulness-Based Stillness Meditation, but it can be integrated into everyday life as a stand-alone practice. At any time throughout the day, you can stop the forward (imagination) or backward (memory) movement of the thinking mind by simply checking in with yourself. Just for a minute or two, ask yourself, "How am I feeling inside? How am I doing?" and then allow your breath to flow as you move your compassionate curiosity down along the centerline, the feeling centerline of your being. Drop any story of judgment, analysis, speculation or anticipation, and simply feel the sensations inside your center. Practiced regularly, this simple technique will enhance your self-esteem and self-love. It will also enable you to digest and integrate your experience, and to heal the impact of change, loss and disappointment.

If a specific issue or relationship is troubling you, for a while drop the cognitive aspect of trying to analyze, find solutions, justify, rehearse and rationalize, and just feel inside. Patiently stay with the feelings and make your experiential reality important. Trust the feeling centers and allow them to do their work. If you courageously accept any discomfort and face the "beautiful intensity" inside your center, you will learn not to fear your emotions. You will learn that your essential nature is bigger than your emotions and the silent presence of awareness can enfold any difficult emotion with deep compassion.

STEP 4

STILLNESS

CHAPTER 11

MINDFULNESS OF THOUGHTS AND STILLNESS

Water if you don't stir it
will become clear.
The mind left unaltered
will find its own natural peace.
—SOGYAL RINPOCHE QUOTING THE GREAT TIBETAN MASTERS
OF THE PAST, *The Tibetan Book of Living and Dying*

The first two steps of Mindfulness-Based Stillness Meditation (MBSM) help us to relax deeply in both body and mind. With our mind less troubled and more relaxed, we experience less impact from our doubts, worries, fears and anxieties. With our increased sense of calm and ease, quite naturally we become more aware, more mindful. The third step of MBSM, mindfulness, teaches us to pay attention to the present moment deliberately and nonjudgmentally through practicing the specific techniques of Mindfulness of Breath, Mindfulness of Body and Mindfulness of Emotions.

One of the great strengths of mindfulness is the benefits it brings to everyday life. By practicing mindfulness we learn to give our full attention to whatever we are doing, to be less judgmental, to be less reactive. Then we begin to feel the freedom this brings. Worries, fears, anxiety all begin to drop away. Quite effortlessly. We do not have to think about it, to work at it. With ongoing practice and by becoming more mindful, we become more present, more alive. Life becomes more joyful, more satisfying, more complete.

To complete our study and practice of mindfulness techniques, we will move on, again quite naturally, to Mindfulness of Thoughts. Through this final step of Mindfulness-Based Stillness Meditation, we learn how to go beyond relaxation, beyond thought and into a simple state of stillness of mind. This experience, this aspect of meditation, has profound benefits for our health and for our capacity to heal, and it is at the heart of the spiritual path—the pathway to experiencing the essence of who we really are. With all this on offer, it is easy to understand why stillness is so valuable and is at the zenith of our four steps into profound meditation.

We will start with the techniques that help us into the experience, and then in chapter 12 we will discuss what stillness really is, how it relates to meditation specifically and why it is so important.

EXPERIMENTS TO PREPARE FOR STILLNESS

Just as in recent chapters we have learned how to use the breath, the body and emotions as a focus for mindfulness, now we learn to use thoughts. And, by directing our mindfulness to our thoughts, we will discover how mindfulness leads quite naturally into stillness.

Put simply, Mindfulness of Thoughts is paying attention to what we are thinking, deliberately and nonjudgmentally. An effective way to learn how to do this, and particularly to experience how mindfulness leads into Stillness, is to practice a series of simple exercises (or you might like to think of them as experiments). These exercises were developed by Ian and first described in his book *Meditation: Pure and Simple*.

This series of exercises is best experienced. For each exercise read the instructions and then do it. Read and practice each exercise in turn. Resist the temptation to read ahead to the next exercise before you have completed the previous one. They are all short and easy. They are best done sitting, either in a chair or on the floor, but if this is not comfortable you can practice them lying down. For most people, these exercises work best when they are done with the eyes closed. Altogether, give yourself around forty minutes, perhaps up to an hour, so you can take your time and receive the benefit of doing the series of exercises in one sequence. If this is not convenient, however, do them as you can.

Approach these exercises with an open and curious mind, eager just to observe what happens—as if each one is an experiment. Each exercise is short, simple and interesting. Aim to let go of any expectations and judgments. Be curious, alert, attentive.

Once you are ready, adjust your position, relax into your posture and begin.

OBSERVING OUR THOUGHTS

EXPERIMENT 1: NOTICE THE THOUGHTS

Close your eyes and, just for a minute or so, notice what you are thinking about. What thoughts are coming into your awareness right now?

For about one minute, simply aim to be aware of your thoughts, what you are thinking about.

What did you notice?

Quite curiously, many people find when they do this first exercise that they have trouble finding even one thought! It is as if their thoughts have just disappeared. Where did they go?

Darrell had been meditating for years. While he had maintained a good routine and felt some benefits in his personal life and at work, Darrell complained of being frustrated by intrusive thoughts. He had tried all types of meditation techniques aimed at getting rid of the thoughts but they still came and they still bothered him. He expressed a sense of failure with his meditation.

After Darrell did this simple experiment in his meditation class, he opened his eyes in amazement. He was stunned! "I couldn't find a thought," he said, almost in disbelief. "There were no thoughts there." Darrell's voice trailed off, "I have been trying for so long to get rid of them. Where did they go?"

Three ways to still the mind

Darrell was not alone. In his group, many others had the same experience, and this is a typical result. It was explained to the group that there are three ways we can still the mind.

1. The direct approach

With this approach, we simply stop thinking! Just as we might tell our body to stop what it is doing and be still, we tell the mind to stop thinking and be still. Not many beginners can actually do this, but in theory it is possible. In the interim, however, concentration and mindfulness, when used together or alone, do reliably settle the mind. These two principles are actually the basis of all traditional meditation techniques.

2. Concentration

By focusing our concentration on just one thing, there is no room in our minds for other thoughts. Traditionally, the most common things to use as the focus for concentration are the breath, a mantra (which is a sound or group of words like a prayer), a particular object, or images created from within one's own mind. However, just about anything you can think of—and probably many things you would never have thought of—have been used in some tradition or another as an object of concentration and meditation.

We applied this principle of concentration earlier when we focused on the feeling in the body during the Progressive Muscle Relaxation exercise. That exercise is a great focus for concentration as well as being inherently relaxing in its own right. By concentrating on the feeling of relaxation, we get not only the benefit of the physical relaxation but also the relaxation of the mind that comes along with it.

3. Mindfulness

When it comes to stilling our minds, the third technique that works, as the first experiment often demonstrates, is mindfulness itself. In this case, Mindfulness of Thoughts. It seems that when we do give our full attention, nonjudgmentally, to our thoughts, they quite simply dissolve and we are left with a still mind. How can this be so?

Remember that the instruction was to approach this simple exercise as an experiment, and just for a minute or two notice what you were thinking about. In the nature of an experiment, with that gentle curiosity, we look into our minds to observe what is going on. What we experience when we do this is the truth of the mind, and that is that the mind has two aspects. There is the active, thinking aspect, which we are so familiar with, and then there is the spacious, still aspect that you may have had some experience of when you did the previous exercise.

Stillness is ever-present

As we shall come to realize more and more clearly as we continue with these experiments, this stillness of the mind is there all the time. We do not have to create it or make it happen; it is simply there, inside us, all the time. In the same way, there is a natural stillness or silence in any given room all the time. Of course, if there are lots of people milling about and talking, the room appears very noisy, very busy. But we know that if everyone was to leave the room, or if they were to stop talking and to stop moving and to be still, then the natural silence, the stillness in the room, would be very obvious once again. It was always present, it is always present; it is just that noise and busyness mask it.

Without the benefit of a trained mind, our attention tends to go quite naturally to the noise, missing the fact that the stillness is not only ever-present but that it actually provides the space through which the noise travels. If the room was full of noise, we would be unable to hear, to discern an individual voice. If the room was full of concrete, we would be unable to move in it. So it is that stillness, with its associated spaciousness, that makes sound and movement possible.

Commonly we are so busy thinking and doing things that we fail to notice our own inner stillness. When we do stop for a moment, our thinking can be suspended and the stillness is revealed with its accompanying sense of spaciousness.

Another good analogy for this stillness of the mind is the sky. This is a commonly used metaphor in Dzogchen. The natural state of the sky is that wonderful blue canopy with which we are so familiar. Yet on any given day, clouds may roll in and obscure the blue sky—sometimes peaceful, white, fluffy clouds; sometimes dark, ominous storms with thunder and lightning. However, we know from experience that all clouds simply do come and go. Eventually they clear, and there it is again, that beautiful blue sky—vast, pristine and with the sense of the infinite about it. And no apparent boundaries or borders. How interesting it is that even after the worst of storms, the clouds eventually clear, and not only is the blue sky revealed once again but we can see that it is unstained. The very nature of that blue canopy is that it is so pure and pristine, so infinite, that nothing sticks to it. It is unstainable. Inviolable.

Our mind, then, has this same dual nature. There are the active thoughts, of course, which, like the clouds, come and go quite regularly. Then there is the more passive stillness, which is ever-present, calm, pure and serene, just like the sky.

The nonjudgmental observer

Jane echoed many meditation beginners' experiences when, only a few weeks after beginning to meditate, she said:

> I cannot believe how busy my mind is. I never realized how many thoughts were occupying my head. How constant they are. But then, it has only been since I started attempting to meditate that I realized that I was actually thinking. I have come to realize there is a part of me that is capable of being aware of the thoughts, of being able to observe the thoughts. And how many of them there are!

Like Jane, most people get caught up in their thoughts. We tend to react, to judge, to become fascinated by and immersed in the stories that our thoughts present to us. This is a bit like when we go to watch a movie. As we sit down in the theater, we are aware of being in our seat with other people around us and we are aware of the movie screen in front of us. As the lights dim and the movie begins, for a few moments we are aware of watching the movie on the screen. Then usually quite quickly we forget we are in our seat in the cinema. It is like we have become caught up in the movie itself. Maybe from time to time we snap out of it and remember that we are in the cinema, only to become lost in the movie once again. Mindfulness of Thoughts can be compared to remembering we are in our seat watching the movie of our own minds, the movie of our own thoughts.

But there is more to it than just watching our thoughts. Mindfulness of Thoughts gradually helps us to let go of the reactions and the judgments, and to distance ourselves from the stories that our thoughts create. By using the approach of an experimenter, we become an impartial or nonjudgmental observer, and the nature of our mind begins to become more obvious. We come to realize through direct experience that our mind does have this background of stillness like the blue sky, as well as active thoughts that come and go, just like clouds traveling across the blue sky.

The curious fact is that the more we are able to simply be aware of our thoughts, to notice them and to not react to, judge or indulge in them, the more they clear and the more the stillness is naturally revealed. Mindfulness of Thoughts—just allowing any thoughts to come when they are ready and to go when they are ready, without engaging with them—naturally leads to the thoughts settling. This is a direct way to experience the natural stillness of our mind.

Jane was suitably impressed by this first simple experiment:

I have been trying so hard to experience the stillness. By concentrating on my breath I had experienced some calmness, but really there were only fleeting moments of stillness. My mind kept turning over. Now, when I go looking for my thoughts, it is as if they have all disappeared. It almost seems perverse or crazy, but wonderful at the same time.

It is as if, when we stop trying, when we remain alert and pay attention to thoughts, and let go of judgment and reaction, everything changes. The thoughts do clear and we do experience stillness. A natural, peaceful, calm and deeply reassuring stillness.

In a sense, what could be easier? Well, that probably depends on whether this first experiment did have that effect for you or not. For many, simply observing their thoughts does lead to a direct experience of the stillness of no thoughts. If you are one of these people, you now have a reliable technique for settling your mind and experiencing stillness. Simply relax and then observe your thoughts. Let them come and go, free of judgment. You will probably notice some stillness and then some thoughts will rise again. Just notice them and let them pass, a bit like noticing white clouds drifting by on a blue sky. They just come when they are ready and go when they are ready. Quite effortlessly. We just feel the ease of it. There is a natural simplicity to it. Then, it is almost as if we can enter into and rest in the stillness.

When thoughts keep coming

More on the stillness later, but for some, all that this first experiment reveals is an awareness of thoughts—lots of thoughts. Some people who try this first experiment notice one thought after another, with no semblance of stillness. Then there are those who do experience something of the stillness, yet it is only transitory. The stillness lasts for just a few moments and then the thoughts crowd back in. What to do?

Having gone into such an extensive discussion following our first technique to do with Mindfulness of Thoughts, let us move on to the next series of linked exercises. This will help us to become more aware of our thoughts and how we can work with them. With a little more practice, we will learn how Mindfulness of Thoughts can lead even more reliably into stillness, that state of awareness beyond thought. The following experiments will help with this and will also help reveal our thoughts more fully.

How do we know we are thinking?

This time, we will perform a short experiment with the aim of discovering how it is we know we are thinking. The typical response to this question is, "Well, I'm just thinking. The thoughts are there and I noticed them." Yes, but how do you know they are there?

Three ways of noticing our thoughts

There are actually three main ways we notice our thoughts. The first is when we see them like a sequence of pictures similar to a short movie or a video clip. Some people are able to observe these pictures very clearly, almost as clearly as they see things in daily life. For others, the pictures are less distinct, more fuzzy, but still clear in their intent and meaning.

The second way in which we think is by having an ongoing conversation in our head. We "hear" ourselves thinking the thoughts—"Maybe I will do this, maybe that"; "I remember when she said so and so"; "Perhaps next week I will go and visit such and such."

The third possibility is that we feel ourselves acting out our thoughts in our mind. This is as if we were actually doing things, acting out our thoughts and feeling ourselves doing them.

The first way, seeing pictures, is called the *visual way of thinking* and is the most common way of becoming aware of our thoughts. Slightly less common is the *conversation* or *aural mode*, while the least common is the *kinesthetic*, that which involves a feeling sense.

While everyone uses all three ways from time to time, and it is not uncommon to use two or even three modes at once, most of us tend to predominantly use one mode or another. This means that as individuals we tend to be primarily visual, auditory or kinesthetic in our way of thinking.

While this information is interesting and has practical implications when we study how the mind works and how to improve communication between people, for our purposes, simply being aware of how we think is of great help in developing Mindfulness of Thoughts.

So now we turn to the next experiment, which, like the first one, only takes a minute or two.

EXPERIMENT 2: HOW DO THOUGHTS APPEAR?

Take up your position as if you were about to meditate. Close
your eyes, and this time, just for a minute or so, think about
what you are planning to do once you finish reading today.

The key point of this experiment is that, as you think of
what you will do later, notice how those thoughts are coming to
your awareness. Are you seeing them? Are you talking to
yourself about the possibilities? Are you feeling yourself doing
what you plan to do in real life later in the day?

This experiment is simple: think about what you will do
later in the day, and notice how you know that you are actually
thinking.

Take a minute or two and then come back to the book.

How was it? Are you seeing, hearing or feeling your thoughts?

Just to be clear about this, there is no particular significance in
which group you fall into. One is not better than another. There is
certainly no right or wrong. They are just different. So just as some
people have black hair and brown eyes, some people are visual, some
auditory, and still others kinesthetic in their way of thinking.

Also, most people do find these short exercises, these experiments,
interesting and fun, and it is best to approach them in a lighthearted
way. Simply be curious to become more aware of what is going on in
your mind. It is not unusual for there to be something of a feeling of
amazement as we get to know our mind and how it functions.

Now, while this second experiment helps us to simply become more
aware of our thoughts, the next experiment takes this a step further.

THOUGHTS AS SEGMENTS

Obviously a thought has to start somewhere and finish at another given
point. Realizing this, it is clear that each thought that comes into our

mind is like a unit unto itself. It has a beginning, a middle and an end. Each thought is like a unit or a segment.

The aim of our third experiment is to become aware of this fact. Again, our intention is to be more aware and more mindful of what it is to be thinking. This experiment, just like the previous ones, only takes a minute or two.

EXPERIMENT 3: THOUGHTS AS SEGMENTS

Take up your posture and close your eyes. This time, without aiming to think of anything in particular, notice when a thought first comes into your awareness, how it runs its course and then how it finishes. There is no need to dwell on the content, just adopt that attitude of being curious to observe, to be aware when any thoughts actually do turn up.

Then notice how each thought is like a segment or unit, with a starting point where you first become aware of the thought, a main body, which is the content of the thought, and an end point, which is when you know that the thought is over and finished.

So how was this latest experiment for you?

A stream of thoughts that settle

With the last experiment, most people do notice how each thought is like a segment or individual unit. For them, the starting point, main body and end point of most thoughts are fairly clear. However, for others, the stream of thoughts they notice is like a torrent tumbling through their minds. If you are one of these people, do not worry. You are certainly not alone and there is a simple solution. Just be patient. Do what you can to avoid becoming frustrated. Particularly resist the temptation to beat yourself up about it.

A busy, high-powered lawyer, Jacqui was paid to think. Jacqui also had two teenage children and a hardworking husband. There were lots of demands on her time and energies. A self-confessed "adrenaline junkie and stress-head," Jacqui turned to meditation, desperate to find a little peace and balance in what felt to her to be an ever more demanding world.

Jacqui's experience of life had become so uncomfortable, and she felt on the verge of being out of control so often, that she applied herself to learning meditation with the same zeal she did everything else in her life. She quickly mastered the capacity to sit still and to relax the body. This brought some calmness to her mind and to her life, but when she did these Mindfulness of Thoughts experiments, her reaction was strong and exasperated. "My mind is like a washing machine," she reported to her group, with a tinge of disgust. "There are so many thoughts, one on top of the other. I can't even see where they start, let alone where they finish. One just rushes into another. I must be hopeless at this." The frustration was palpable, a sure sign of the anxiety and tension Jacqui was experiencing.

The thoughts that often seem to rush headlong into our mind can be likened to a mountain stream. High in the mountains, the stream tumbles over rocks and plunges down valleys. It is turbulent, fast, jumbled. But as it descends, the mountains give way to gentler slopes. The stream is still flowing fast, but there is less turbulence, less chaos. Farther on, the stream reaches the flat plains and swells into a larger river. The river begins to meander gently, quietly navigating bends, its surface becoming calm and smooth. Finally the water makes its way to the sea, and merges into something vast and deeply tranquil. While waves may rise and fall on the surface of the sea, we know that just below the surface all is peaceful and calm.

Jacqui found that this metaphor gave her confidence to persevere. She determined to maintain the intention of just observing her thoughts, aiming to be free of reaction or judgment. She could understand the notion of becoming an impartial observer, and learned to differentiate between the times when she was able to simply be aware and those other times when she lost it and became caught up in her thoughts and re-actions once again.

After just a few weeks of this practice, this mind training, Jacqui told the group:

> There is really quite a difference. Although there are still lots of thoughts, I seem less caught up in them. It is as if I really am able to be aware of them. It's a bit like watching a B-grade movie on late-night television (which I used to do to try and relax) and being quite dispassionate about the story and its outcome. That sense of curiosity is there; I can be curious to notice the thoughts but I am not too concerned with their actual content.

Jacqui went on:

> It's like the thoughts have lost their power over me. I used to worry about every little thing. I took every thought that came into my head seriously and got wound up by it. It was exhausting. Now it is as if so many of my thoughts are of no great conse-quence. While I can pay attention to what is important, so many thoughts seem to be just that, they are just thoughts, and there is no need to worry about them.

Then Jacqui added another important point:

> What is really exciting, though, is that the washing-machine ef-fect is definitely slowing down. I feel like I am out of the high mountains and into the middle slopes. While there are still lots of thoughts, I am getting the sense of how one thought does lead into the next. That segment thing is starting to become quite obvious, and it even seems like there are a few gaps between the thoughts where not much is happening at all.

What Jacqui is alluding to here is in fact the next key point in these exercises. Once we start to notice how each thought is like a segment or a unit, we may well start to notice how there is often a gap between one thought finishing and the next one starting.

THE GAP BETWEEN THE THOUGHTS

In the following exercise we aim to notice the gap that often occurs between thoughts. It may be useful to spend a little longer on this exercise compared to the earlier ones. Simply observe your thoughts, aim to notice them as segments and then pay attention to the gaps.

EXPERIMENT 4: THE GAP BETWEEN THE THOUGHTS

Take up your meditation posture again and close your eyes. For a few minutes, aim not to think of anything in particular. . . . Just allow thoughts to come when they are ready, to go when they are ready. . . . Simply being interested to notice how each thought is like a segment or unit. It has a start, a middle and a finishing point.

Then notice how it may well be that after one thought finishes, there is a gap before the next thought starts. . . . There is no need to belabor this. You do not need to make anything happen, or do anything in particular, except to maintain that attitude of mindfully observing your thoughts. Aim to be patient . . . just allowing any thoughts to come when they are ready, and to go when they are ready. . . . And be curious to notice any gaps when they actually do appear.

What did you notice? If this is the first time you have done this exercise and you did notice some gaps, then you are making real progress.

If the gaps are yet to open up for you, then persevere. Be patient. Allow the torrent of your mind stream to flow, to run itself out, to reach a quieter state. This can be a bit like allowing the B-grade movie that Jacqui mentioned to just play itself out. Eventually it finishes. If we are patient, if we maintain the stance of mindfulness by paying attention nonjudgmentally, if we just hang in there, the thoughts will slow, the gaps will appear. Quite naturally. Quite effortlessly.

This brings us to another crucial observation Jacqui made. In the gap between two thoughts, there is an absence of thought. Obviously, in the gap between two thoughts there is a moment of silence or stillness as we call it. So now we will turn our attention more particularly to the stillness.

STILLNESS AS THE EVER-PRESENT BACKGROUND

Now we aim to become more aware of those two aspects of our mind—the still, quiet part and the active, thinking part. The next exercise (on page 228) requires a little more introduction. What is of particular interest here is the stillness. As we start to notice the stillness in the gaps between the thoughts, two things quite naturally evolve: bigger gaps, and longer stillness.

First, if we can manage to just observe the stillness, the gaps get bigger. By not reacting, not judging, not trying to analyze the nature of the gap or the stillness, by just being content to continue to observe it, the gaps quite naturally will get bigger; the thoughts will tend to come less frequently. At the same time we may well notice that we are becoming more present. In this state of mindfulness we are less concerned with what happened in the past and what might happen in the future. Quite naturally we become more attentive to what is happening in the present moment. Our attention is more taken up by our present moment experience; when, in the present moment experience of this particular exercise, we give attention to observing our mind, what we see is its natural state.

Remember that this natural state can usefully be compared to the sky. In our mind there is a background of stillness, a constant, expansive, borderless stillness somewhat like the blue sky. Then there are the thoughts that come and go, moving through the stillness like white clouds floating across the blue sky. For many people it works well to experience the gaps between the thoughts and the stillness as being like a background across which the thoughts travel. However, it may be helpful to know that stillness and spaciousness are very closely related.

As another option, it may work for you to be aware of the space between you, the observer, and the thoughts you are observing. In the same way that when we are watching TV there is a clear sense of space between us and the television, we can be aware of ourselves—the observer—our thoughts and the space between the two. You may also have a sense of the space around your individual thoughts—above them and below them, not just between them and behind them. If this is so, then as we progress with these experiments, we can substitute "space" for gaps. In other words, rather than using the gaps between thoughts as your entry point to experience the stillness, you can use the space around your thoughts.

Two aspects of the mind: stillness and thinking

Having turned our attention inward, away from the mind's usual preoccupation with what is going on outside of our mind, we are now effectively investigating the nature of the mind and its thoughts. In doing so, the two basic elements of the mind are not only revealed, but they become clearer.

As mentioned, the mind has what can be described as a constant ground state of stillness, and a more obvious, day-to-day activity of thinking. Now, after all, the mind's function is to think. The mind's job, as it were, is to present us with thoughts and to use those thoughts to good effect. But it does this thinking within a context of ever-present stillness. The delightful fact is that we can become aware of this stillness through our own investigation, our own direct experience.

With our next experiment, the aim is to become aware that the stillness we experienced in the gap between the thoughts, or in the space around our thoughts, is in fact more like a constant presence than just a chink between a couple of thoughts. With this exercise, the intention will be to allow any thoughts to come and go while you simply observe them mindfully. As the gaps and the space become more apparent, it is as if you move into the stillness, aiming to experience it more directly as the constant presence that it really is. This is a bit like watching white clouds drift across the blue sky, realizing that the sky is the vast, virtually infinite canopy that it is, and that the clouds are just transient; they come and go, and the gaps between them provide glimpses of the blue sky. And now it is as if we turn our attention from the clouds to the sky. We let go of the clouds and hold our attention on the spaciousness of the blue sky. We move our attention from our thoughts to the stillness.

In practical terms, there can be a sense of movement in this. It is as if we move forward through the gap between our thoughts and into the spaciousness of the stillness, as if we have taken off in an airplane from the ground, passed through a gap in the clouds and are now experiencing the full canopy of the sky. Many of us will have had this experience while flying out of an airport on a cloudy day. From the ground, the clouds may appear thick, even impenetrable. As the plane rises into the sky, there is often turbulence as we pass through the clouds. Sometimes it seems as if we almost bounce in and out of the clouds until we are finally above them. Then, if we look up, there it is again—the vast blue canopy of the sky. It was always there, it was just that we could not see it from the ground; the clouds obscured it.

Another fascinating thing about flying is that when we do get high enough and look down, the clouds can seem so small and so inconsequential. So it can be with our thoughts. Sometimes, when we first begin, they are so thick and come and go so fast that we have no sense of stillness, just one thought after another. The techniques we are experimenting with are like the airplanes of our mind. They give us wings. They give us the capacity to rise above the thoughts; perhaps even to go beyond the thoughts and experience that more profound, vast stillness. And often when we do this, just like looking down from the plane on the clouds below, from the vantage point of stillness, any thoughts that do arise can seem of little concern. They do not distract us or disturb us. In the stillness, we experience a profound sense of peace.

A note of caution before we proceed with the exercise: we need to temper the natural desire to experience all of this with the mindfulness that is required to actually allow it to happen. What helps is to combine the positive intention to do the exercises as described with the right attitude—one where we deliberately let go of expectations, judgments and reactions. Approach the exercise with that open curiosity we have spoken of so often.

Now we can put it all together. Once you are ready, take a few minutes for this next experiment. The aim is to notice the stillness as the background across which the thoughts travel, in the same way white clouds travel across the blue sky. Again, first read the exercise and then put the book down for a few minutes while you do it.

EXPERIMENT 5: STILLNESS AS EVER-PRESENT BACKGROUND

Take up your meditative posture, close your eyes and, without intending to think of anything in particular, simply allow any thoughts to come when they are ready, and go when they are ready. . . . Notice how the thoughts are like segments or units unto themselves, with a start, a middle and an end.

Pay particular attention to how, as one thought finishes, there is often a gap before the next thought starts. . . . As you notice this gap, notice the silence, the stillness in the gap.

Then it is as if you move into the gap, becoming aware of how the stillness is like an ever-present background across which the thoughts are coming and going.

It is our experience that most people are able to do this either on their first attempt or after only a few practice sessions. However, remember that for some, being aware of the spaciousness around the thoughts may be more useful than the technique of focusing on the gap between the thoughts with the intention of revealing the stillness as a background.

When you do notice the stillness, you will probably notice several things. First, how peaceful and calm it is. Also, while it is true that when your mind is still it is empty of thoughts, it does not feel like you are in a void or in some deep, dark hole. Quite to the contrary, the usual experience is one of aliveness, of being in a creative space full of possibilities. It is a very pleasant feeling. What you may also notice is that this stillness itself has a sense of place; the stillness is somewhere, not nowhere.

WHERE IS THE STILLNESS?

Now, if you cannot remember this or you did not notice it as you experienced the stillness, take a few more minutes now to repeat the exercise, this time investigating for yourself where this stillness seems to be most obvious to you. Where is it located?

EXPERIMENT 6: WHERE IS THE STILLNESS?

Take up your meditative posture, close your eyes and, without intending to think of anything in particular, simply allow any thoughts to come when they are ready, and go when they are ready. . . . Notice how the thoughts are like segments or units unto themselves, with a start, a middle and an end.

Pay particular attention to how as one thought finishes there is often a gap before the next thought starts. . . . As you notice this gap, notice the silence, the stillness in the gap.

Then it is as if you move into the gap, becoming aware of how the stillness is like an ever-present background across which the thoughts come and go. Now, notice where this stillness seems to be most obvious to you. Where is it located?

Most often, people describe the stillness as being like a screen in front of them. Often this screen is two-dimensional like a big, flat movie screen, but not uncommonly it is three-dimensional, having depth as well as width and height.

The stillness can appear in a wide range of places, depending on the individual. Sometimes it is external—in front, to one side or above or behind the person. Sometimes, but much less frequently, it seems to be internal: maybe in the head, just behind the eyelids, or in some other part of the body. But again there is no right or wrong in this; people are different in so many ways. What is useful here is merely to notice where the stillness is most obvious to you.

What comes next is the realization that you and this stillness are still somehow separate. While you may now have a good awareness of the stillness and where in space it seems most noticeable to you, there will probably be this sense that you are observing the stillness. In other words, you are in one place, and you are observing the stillness which is in another place. There is you, the observer, the stillness being observed and then there is the activity of observing. With an observer and a thing being observed, it means there is a duality. Two things. You and it. And as well as those two things there is the activity. You are performing the activity of observing.

WHERE IS THE OBSERVER?

Now it gets really exciting. There is the possibility of going beyond this duality and this activity, and experiencing a more profound oneness. To help make this possible, what we need to do first is to locate that observing part of ourself. This is a very quick experiment—it should take less than a minute.

EXPERIMENT 7: WHERE IS THE OBSERVER?

Sit as if to meditate, close your eyes and notice where the observer part of you is located. . . . This part of you will feel like your central point, the center of your being.

Where is it for you? For many it feels as if their observer part is located in that area between the eyes and a little into the forehead. For some it is external to the head, perhaps above, behind or a bit in front. Others locate it in the region of their throat, or in the heart or mid-chest region. Again, remember that people are different and what is important is where you feel this observer part to be located.

The complete practice of Mindfulness of Thoughts and Stillness

Having now a sense of where the observer is, and where the stillness is, we aim to bring the two together.

For this exercise, you can either have the sense of moving into the stillness and merging with it, or you can imagine the stillness coming to you and enveloping you. Either way, the intention is to join with the stillness. A sense of joyful surrender helps with this, like melting into the comfort of loving, trusting arms. It is as if we become absorbed in the feeling, the presence, the radiance of the stillness. We aim to let go of any sense of boundaries, any sense of it and us, and to simply let go of all attachments, all concerns, everything. We aim to simply let go and be in the stillness. In a profound sense there is nothing we have to do. We simply let go and rest in the stillness.

Now we are ready to put all these preparatory experiments and techniques together into the one exercise. This is a key exercise that you may well choose to do regularly. It provides a reliable means for using mindfulness to move beyond busy and potentially distracting thoughts, and into a simple stillness. This exercise is based on combining the experiments we have already practiced individually. It becomes one repeatable process that flows into stillness.

EXPERIMENT 8: MINDFULNESS OF THOUGHTS AND STILLNESS

Take a few moments to adjust your position and settle into your posture. . . . Feel your body relaxing once again . . . the muscles softening and loosening . . . relaxing and releasing. . . . Maybe a deeper breath or two helps. . . . Just simply letting go . . . quite effortlessly . . . quite effortlessly.

Now, without aiming to think of anything in particular, just notice whatever thoughts come into your awareness . . . simply allow the thoughts to come when they are ready, and go when they are ready. . . . And notice how the thoughts are coming into your awareness. . . . Perhaps you are seeing them as pictures . . . or hearing them as words . . . or perhaps you are feeling them . . . or a bit of both. . . . Just noticing how these thoughts are coming into your awareness.

And notice how each thought is like a segment or a unit . . . each with a beginning, a middle and an end . . . noticing the segments or units. . . . And now notice how, as the next thought finishes, there may well be a gap between that thought finishing and the next thought starting. . . . So hold your attention on the gap between the thoughts . . . notice that in this gap between two thoughts is a moment of stillness . . . and then it is as if you move into the gap, into the silence . . . then there is the sense that the silence, the stillness, is almost like a background across which the thoughts are traveling . . . a bit like white clouds drifting across a blue sky. . . . There is a silence, a stillness. . . . It is like the sky, it is there all the time . . . vast . . . spacious . . . infinite . . . like a background across which the thoughts travel. . . . The thoughts are like clouds, white clouds drifting across a blue sky. . . . They just come when they are ready . . . and go when they are ready. It is as if you move your attention from the clouds to the sky . . . hold your awareness on that stillness, that background. . . .

And now, become aware of where that stillness is most obvious to you. . . . Where is the place in which the stillness is most obvious . . . ? Perhaps it is like a screen in front of you. . . . Perhaps it is to one side, or in some other place. . . . Or perhaps it is within you somewhere. . . . Just noticing where this stillness is most obvious.

And be conscious now of your own central point . . . being aware of where your own central point is located. . . .

And now bringing together these two places, the stillness and your central point . . . either by having a sense of bringing your own central point into that place where the stillness is most obvious . . . or feeling the stillness moving toward you, wrapping around and through you. . . . There is a sense of merging . . . of bringing these two places together . . . of unifying . . . becoming as one. . . . It is almost like a melting . . . a merging . . . a union . . . perhaps a sense of relief . . . a sense of coming home . . . a sense of joining . . . a sense of resting . . . deeply . . . profoundly . . . a direct experience . . . resting in that presence for a few moments now.

When you are ready, gently open your eyes once again.

Many people find this exercise very useful. Maybe you will find it enough to just practice these exercises once to get a real experience of stillness before moving on to the next stage, the complete practice of MBSM. However, many people do find merit in this technique in its own right. So just as we may practice the relaxation or the mindfulness techniques regularly, if the Mindfulness of Thoughts exercise helps you to have a more direct experience of the inner stillness, then maybe it is an exercise to do repeatedly. Certainly, some people use it as their main practice.

What you can do very effectively with this exercise is to develop a real awareness, a real familiarity with the stillness. And as you practice more, you are also likely to find that thoughts, along with other potential distractions such as external sounds or internal feelings or emotions, simply do not disturb you. You will develop the capacity to be aware of the stillness and the thoughts and the emotions and the sounds, and to be calm and present to them all. However, before we bring our four steps of preparation, relaxation, mindfulness and stillness into the one complete practice, let us make a deeper inquiry into the nature of this stillness we have been discussing.

CHAPTER 12

STILLNESS AND THE NATURE OF MIND

Profound peace
natural simplicity
uncompounded luminosity
—THE FIRST WORDS SPOKEN BY THE BUDDHA
AFTER HIS ENLIGHTENMENT

It is just purely a stillness of the mind,
Not asleep, not unconscious, not drowsy, quite clear, but just a stillness.
—DR. AINSLIE MEARES, *Relief Without Drugs*

EXPERIENCING STILLNESS

In many of the more mystical or esoteric meditation traditions, the experience of stillness is merely alluded to. What can we say of it that is useful?

When we begin to experience something of the stillness we have been referring to, we enter into a state of open and undistracted awareness. This state has been discussed earlier, particularly in relation to mindfulness. It is where we are fully present and aware of what is happening in and around us. We are open, free of judgment and reaction, simply curious and engaged with whatever is happening in our lives in this particular moment.

When we are able to bring this open and undistracted awareness to our meditation practice, quite quickly we notice two things. As we pay attention to our present moment experience, deliberately and non-judgmentally, we quite naturally come to realize that there is both stillness and movement.

Movement in this context is used to describe in a collective sense anything that happens, anything you notice. For example, a thought is a movement in the mind, and a sound is a movement, as is an emotion. All these things come and go, they pass on by, they are not permanent or fixed. They move; hence the word *movement*.

So there is stillness and there is movement. And when we can rest in that state of awareness, just being aware of what is, without any judgment, without any reaction, without becoming caught up in the movement or the stillness, just resting in the pure awareness, then we are completely at peace, completely at ease and completely aware and undistracted.

If we are aware of the stillness, we are calm and peaceful. If some movement arises—if a thought comes into our awareness—just the same, we are calm and peaceful. An emotion arises and we become aware of that too, free of judgment, free of reaction. With time and practice we develop a real equanimity, the capacity to remain unaltered in our state of mind in the face of stillness or movement. This is the state of "one taste," where the taste, the experience, is the same whether we are experiencing stillness or movement. And it is in this state of one taste that we feel calm and at peace, whatever comes our way. Imagine that! Calm and peaceful in the face of all that life brings. And joyful and content. Real happiness. Real inner peace.

Stillness in daily life

So what is it like to be constantly calm and peaceful? Pretty dull, some might imagine—where are the highs and lows, the peaks and troughs, the spice of life? Well, it may be true that if you want to live your life like a character from a soap opera or some volatile melodrama, this equanimity is not for you. But if you prefer a sense of deep contentedness and the ability to be open to the range of life experiences, and to have the capacity to engage in these experiences with intimacy, good humor and joy, then this might be just what you have been looking for.

Some may imagine that meditation leads to a laid-back, drowsy, "whatever" sort of attitude. In fact, it is quite the opposite. Out of meditation grows a natural and profound sense of compassion, and a desire to be useful in life. Experiencing stillness leads to enthusiasm, vigor, compassion and love.

THE NATURE OF STILLNESS

There can be quite a wide range of experiences that come under the banner of stillness. However, in broad terms, there are two types of stillness: stillness of the ordinary mind, and the more profound kind of stillness associated with the true nature of mind.

Stillness of the ordinary mind

By ordinary mind we mean the thinking mind. Commonly this is the mind that we are most familiar with. Stillness of the ordinary mind is best defined as an absence of thoughts. It is when we are awake and conscious but not thinking of anything. When we experience this type of stillness during meditation, it is like our mind has taken a break from thinking. In this sense it is like a deep rest for the mind. It is easy to appreciate how this type of stillness can be deeply relaxing, deeply healing and deeply regenerative. It is just the same as when we give our body a rest, relaxing our muscles and allowing them to recuperate after a hard workout; when our mind settles, it experiences these same regenerative benefits.

The function of our ordinary mind is to think, so it is helpful to realize that it is normal to have thoughts in our mind. In exactly the same way, it is normal for the sky to have clouds appearing quite regularly. With our mind, it is not the thoughts that are the problem, it is what we do with them. As we have previously explored, there are a variety of difficulties associated with excessive thinking, including worrying, fears and anxiety. Giving the mind a break from all this is an obvious delight and benefit that accompanies stillness.

Of course, the challenge is that, until we train the mind, stillness does not come so easily. Again, as we have discussed, some meditation schools use concentration as a means to cut through the thoughts and arrive at stillness. Other schools use mindfulness, allowing the thoughts to come and go, waiting patiently and nonjudgmentally for our mind to settle. With our technique of Mindfulness-Based Stillness Meditation we use both concentration and mindfulness. As we are learning to practice these techniques, it is most likely we will first experience stillness as this stillness of the ordinary mind.

Commonly, people who provide feedback on this experience will say, "I am not sure if I was asleep or awake. I do not think I was asleep; I know I was not thinking of anything, but I am not sure what happened." A hint here is that the experience of stillness of the ordinary mind is often somewhat dull, in the sense that it is rather vague and nebulous; somewhat reminiscent of daydreaming or that rather nice reverie that comes just before sleep. Stillness of the ordinary mind also rarely lasts for long. It is a bit like the sky without clouds: sooner or later more clouds—thoughts—will turn up. Another observation often made is that in this stillness our perception of time can change quite dramatically. Time is related to movement. When things happen, we notice things changing and moving, and we get a sense of time passing. When we are still, sometimes time goes inordinately quickly, whereas on other occasions it seems to pass very slowly.

What is important to emphasize is that this type of stillness is almost always accompanied by deep physical relaxation, a very calm state of mind and a good feeling. People invariably enjoy it, and it is very helpful for all aspects of our health and well-being, as well as being profoundly useful in creating the inner balance that leads to natural healing. So from that point of view, this type of stillness is very effective, and well worth being able to experience and rest in while meditating.

However, for those on the spiritual path, this type of stillness has less value. There are two reasons for this. The first is the dull state of mind that this stillness involves; the second is that this stillness is often mistaken by inexperienced meditators for enlightenment. Absence of thought is associated with a good feeling and it can give a sense of an altered state of consciousness, but if we are seeking a more profound and direct experience of the true nature of our minds, then we need to go beyond the ordinary mind and we need to go beyond the stillness of that ordinary mind.

Stillness and the nature of mind

What is the difference, then, between the ordinary mind and the true nature of our mind? And what do we mean by "nature of mind"?

If we reflect upon these questions for a moment, what we are really asking is: Who are we really? Is there a difference between how things commonly appear and how they actually are? What is the truth of who we really are?

Asking these questions and seeking their answers is a bit like a physicist looking at a cup and asking, "What is it really?" It looks like a cup: solid, functional, permanent. The cup looks real enough, it holds water reliably enough, we can put it away in a cupboard and go back for it later. You can give it to me and it works quite nicely as a cup for me too, thank you very much. But if a physicist were to break the cup down to examine it more closely, it could be reduced to dust quite quickly and easily. No more cup, no more capacity to hold water. Broken into pieces, the cup's lack of real permanence is clearly revealed. And by examining the dust more closely, the physicist will find smaller and smaller pieces—molecules, atoms, nuclei, electrons and so on, until, as we know, it is clear that the cup is made up of pure energy. There is nothing in the cup that is either truly solid or permanent or that exists independently in its own right. There is nothing permanent about the cup. Yet clearly the cup does exist. So the cup has an appearance in the relative, physical world, and as such it functions quite nicely in the way that we expect cups to function. But in absolute terms it is quite empty of anything real or solid or permanent.

Who are we really?

What, then, of us human beings? Our bodies are like the cup: real enough in one sense, but ultimately made up of matter that, when broken down, is essentially concentrated energy. Even more quickly than the cup, our physical bodies are changing all the time. Old cells are dying, new ones being reproduced. Our body today is different from the one we had a year ago, or ten years ago. This body we have now is dramatically different from the body we had as a young child. So if this body we have now is changing all the time, who are we really?

Of course, just as our physical body is changing all the time, so too are our emotions and thoughts. These can seem real enough, solid enough, when we are experiencing them. Like the cup, our emotions and thoughts can be useful and they can be quite obvious to other people. But if we examine them closely, like the cup, we find them to be quite insubstantial and definitely impermanent. Our emotions and thoughts clearly come and go quite rapidly.

The direct perception of truth

So when we talk of the true nature of our minds we are inquiring as to whether or not there is some more absolute, enduring aspect at the heart of our being. While all the great spiritual traditions offer answers in response to these inquiries, and while we may discuss some of these here, the real answers, the only truly satisfying answers, will come from your own direct experience. This is a key promise of meditation: the possibility of the direct perception of who we really are, and the true nature of our mind.

This perception, the experience of an absolute truth in relation to the nature of our mind, is to be realized in the deep stillness of meditation; in the stillness beyond the thinking mind. The curious thing is that for almost everyone this experience will have the qualities of a revelation. It seems like a revelation because commonly we have lost touch with who we really are, the true nature of our mind, and now we come to reexperience it. It is like coming home. Coming home to our true self.

To be clear, when we experience this true nature we are not manufacturing an experience or creating something new. All that we are doing is becoming aware of an aspect of ourselves that was always there, is always there, will always be there; only for most of us it has been obscured from view.

Meditation is the path

A useful analogy, again, is that of the blue sky and the clouds. The blue sky is the absolute nature, the clouds are the obscuring thoughts. Meditation has us traveling past the clouds, past the thoughts, to reveal the true nature of the sky, the true nature of our mind.

In meditation we begin to reacquaint ourselves with this inner essence, this true nature of mind. As we do so we begin to realize that in a very real sense so much of our suffering has resulted from overidentifying with the wrong "bit" of ourselves. We think we are this body, these emotions and these thoughts. We overidentify with what we commonly call our ego and, as a consequence, fear for its vulnerability. We fear for its having its needs unmet, its being hurt and for its aging and dying; all of which will surely happen sooner or later. No wonder we suffer!

THREE MAIN QUALITIES OF NATURE OF MIND

When we begin to have glimpses of the true nature of our mind, we begin to realize it has very different characteristics from the fragile and impermanent thinking mind and its attendant emotions. Drawing upon the Dzogchen teachings, especially those given by Sogyal Rinpoche, it can be explained how the true nature of our mind has three main qualities: emptiness, awareness and compassion.

1. Emptiness

Like the cup, ultimately our mind is empty of anything solid or permanent in the usual sense of these words. However, clearly we do exist, and this "emptiness" does not mean there is a void or black hole in our heart's essence. In fact, this emptiness is all-pervading and makes so much possible. It is better described as being like an "immanence."

Imagine if you were in a room with no space in it, or if you were in a swimming pool full of concrete. How could you move? What could you do? Who would be able to hear you? Clearly we need the space in the room or the pool so that we can move about or so that sound can travel. Similarly, earlier we used the metaphor of the black writing on the white page. If the paper was all black, you would be unable to discern the words. It is the "emptiness" of the white page that makes the words visible. And in so many ways it is the emptiness, or the space or stillness, that makes life possible.

2. Awareness

The second quality of the nature of mind is the capacity of awareness. We are capable of recognizing—we can see, and we can hear, smell, taste and touch—as well as thinking, learning, understanding and knowing. However, when we use this awareness to overidentify with our ego, it brings us anxiety, uncertainty, pain and suffering. And when we use this awareness to recognize our true nature and live in the light of that awareness, it brings peace, confidence and true happiness.

Now, importantly, this awareness is present within us all the time. We are aware of reading this book. We are aware of what we did yesterday. Even when our emotions are strong, we can also be aware of them. We can be aware of thinking. Maybe this is all simpler than we might have imagined?

3. Compassion

The third quality of the true nature of mind is that which spontaneously flows out of this empty essence and awareness. In the Buddhist tradition this natural outpouring is called compassion, which is the wish for all people to be free of suffering. In other traditions, notably in Christianity, it is called love—the wish for all people to be happy. And not just happy in that fragile sense of worldly happiness, but happy in the true and sustainable sense of inner happiness, the happiness that is the product of realizing the true nature of our mind.

FAMILIARITY AND CONFIDENCE

There is a difference between meeting people for the first time and actually getting to know them. We may have been introduced to various people and be able to remember and recognize them when we meet again, but that is quite a step from actually having a long-term relationship, really understanding and knowing someone.

In the natural progression of our meditation experience, we may well be fortunate and have an introduction to the nature of our mind. In Tibetan one of the common words for meditation is *gom*, which means "getting used to." What we are getting used to, what we are becoming familiar with, is the nature of our mind. Sogyal Rinpoche explains that the key point of Dzogchen meditation is abiding by the recognition of the nature of mind. Abiding means that after first recognizing this state, we then simply rest in it, until we become familiar with it.

As we become familiar with the nature of our mind through meditation, we also develop a capacity for open, nonjudgmental awareness, and the capacity to rest in or maintain that state of awareness, so that it becomes both known and increasingly stable. Using our analogy of relationship, this is similar to the difference between being introduced to someone in a way that you might recognize them if you saw them again, and really getting to know them. As our meditation matures and deepens, our awareness of the true nature of our mind, and in that sense our awareness of the truth of who we are and what life is, becomes ever more constant. We develop what is described as "confidence in the view." "The view" is our spiritual awareness and we can only gain confidence in it through gaining familiarity with the direct experience of the true nature of our own mind.

What also happens as our practice develops is that we realize the important difference between having a thought and thinking. We have a thought; thoughts come and go. This should not be surprising. After all, the nature of the ordinary mind is to have thoughts; that is what it does. But we can learn to be aware of these thoughts, so that rather than getting caught up in them along with their companions of hope and fear, anxiety and stress, we simply observe them.

Sogyal Rinpoche explains, "As long as you are aware of what is going on, without distraction, then it is meditation." So once you have grasped the truth of this, the method in meditation is the same regardless of what occurs. Whatever thoughts occur to you while you are meditating, whatever sounds come to your awareness, whatever bodily sensations, whatever emotions, you just notice them. Simple as that. You notice them free of judgment, free of reaction or commentary. You notice them with full open awareness.

As time goes on and your practice develops not only will remaining undistracted become easier, but also you will come to realize that difficult thoughts, emotions and sensations can actually be helpful for your meditation. As you become better able to deal with these challenges to your meditation practice, you strengthen and mature your capacity to remain undistracted. This is why we encourage you to learn the earlier steps of MBSM: preparation, relaxation and mindfulness. Through this method, the experience of stillness is developed in an accessible and reliable sequence, creating the right conditions for the recognition of the nature of mind. By following this method, your relationship with your own mind has the possibility of developing from that introductory phase of early recognition into a mature and stable knowing.

As your meditation develops so will your capacity to remain for longer periods of time in a state of open and undistracted awareness, leaving you free to rest in the natural clarity of your own true nature. You will have confidence in the view.

Coming home

What happens when we do begin to experience the true nature of our mind, with its empty essence, its awareness and its compassion? Well, often the first thing is a sense of sheer relief. It is like you have been lost and found your way home. Then there is a sense of familiarity. Again it is like coming home; coming home to who you really are. Knowing you have found what you were looking for brings contentment and satisfaction. A gentle smile that comes from deep within. And next the good humor that follows when you have a certainty, a confidence, a knowing of something really important. And out of all this emerges a deep concern for the welfare, the good health and the happiness of self and others. There comes a gentle but resolute compulsion to do all that is possible to look after yourself and as many other people, creatures and aspects of the environment as possible.

This connection with the essence of who we are is the radical healer. It brings love of self and love of others, which leads to the type of transformations we call healing. Healing of bodies, healing of relationships, healing of minds, healing of spirit and even the potential for healing the planet. Radical healing. Profound healing.

This connection with the true self permeates our life. It becomes like a point of reference. It is the ultimate refuge and a safe haven into which we can confidently retreat, as well as a source of inspiration and energy for good. The more we identify with it, the more we are aware of it, the happier, the more effective and the healthier we will be.

All that is required is that we study and practice; learn what to do and then do it. Through meditation, all this is on offer.

CHAPTER 13

THE COMPLETE MINDFULNESS-BASED STILLNESS MEDITATION TECHNIQUE

All of man's difficulties
are caused by his inability to sit quietly in a room by himself.
—BLAISE PASCAL, *Les Pensées*

To complete Part I, let us bring together all the elements of preparation, relaxation, mindfulness and stillness into the main meditation technique we recommend for regular practice, Mindfulness-Based Stillness Meditation (MBSM).

This key meditation practice builds on all the exercises we have been learning and practicing. The complete technique aims to help us to naturally progress from establishing a good posture in a conducive environment to gently relaxing the body and calming the mind. Then as we go with the relaxation, the mind becomes more calm and settled and we turn quite effortlessly to mindfulness. We simply become more aware, less judgmental. We mindfully give attention to our breath, and in doing so relax and settle a little more. Then we give our nonjudgmental awareness to our body, simply noticing how it is at that particular time. Whatever emotions we may become aware of, we notice them too, just as we do our thoughts. We allow them to come when they are ready, to go when they are ready. Free of judgment, free of reaction, with a gentle, open curiosity. Open and undistracted awareness.

And as we impartially observe all this, we begin to notice a stillness. Maybe it is first noticeable in the space between our thoughts. Maybe around the thoughts. Maybe throughout our being. We notice the stillness. And we notice the movement. Things come and go. We remain undistracted. Awake. Alert. Curious. Open. Nonjudgmental. In a state of deep, natural peace. And we simply rest in that state of open and undistracted awareness.

Now perhaps you can use what is written above as a guide into the practice of Mindfulness-Based Stillness Meditation. Or perhaps you would benefit from learning a more formal script. You may like to try both and find out what is most useful for you. Either way, the aim is to learn how to use the progression described above from preparation, through relaxation, into mindfulness and on into stillness.

Here, then, is the more formal script for Mindfulness-Based Stillness Meditation. Allow at least twenty minutes for this exercise.

MINDFULNESS-BASED STILLNESS MEDITATION— THE COMPLETE PRACTICE

Take a moment to adjust your position. . . . Gently close your eyes and settle into your posture.

Now, in your own way, take a few moments to relax your body. . . . Feel the muscles softening and loosening . . . relaxing and releasing . . . just simply letting go. . . . Perhaps a deeper breath or two helps.

With your eyes gently closed, become aware of the space before your eyes . . . just simply rest your attention there. . . .

Now pay attention to any sounds outside the room . . . just listening . . . with a gentle curiosity. . . . Let the sounds come and go . . . no need to judge. . . . Now any sounds inside the room. . . . Now the sound of your own breathing . . . even if very soft . . . just listening.

As you bring your awareness to your breath, notice what sensations there are as you breathe in . . . and as you breathe out. . . . Feel the air touch your nostrils. . . . Feel the slight movement of your chest and your tummy. . . . Listen to the gentle sound of your breathing . . . just being aware of the breath.

Next, bring your awareness down to your feet. . . . Move your awareness through your feet. . . . Notice any sensations in your feet. . . . Just feel them . . . feeling into your toes . . . your heels . . . the surface of your feet . . . all through the feet. . . . And as you feel into your feet, feel the flow of your breath . . . simply coming and going . . . just watching . . . quite effortlessly.

Now bring your awareness to your shoulders . . . Notice the feeling in the muscles of your shoulders . . . the base of your neck . . . a pressure or a tingling. . . . Just feel it . . . simply noticing. . . . And as you feel into the muscles of your shoulders . . . feel the flow of your breath . . . simply being aware of the breath.

As you are aware of the space before your eyes, become aware of any sensations in and around your eyes. . . . Move your attention through your eyebrows . . . and across your forehead. . . . Notice whatever sensations are there. . . . As you feel through the eyes and across the forehead, feel the flow of your breath . . . just resting in the awareness.

Now, with a willingness to get in touch with how you are feeling inside, bring your awareness to your center . . . the feeling centerline of the body. . . . Feeling into the throat . . .

feeling into the center of the chest . . . feeling into the solar plexus . . . and feeling into the tummy . . . resting your attention along the whole feeling centerline of your being. . . . Keep the feelings company, with curiosity and compassion . . . just simply being aware. . . . And as you notice the feelings in your center, feel the flow of your breathing.

Open your awareness to the whole body. . . . Notice whatever sensations are coming into your awareness at this particular moment. . . . Perhaps the awareness of the space in front of your eyes. . . . Perhaps the feeling of the breath. . . . If any thoughts come to your awareness, just let them come and go. . . . Watch the thoughts coming and going.

And notice the background of stillness . . . the background across which the thoughts travel . . . like white clouds drifting across a blue sky. . . . Just noticing whatever comes and goes . . . just noticing. . . . Being aware of that still and silent presence . . . simply resting in that stillness.

MINDFULNESS-BASED STILLNESS MEDITATION: THE METHOD SUMMARIZED

To make all of this even simpler, to highlight the essence of this approach and to summarize how we might practice in daily life, here is the MBSM in brief.

Step 1: Preparation

In a conducive environment, take up a conducive posture, turn your mind inward and relax.

Step 2: Relaxation

Use the simplest, most practical technique that helps you to relax your body. Allow your mind to go with it. Let go. Effortlessly.

Step 3: Mindfulness

As a natural sequence you could flow on to use the focused applications of mindfulness of sound, mindfulness of bodily sensations, emotions, thoughts and stillness. Or you could use the more open mindfulness that leads into simple, undistracted awareness—simply notice with bare attention whatever comes to your awareness, whether it be sounds, sensations, emotions, thoughts or stillness; whatever happens, simply be aware, open and present.

Step 4: Stillness

As you rest in this undistracted awareness you notice the movement—the activity or phenomena that occur within you and around you—and you notice the all-pervading background of stillness. The stillness becomes increasingly familiar. You smile as you are warmed by the comfort and ease that flows with this knowing, this experience of the essence of meditation.

Putting MBSM even more simply!

Having prepared well, we relax.

Relaxing deeply, we become more mindful.

As our mindfulness develops, stillness is revealed; naturally and without effort.

We rest in open, undistracted awareness.

This is Mindfulness-Based Stillness Meditation.

Meditation: the direct approach

In chapter 1 we explained how meditation could be practiced using the direct approach of no method, or the gradual approach, which relies on learning and using techniques. Having described the specific techniques of MBSM in great detail, let us conclude by restating the essence of the direct approach to meditation.

There is nothing to do. Simply be aware.

Open. Undistracted. Aware.

It is as simple and as difficult as that.

SOME REMINDERS

Some final reminders for your ongoing MBSM practice:

- Aim to practice regularly.
- Practice most often in an ideal, conducive environment, but remember the value of developing your practice using less comfortable postures and more challenging circumstances.
- Ensure you relax physically as a prelude to any meditation practice. Take time to develop the capacity to relax quickly and deeply.
- Use your concentration to assist your mind to become more calm and stable. It may well be useful to practice and develop your concentration by focusing on the breath. Remember, however, that by concentrating on the feelings of relaxing your body, as you do in the Progressive Muscle Relaxation exercise in chapter 4, not only will you get the benefit of relaxing your body, but your mind too will become calm.
- Develop mindfulness—the ability to pay attention deliberately and nonjudgmentally. Practice mindfulness by using the techniques that focus your attention on your breath, your body, your emotions and then your thoughts.
- As you become more mindful, you will become more aware. Quite naturally you will become aware of the ground state of stillness, and the movements that take the form of sounds, physical sensations, emotions and thoughts.
- Develop the capacity to remain calm and peaceful; aware and undistracted by whatever is present in your moment-by-moment experience.
- Put all this together. Practice regularly using the MBSM technique.
- Enjoy!

MILESTONES INDICATING PROGRESS

As you start your own practice, you will no doubt ask: How do I know how I am doing? How do I know if I am meditating well? Ian remembers asking Dr. Meares this question. The reply he got was rather blunt and to the point: "You know you are meditating well when you do not have to ask the question." What can be understood from this is that we reach a point in our meditation practice where we have an inner knowing that leaves us confident that all is well, that the meditation is going well.

However, particularly when relaxation is used as a lead-in to meditation, there are a series of key indicators of progress that are worth being aware of. Of course, by providing a measuring stick for meditation progress, there is a risk we will become judgmental, wanting to achieve a particular "level," or becoming despondent if we do not seem to be making progress. Therefore we have to remind ourselves yet again of the need to approach all this in the right state of mind. However, many people find it helpful to use the following information as one would use a series of signposts or significant milestones that appear during a journey. If we have a sense of where we are traveling to and know what signposts or milestones to expect, when we see them we can simply relax, knowing that we are on the right track and heading in the right direction.

This information was collated by Ian using a series of extensive questionnaires filled out by many people who were taught to meditate over several years in the late 1980s. The experiences recounted here match common experiences described by some of the great meditation traditions. In our experience many people do advance in a steady progression through all of these experiences, but it is also not uncommon to leapfrog some milestones. Just because you do not have one or another of these experiences does not mean you are not meditating well.

1. Motivation and intention
By reading this book you have already reached the first milestone. You have taken the first step of acting on your motivation to learn to meditate. Attending a group or finding an individual teacher would be another indicator of your intention to get started.

2. Establishing a practice

This second milestone is reached when you actually start to practice. Of course, a regular daily practice is ideal, but every little bit counts.

3. Being able to sit still

Most people who start need to overcome some feelings of restlessness; they need to learn to sit still. The best way to do this is to use your willpower. This is a step in meditation where determination really works. Tell yourself to keep still, resist the urge to fidget, scratch or move, and usually within a few sessions staying still will become easy. Once you can sit still, you have accomplished another milestone.

4. Feeling heavy

As we begin to relax physically, often the body begins to feel heavy. This feeling usually affects the limbs, especially the arms. During this stage some people report that their arms feel so heavy they doubt they could lift them even if they wanted to.

5. Feeling lighter

As we relax more, heaviness often gives way to lightness. Sometimes people feel as if their arms are floating; sometimes the whole body. For some, this sensation can feel as if they are floating in space. This is much less common, however, and while it feels good for some, for others it is a bit disconcerting—sometimes even scary.

Generally, by concentrating on the PMR, using the MBSM technique, we stay well grounded, and while the feeling of lightness does often come, it is a lightness of body that we experience, not a disconnected, troubling feeling. The lightness most people experience is very pleasant, very comfortable.

6. Temperature changes

Often as we begin to relax and to meditate, we move through a phase where we feel hotter or cooler. For a small percentage of people, the feeling of heat can be accompanied by sweating. Sweating is more common if there is a localized area of illness or injury, but some very healthy people do sweat for a while too. Sometimes hot flushes are experienced.

If there are persistent feelings of cold, then warm clothes or a blanket are recommended. Usually the feelings of temperature changes come and go fairly quickly, both in individual sessions and during the practice generally. These sensations are rarely around for more than a week or two.

7. Sexual arousal

This is not so often discussed, but it is not uncommon for beginners to have some experiences of sexual arousal. While this is more common when techniques are used that focus on energy centers, particularly the chakras and their activation, it can occur when we simply relax. While often disconcerting because it is usually unexpected, this experience is another one to simply observe. It usually passes quite quickly, and is an unusual phenomenon for more experienced meditators; maybe that is a little disappointing for some, but it is the truth of the matter!

8. Feeling the same all over—the hollow-body feeling

As we relax more deeply, more completely, we reach a point where we can scan our attention through our body and it feels the same all over. At this point we will have a clear sense of our body's outer boundaries, as in the sense of where our skin is, but inside, everything feels "hollow." Now this "hollow" is not like an empty void; it is not a nothingness. On the contrary, it feels luminous and vibrant. It feels very much alive and, again, very pleasant.

9. Changes in body awareness

There are two versions that commonly occur during this stage. The first is that we lose awareness of parts of the body, usually the hands and forearms. We can be sitting there, quite awake but not able to feel those parts of our body. Of course, if we were to open our eyes our body parts would be there, but it feels as if they are not.

Less frequently, people feel as if their body is expanding and becoming larger, as though it was being pumped up like a balloon, and becoming fuzzy around the edges.

10. Loss of body awareness
If we simply relax into and go along with either of the two changes in body awareness mentioned above in point 9, the next thing is that we lose awareness of our body altogether.

11. Transitional experiences
By now, if we are experiencing a loss of body awareness, we are deeply relaxed and our mind is becoming very calm and relaxed as well. We now enter into what is called the transitional phase, which occurs in that realm between an active mind and a still mind. If the stillness we enter into is the stillness of the ordinary mind, just an absence of thoughts, then our experience is likely to be rather dull and nebulous. If we are more alert, more mindful and more aware, then maybe we enter into the stillness beyond thought. The transition occurs as we move from awareness of the thinking mind into that awareness beyond thought, the awareness of stillness. In this transitional phase, inner phenomena often, but not always, come to our attention.

The most common phenomenon is the appearance of inner light. This light will almost always be iridescent, of a primary color like blue or red, though it could also be white. Usually the lights move. Most frequently they pulsate, often starting off in the distance and then moving toward us, only to fade away or to recede into the distance before pulsing back again. Sometimes they do the opposite, starting as a field of colored light in front of our eyes, and then receding and pulsing back and forward. For others the light may move from side to side or swirl around.

The common reaction when we first see these lights is to be pleasantly surprised, to realize that something interesting is happening and to try to analyze what the lights mean! This, of course, activates the thinking mind; we come up out of the depth of relaxation in which the lights appeared, and so the lights disappear. Then, if we consciously try to make them appear again, we are using our thinking mind, and so we do not relax enough, we do not let go deeply enough and the lights do not reappear.

These inner lights are classic signposts and they can be very instructive as our meditation progresses. What their appearance tells us is that we must be deeply relaxed in both body and mind. Whatever has got us to that point of deep relaxation is working well.

Also, the lights demonstrate to us very directly that if we use our thinking mind we come out of that deep relaxation. At the same time, we come to learn that if we simply relax and go with the feeling of deep relaxation, we can move on past this transitional phase where the inner light appears, and into the deeper realm of stillness.

While inner lights are the most common phenomenon in this transitional phase, some people see images, like faces, and some hear music or other sounds. However, these phenomena are much less common than the frequently observed inner light. It is best to treat them all in the same way: simply be aware of them, resist the temptation to analyze or judge them, let go a little more, relax more deeply and flow on into a deeper stillness.

12. Infinite space

Having moved through the transitional phase described, the next most common experience is to lose awareness of one's body and to have a sense of being in infinite space. This "space" is not a void or an emptiness. It is commonly dark, yet it has a feeling of luminosity and what is best described as an immanence. It feels as if it is a very creative, very alive space, yet empty of anything definable or recognizable as a specific object. Infinite space: vast with no borders, no boundaries and accompanied by a very expansive, warm, contented, blissful feeling.

13. Infinite consciousness

This feeling of infinite space can flow on to become a feeling of being connected to, or part of, an infinite consciousness. It is as if the luminous space described becomes more directly, more tangibly ripe with creative potential. This becomes a more mystical type of experience, a more direct experience of a spiritual truth. For some people this mystical feeling can be accompanied by visions. For all, it is a transcendent and transformative experience.

14. Oneness

The experience of infinite space, and the experience of infinite consciousness, significant and wonderful as they both may be, still involve a duality. In other words, while these two experiences can only be found in the realm of stillness beyond the thinking mind, there is still a part of us that is observing the experience. There is a sense that I am experiencing, or I am observing, infinite space. I am experiencing or I am aware of infinite consciousness. There is me, and there is the experience. A duality. That which is the observer, and that which is observed. In this state of stillness, that duality may be quite subtle, but it is a duality nonetheless.

Meditation reaches its end when we transcend that duality, when there is simply a pure awareness. The duality merges into a state of union, and there is the direct experience of unity, a oneness.

We have already discussed this stillness and the sense of oneness. Even a glimpse of this oneness, even a moment, or just a fleeting sense of what it is like, is deeply reassuring. Maybe this is just like being introduced briefly to a new person and we are yet to get to know them well; to become familiar with them. But even in a brief experience of that oneness we come to experience a profound inner truth, the truth of who we really are, and the truth of what is in our heart's essence.

It is tempting, as a beginner, to become eager and impatient at the prospect of experiencing all of this. So again, remember to temper this excitement with the knowledge that in meditation what will help us to advance is to avoid trying too hard, to avoid making it a source of a stress, to avoid judgment and to concentrate on just doing it.

Where these signposts can be helpful is that, when we do experience them, we can take comfort that we are heading in the right direction. They tell us we are progressing, and that we simply need to use the techniques and support them by letting go of judgment and reaction, and taking comfort in the knowledge that the techniques do work and that we just need to go with them.

OVERCOMING DIFFICULTIES: THREE PIECES OF ADVICE

Judith came to a cancer group full of anxiety about her situation. She had completed her medical treatment successfully and had a good prognosis. However, being a young mother with two children aged seven and four, Judith was struggling with the pressures of returning to work, keeping up a social life as well as being a wife and mother.

So Judith had a modest level of anxiety. She was nervous and irritable. She was not sleeping well, and was tending to alternate between going off her food and bingeing. She felt distant from her husband, Mark, and guilty that sometimes she would spoil her two children while at other times she would snap at them with uncharacteristic fire.

New to meditation, Judith was typical of so many people. She enjoyed learning about it, enjoyed being led into meditation, and she enjoyed practicing with the group she was in. She was strongly motivated and held high hopes for what meditation could do for her. However, within a few weeks, her regular report to the group was that she could not do it! She clearly had her own expectations of what "it" was, and soon convinced herself that she was not experiencing "it" and was probably a hopeless case. Judith had decided that she was one of those people who would never learn to meditate.

Judith was helped to overcome this common beginners' difficulty by three pieces of advice.

1. Realistic expectations

The first piece of advice to Judith was to establish realistic expectations. Of course, when we start something we have expectations. It is natural to hope for a good outcome and to also have some fear of failure. So in Judith's group, we talked more about what were *realistic* expectations. We talked of the signposts, and of the value of trusting the techniques and being patient.

2. Letting go of expectations, developing mastery

Our second piece of advice for Judith was a more radical solution to this problem—radical in the sense that it strikes at the core of the problem and is a more profound and complete solution. The advice was to consider that the solution to unrealistic expectations is to progress to that more advanced stage where we can let go of the expectations themselves.

Mastery is when we do something purposefully, when we do it with intention, but free of expectations, free of judgment. Judith could understand the theory of this, but as a beginner, she was grappling with that natural inclination to want, and to expect, immediate results.

3. Ask for feedback

The third of the solutions offered to her was the one that Judith said helped her the most to move forward and to have some confidence in her meditation. Over a cup of tea after her sixth week at the group, she was asked about her life.

One of Judith's strengths over the six weeks had been her commitment to regular practice. She had been managing to organize her children and her life so that she had regular time for meditation. For twenty minutes each day, nearly every day, she was actually practicing.

"So how is your life going? How are you sleeping?" she was asked.

"Well, now that I think of it, I'm sleeping better. I'm going to sleep quicker and I haven't woken up during the night for the last couple of weeks."

"How about the irritability?"

"Well, yes," she said, almost surprised to realize it. "I haven't yelled at the kids for a while . . . and Mark and I are arguing less. And actually," she continued, beginning to smile a little now, "my eating patterns are better. I'm just happy to eat like the rest of the family, and the bingeing has stopped. . . . Maybe the meditation is working after all!"

Judith's story is such a common experience among beginners. Beginners often have a sense of very real problems in their lives and an earnest commitment to do something about them. Often this need is then coupled with high expectations, and then comes the self-judgment of not meeting those expectations—because they feel there is either something wrong with themselves or with the way they are meditating.

Perhaps the best way to gauge the success of your meditation is to ask your friends or your family. In Judith's case, the positive changes were palpable. When she asked those around her, everyone commented that it was obvious how much more at ease she was, how much calmer. All of this was so noticeable to her friends, even while she was at that beginner's stage of feeling hopeless at "it."

Now for Judith, this all flowed fairly quickly and smoothly. For some it may take longer. As we discussed earlier, meditation releases repression. As repression lifts, things can become a little more volatile for some people. This is well understood in traditional circles. So if in the early stages of meditation you find yourself a little more excitable, more uncharacteristically expressive of emotions and thoughts, this may well be a useful and natural phase. Be heartened to know that as you continue with your practice, a more natural ease will come to your state of mind and emotions.

So again, aim to trust the process. For thousands of years, millions of people have used these techniques in a way that is predictable, reliable and effective. And the major part of what makes these techniques so predictable, reliable and effective is the necessity to temper our excitement, our anticipation and expectations with the intention of mastering the techniques. Mastery is what it is like when we can do these things confidently with purpose and focus, free of expectation and judgment. All we need now is to do it—regularly!

PART 11

OTHER APPLICATIONS

Learning to meditate is one of the greatest gifts we can give to ourselves, and maintaining a regular practice of meditation is one of the kindest things we can do for ourselves and for others. Perhaps the best motivation for learning to meditate is to be a happier, healthier, more present and more useful human being.

Part I provided a general introduction to meditation along with a specific introduction to Mindfulness-Based Stillness Meditation, the method found most useful by the authors for introducing and developing a meditation practice. MBSM's four steps—preparation, relaxation, mindfulness and stillness—now lead us into an introduction to the two aspects of the mind.

First there is the more active aspect of the ordinary mind that has to do with our thoughts and thinking, remembering and planning, along with all of our hopes and fears, and a preoccupation with self. This "thinking part" is directly connected with many of our emotions. Then there is the more fundamental nature of the mind, that seemingly more passive aspect that has to do with stillness, a creative immanence and a sense of the infinite, along with a natural inclination to be committed to the welfare of others.

As described in Part I, many of us are overly engaged with and influenced by our thinking mind, and have lost touch with the true nature of our mind. It is almost as if we have become lost in the activity of our minds, lost in the external "doing" of our life. As a consequence of that, we have lost touch with our inner essence, the truth of who we really are and the deeper nature of our mind.

Meditation, then, involves turning our thoughts inward. Turning our attention away from the external "doing" toward the internal experience of "being." In this sense, meditation can be described as bringing the mind home. It is as if our mind has been lost, wandering around in a challenging world, when all the time what it was really looking for—peace and happiness—was there inside us all the time. It is as if we have been looking for the right thing in the wrong place. Now, courtesy of meditation, we can turn our minds inward and begin to look in the right place!

So is what we have learned in Part I enough? Is it enough to relax, to become more mindful and to experience something of the stillness? Will this provide us with all that meditation has to offer? Particularly, is it enough to experience undistracted awareness and the true nature of our mind?

Well, certainly in theory it would seem so. Dr. Ainslie Meares was clearly of the view that the type of meditation described in Part I was a veritable panacea. And many of the great spiritual traditions are content to focus on the simplicity of silent meditation. Curiously, however, the Buddha detailed around 84,000 techniques for training the mind, many of these being different meditation techniques. Why so? The answer he gave around 2,500 years ago was quite simply that people were different. While he said it was possible to outline what worked best for many people, no particular technique worked well for everyone. And most of us will require help with different methods for different needs at different times in our lives.

As we begin to understand our mind more fully, we can begin to take charge of it. We realize that we can begin to train our thinking mind and use it like the invaluable tool that it is. And we can use it to help us to be happier, healthier, more present and more useful, while at the same time maintaining our own integrity.

In theory, the experience of the essence of meditation may well lead to all these qualities naturally arising. However, in the practical experience of the authors, and based on knowledge that people are different, it is useful to explore more possibilities for training the mind and using particular meditation techniques in more specific and individualized circumstances.

This, then, is the aim of Part II. Our intention is first to understand more about how the thinking mind works. Then we can draw on this knowledge to use the potential of our mind more effectively. We will consider how we can train the thinking mind in a way that we can use it more constructively. In the following chapters we will explore specific applications for meditation—disease prevention, healing, well-being, pain management, contemplation and meditation's age-old traditional use as the key technique for spiritual realization.

Finally, we will put all this together with a few words on integration—how we integrate the benefits of meditation into our daily life.

CHAPTER 14

MEDITATION AND MIND-BODY MEDICINE

A state of dynamic harmony between the body, mind and spirit of a person and the social and cultural influences which make up his or her environment.
—World Health Organization definition of health

I know I probably have as good a team of doctors as any, yet they tell me there is nothing much that can be done medically for the widespread cancer I have been diagnosed with. What can meditation do for me?

I am progressing quite nicely and the treatment I am receiving for chronic illness seems to be helping. What can meditation do for me?

Age is starting to creep up on me and I am becoming more concerned about my memory and my mobility. I imagine that it might be possible to have a healthy and vibrant old age. What can meditation do for me?

Actually, I am pretty fit and life is treating me well. I just feel it could be better. Perhaps there is something to this notion of wellness. What can meditation do for me?

I am interested in peak performance; getting the best out of my potential. What can meditation do for me?

These are the sorts of questions we are asked all the time. The short answer is that meditation has a great deal to offer in terms of preventing illness, facilitating healing and catalyzing a heightened state of well-being. At the time of writing there are well over four thousand research articles published in English-language medical journals around the world attesting to the therapeutic benefits of meditation for a wide range of physical and psychological conditions. This evidence base is now so strong that asking what meditation can do for you is similar to asking what surgery can do for you. It is now well established that meditation has useful application in a very wide range of conditions. It also appears to be compatible and synergistic with most other forms of treatment.

While we have made many references throughout this book to the health benefits of meditation, in this chapter we will enter into a more detailed examination of meditation's role in mind-body medicine. The scientific literature relating to therapeutic meditation is now so vast that to present a comprehensive review of it all is another book in itself. For those interested in research, refer back to pages 12 and 13 for the details of where all the current research on the therapeutic use of meditation from journals around the world is freely available online in up-to-date form. In this book the aim is to satisfy the need for a practical understanding of what meditation does have to offer, how it functions as a therapy and what methods are useful as therapy.

To be clear, what follows is not intended as specific medical advice. For any individual considering using meditation to treat a specific medical condition, including mental illness, it is necessary to do so in consultation with medical or other appropriate health practitioners. Having said that, it is the opinion of the authors that based on their extensive clinical experience as well as the burgeoning research evidence, meditation is the foremost self-help technique available when it comes to our health, our capacity for healing and our potential to experience high-level well-being.

FOUR WAYS OUR MIND IMPACTS OUR HEALTH

Mind-body medicine is the study of how the mind affects our health, and the teaching and practice of mind-based techniques that positively affect health outcomes. Health, as we use the term here, relates to:

- our capacity to be free of physical and mental disease
- our quality of life
- our potential to be well in spirit

There are four substantial ways in which we can use our minds to directly affect our health:

1. through the choices we make
2. through the healing potential of meditation itself
3. by applying imagery techniques to healing
4. by understanding how our state of mind affects our potential to heal

Meditation either is directly involved in or directly affects all four of these avenues of potential for training and utilizing our mind to contribute to our health, our potential for healing and our capacity to experience enduring well-being. We will examine each of the four in turn.

1. Making healthy choices

Healthy choices are all to do with how we use our minds to make decisions and how these decisions impact our health. Obviously it is the mind that decides what we eat, what we drink, whether we smoke or exercise, what drugs we do or do not take and on and on. When the authors talk of "positive thinking," we are referring to how we use our minds in any given situation to consider what choices are available to us, to make effective decisions and then to commit, persevere and follow these decisions through to completion.

This process has nothing to do with the fantasies of wishful thinking. Wishful thinking is where we hope for the best and do nothing about it. Positive thinking is where we hope for the best and do a lot about it. In other words, positive thinking involves understanding the way the mind works, or what we could call the laws of the mind, and using them intelligently to develop clarity of mind and confidence in the decisions we make, and then having the commitment to follow through.

To make good decisions we need a combination of knowledge, a clear mind and access to our own inner wisdom.

Philip was a successful businessman whose life seemed to be full of good things until he was diagnosed with advanced bowel cancer. He was told that his cancer had spread widely, that little could be done for him medically, and that his life was likely to be measured in months rather than years. The impact on him was devastating. He withdrew from his work and his family. He felt his life closing in and saw nothing but a painful, miserable future in front of him.

Two months after the diagnosis, Philip began attending our lifestyle-based self-help group and picked up on meditation. "It is hard to know how it happened, but quite quickly my mind became more settled," Philip reported. He continued to say:

> Perhaps the group helped too, with the discussion and the generally optimistic atmosphere, but it was like a fog cleared and I realized that there was a lot that I could do. I had options. More choices than I had first thought. And my mind has become clearer so that it seems more obvious what I need to do. With this clarity it has been easy to feel committed to what I am now doing. I feel so much better in myself, and so far the cancer seems stable and my doctors are pleasantly surprised with my progress.

How meditation leads to healthy choices

Remember the analogy of the glass filled with muddy water? Just as when muddy water is left undisturbed and the mud sinks to the bottom and we are left with clear water, so too it is for our mind. If we have a major decision to make and our thoughts are swirling around in our head one after another, meditation allows them to settle. When we give our mind the chance to settle, to rest undistracted for even a short while, it clears. With clarity comes the capacity to make effective decisions. With clarity comes confidence, and with confidence, commitment. With commitment comes perseverance, resilience and the capacity to follow through on decisions. This clarity also leads quite naturally to a heightened awareness. We begin to be more aware of what is working well for us and what is not.

Also, as meditation improves the relationship with our self and leads to a healthier and more positive self-regard, we tend to act on what we notice. We are less inclined to do what is not working to our benefit, and more likely to make healthy choices and actually do what is good for us. When we meditate, it gets easier to eat well, to exercise and to look after ourselves generally. A positive snowball effect begins to build.

At the same time this clarity reveals the power of our habits and beliefs in relation to our health. Again, meditation loosens things up. It makes the influences in our lives more obvious, while at the same time it helps us to relax, to be more positive, to break free of unhelpful habits and beliefs, and so to make healthy choices.

Next, it is worth observing that meditation reveals to us in a very direct and experiential way that emotions and thoughts are not permanent and that they do change. This makes it so much easier to have confidence in our ability to deal with the external changes in our lives and to recognize our capacity for internal change. We can begin to let go of old traumas, hurts and unhelpful states of mind, and train ourselves in new and more effective ways of thinking and being. As a bonus of this, meditation is a wonderful adjunct if we are engaged with counseling. Meditation makes therapeutic change more possible; it tends to occur more smoothly and more rapidly.

Finally, the specific technique of mindfulness trains us to be non-judgmental and to live more in the present moment. Both these qualities help with developing clarity and the capacity to act confidently, forthrightly and appropriately in any given situation.

In conclusion, therefore, we can say that meditation works on many levels to facilitate the effective use of the thinking mind to make healthy decisions and to follow these decisions through.

2. Meditation, health, healing and well-being

Techniques like MBSM, which generate deep physical relaxation and mental calm, lead to a state of profound balance and the subsequent natural expression of healing.

When we meditate in a way that includes deep physical relaxation and calming of the mind, we enter into a state of profound physiological rest. With our body relaxed and calm, and our mind relaxed and effectively still, we return to a natural state of balance. In this state, our body is ideally poised to prevent illness, to heal and to be fundamentally well. In balance, our emotions and our mind are at their best, and spiritually we feel confident and at peace.

When it comes to meditation for health, healing and well-being, we are of the view that MBSM is the main event. In our understanding of the research and in our clinical experience, this type of meditation, thoroughly outlined in Part I, meets all the requirements. This is the style of meditation we recommend as a daily practice for everyone interested in good health. While there may be real benefit in the use of the complementary and synergistic techniques of contemplation and imagery, as described in later chapters, if you were to do only one thing, we would recommend the regular practice of MBSM. This may well be all that you need.

Meditation as a therapy

The key to understanding meditation as a therapy is that it is natural for human beings to be in a state of balance. In fact, good health is well defined as a dynamic state of balance. Obviously, for each one of us, our lives will go up and down. In the normal course of events, from time to time we will injure our bodies or face illness. Emotionally, our lives are bound to go up and down, and our state of mind commonly fluctuates among the easy and the difficult times (as we perceive them). The good news is that our body—in fact the whole of our being—is designed to accommodate all of these ups and downs.

The body is incredibly well designed to be in balance and to do all it can to return to that state whenever it does get out of kilter. So while we will discuss the health benefits of meditation techniques such as contemplation and imagery, when it comes to supporting and strengthening our innate capacity for preventing illness and accelerating healing there is a compelling logic to our view that techniques such as MBSM have the most to offer. This form of meditation reliably relaxes the body, settles the mind, enhances awareness and leads to a balance that is ultimately reflected in body, emotions, mind and spirit.

In chapter 6, we set out the physiological changes proven to accompany meditation. Again, the easy way to understand this huge range of benefits is via the concept of balance. If someone has a condition related to an overactive immune system, such as an allergy or autoimmune disease, meditation brings the immune system down into balance and so acts as an immune suppressant. If someone else has an underactive immune system, as people with cancer often do, then meditation brings the immune system up into balance and so acts as an immune stimulator.

This balance is also reflected in meditators' emotional lives. When we are in balance it is easier to feel more at ease with our emotions. We are more able to be authentic and to express emotions comfortably and appropriately. We tend to be more able to give and receive love. Then, too, when we meditate our mind tends to be more in balance and, as we set out in the previous section, more clear and more able to make healthy choices.

Perhaps, for many, the real joy in meditation is the sense of balance that comes into our spiritual life. Perhaps it is a clearer sense of purpose or meaning in our life. Perhaps that sense of connectedness. Perhaps a sense of being a part of something bigger than ourselves. Balance on this level leads to an unshakable confidence and a smile that comes from deep within.

3. Imagery—the will, the mind and healing

Meditation is about creating ideal conditions that allow healing to take place naturally. Imagery is about using the mind more deliberately, more consciously to make healing happen.

This distinction between "allowing" and "making" is a useful one. From the perspective of the ordinary mind, meditation is a passive process in which we return to a natural state of balance, and trust that in that balance the natural processes of healing will flow. We "allow" healing to happen. By contrast, imagery is an active process through which we learn how to use our mind to directly influence the body's capacity to heal. It is an active intervention that relies on our will and is intended to "make" healing happen.

When it comes to healing, allowing and making, meditation and imagery are obviously quite different. However, in clinical experience they can both be useful and are often synergistic. While meditation is recommended as the main practice, imagery is like an optional extra that does not suit everyone but can be very helpful, even pivotal, for some. Therefore these techniques are worth experimenting with to test their merits in your own particular situation. After you practice these techniques a few times, you will quickly gain your own reliable sense of whether they are helpful and relevant for you or not. If they feel useful, keep going; if not, simply continue with the main practice of meditation.

The theory and techniques of healing imagery are detailed in chapter 16, "Meditation, Imagery and Affirmations."

4. State of mind and healing

Instinctively, we know that our state of mind affects our health. It is common sense to think that anxiety, depression, resentment and other destructive states of mind cannot be good for us, while laughter, optimism and happiness are all for the good. Fortunately, our instincts and common sense are now being reinforced with a surge in the amount of research being published on these subjects. Daniel Siegel, whom we mentioned in the Introduction in connection with mirror neurons, offers a useful perspective that adds to the discussion on this topic throughout the book. When it comes to how meditation enhances our state of mind, Siegel summarizes some of the insights he elaborated in his best-selling books *The Developing Mind* and *Parenting from the Inside Out*. In his highly recommended book *The Mindful Brain*, Siegel lists the benefits of developing mindful awareness as being directly and powerfully linked to our capacity for:

- body regulation
- attuned communication
- emotional balance
- response flexibility or adaptability
- empathy
- insight—self-knowing awareness
- fear modulation or extinction
- intuition and its capacity to inform our intellect
- morality and our capacity to enact it

Who would not want to score highly on each of these attributes? And this is what meditation has to offer. Furthermore, the published literature is steadily confirming the ancient wisdom that describes how meditation leads to life-affirming states of mind such as natural optimism, joyful good humor, altruism, compassion, loving kindness and clarity of mind. All that really remains, then, is to begin our meditation practice, to establish a routine and to allow the benefits to flow.

MEDITATION AND HEALING: A PERSONAL STORY

There are many stories that could be told to demonstrate the capacity of meditation, imagery and affirmations to catalyze extraordinary healing. That of Bernice Groeke is perhaps one of the most poignant, and we thank her three daughters for permission to retell it.

Bernice had a melanoma removed from her calf in 1980. Around eighteen months later the melanoma was found in a lymph node in her groin and it too was removed surgically. Another eighteen months later the cancer had spread widely to both lungs. Bernice was told that her situation was now inoperable, that there was no other medical treatment for her, that she was incurable and to go home and make the best of the months she had left.

In 1983 the Gawler Foundation's residential programs were yet to begin. Bernice booked into the twelve-week cancer self-help group and brought her husband, Wain, along. It soon transpired that Bernice had quite a negative mind-set. She told the group that in the past she had felt it her duty to warn family and friends of all that could go wrong; to advise them not to get too excited about new prospects as each one was likely to end in disappointment. No glass-half-full for Bernice: it was reliably half empty! Once the program came to the topic of positive thinking, Bernice quickly realized that she needed to change this life-long trait of hers. She elected to repeat the affirmation "I am a positive person now."

One evening six weeks later, Bernice was sitting in her lounge chair after dinner. One of the melanomas was pressing on her spine and giving her ongoing pain. Wain came to join her and could see that she was rather disconsolate and agitated. When he asked her what was wrong, Bernice replied, "Perhaps the doctors are right. Perhaps I'm just kidding myself. Perhaps I should just accept the fact that I'm going to die and give up on all this other stuff."

Now, Wain was remarkably astute. A dignified and conservative retired gentleman, Wain was attending the group out of loyalty to his wife. He was uncomfortable talking of his own experiences to the group, and uncomfortable with closing his eyes to meditate in public. But he did pay attention. He knew in detail what his beloved wife was attempting. At this point, on this evening, Wain's wisdom provided Bernice with a turning point. He said to her, "Oh, that's interesting. What are you?"

"What do you mean, what am I?" responded Bernice.

"Oh, I thought you were a positive person now." Wain was aware of Bernice's affirmation and he challenged her on it in a gentle, loving way.

Bernice reflected for a few moments and then said, "You're right, I am."

Bernice claims that as she said this, she felt what could best be described as a "physical clunk" inside of her. It was as if a switch had clicked, and from that point on Bernice began to see the positive in every situation that came her way.

Bernice and Wain had a strong Christian faith and were intimately involved in their local church community. Shortly after the "inner clunk," they were visiting church, where Wain was playing the organ while Bernice sat alone in the body of the church praying and meditating. As she did so, her whole perception changed and she experienced a deep, direct mystical experience. This experience gave her more confidence and reinforced her meditation practice. As time went on, Bernice often contemplated the passage "Be still and know that I am God."

Bernice had embraced her new healthy diet enthusiastically, was highly self-disciplined, and combined her own healing efforts with serving others whenever time, energy and opportunity allowed. Six months later her scans revealed the left side of her lungs was clear of tumors, and twelve months later she was given the all clear. That was in 1984.

Once she recovered, Bernice volunteered for the Gawler Foundation. One of her greatest contributions was speaking to individuals or groups, recounting her story and inspiring her listeners with her obvious good health, radiant smile, equanimity, knowledge and enthusiasm for life.

Quite some years ago, Wain died, aged in his late eighties. Friends wondered how this would impact Bernice as she had been happily married for over sixty years. Bernice grieved as you might imagine, but when asked about her future she unexpectedly said, "Well, you know, it is really sad that Wain died and I will miss him terribly, but it will be interesting. . . . I have never lived on my own before. I wonder what it will be like not having to take Wain into account anymore?"

As she wanted to continue to live in the family home, Bernice took in a student boarder from overseas. They became the best of friends. Bernice taught him about life in Australia, and he enabled her to stay at home.

Then, in 2009, when she had reached the ripe old age of ninety-three, Bernice's cancer reappeared and she deteriorated rapidly. Ian had the good fortune to spend time with her a week before she died. He recalls: I was concerned about how she would react to the recurrence, and sure enough when we first met she wanted to apologize to me, as if she had let me or the work down in some way. She was worried that she had done something wrong to bring the cancer back.

We had come to know each other well after all these years. I explained to her that I could understand her disappointment, that I would be pretty angry too if my cancer came back again after all these years. Then I told her that she had done something extraordinary. She had overcome a major illness through her own efforts, with no medical treatment at all. I explained that in my view she had to die of something, and for reasons we could not understand or know, for her it was this way. I knew that she had held her life in great respect and had done everything possible to look after her good health. I suggested to her that it was no big deal that she was dying of cancer, and that for her it was best not to dwell on it. I reminded her of the lives of all the people she had touched and how she had helped so many through her example.

As we talked on, I asked Bernice about her spiritual life. She confided that she had lost something of the closeness to her God that she had felt for so many years. She seemed relieved to be able to put voice to this deep concern. She explained that she felt more concerned about dying now than she could remember at any time in her life. She was not sure what she was going to after she died. Her faith was wavering when she needed it most.

I encouraged her to recognize these doubts and fears as just that, doubts and fears. I told her that dying was like going home. A loving parent is always welcoming, always available. I invited Bernice to think of Christ and notice how He was instantly there in her mind, and how she could feel His presence. She agreed that she could do this. Then I told her how dying was easy, that she had led a good life, she could look back on it with gentle satisfaction and no regrets. To die she only had to breathe out and not breathe in again. It would be easy.

Bernice determined to do what she could to hold Christ's presence in her mind and heart, and when she died to imagine herself leaving her body, leaving this world behind and, while remaining undistracted by thought or emotion, to merge her essence into that of Christ. Bernice told me that she felt reassured and asked if we could meditate together. By now, she was tiring and asked if she could lie with her head on my lap. I was able to gently hold her as we meditated together for a few minutes.

As I left I explained to Bernice that I was not sure if I would see her again, but that I was confident she would be okay. I told her that if she was alive in a week's time I would see her then, and that I would be holding her in my thoughts, prayers and meditations.

Bernice died the day before I planned to see her again. She had lived for twenty-six years after first being diagnosed with widespread, metastatic melanoma. Her funeral was a genuine celebration. As happens at so many funerals, I found out that Bernice had a much wider circle of friends and involvements than I knew of. Hers was an extraordinary life of joyful service. Her story inspired me from the early days and continues to do so. Bernice's life exemplifies what is possible when healing is approached in a dedicated way, and when attention is given to the physical, emotional, mental and spiritual spheres of life.

Whenever I asked Bernice what helped her most, she always smiled in an assured and powerful way. She was a sweet little old lady but quite tough. Her smile had depth to it. "It is the spiritual side of my life," she would say. She recognized the great significance of love for family and the support she received from them, and she acknowledged the importance of diet, attitude, affirmations, prayer, meditation and so on, but it was the spiritual connectedness that underpinned all that she did.

RECOMMENDATIONS

When it comes to health, healing and well-being, MBSM is the main practice we recommend. Follow the techniques and guidelines set out in Part I on MBSM and aim for a regular daily practice. For most health conditions, ten to twenty minutes once or twice daily would seem to work well, while for major conditions like active cancer, consider three long sessions daily of forty to sixty minutes each.

Also experiment with the use of imagery; be guided in this by your own sensibility. The White Light healing exercise, explained in chapter 16, is a powerful addition to MBSM for many people, while the use of affirmations and imagery in a more general context, also set out in that chapter, may lead to better health outcomes for many.

Read, study and learn the techniques. If possible, seek out direct instruction from a qualified teacher. Make a start and remember that the journey of a thousand miles starts with just one step. Start where you are: extraordinary things are possible.

CHAPTER 15

MEDITATION FOR
TRANSFORMING PAIN

*It is not too difficult to extract the essentials of Eastern mysticism,
and to use them to control tension and pain in a way that is
consistent with the full and active life of Western society.*
—DR. AINSLIE MEARES, *Relief Without Drugs*

Most of us experience pain as something quite hurtful, and obviously,
if it is bad enough, pain can be deeply distressing. Acute pain may come
and go relatively quickly, but it is still often intense and very unpleasant.
Chronic pain lingers and is commonly debilitating; if severe enough, it
can verge on being unbearable.

Most of us will have grown up with the attitude that pain is something to be avoided. Many people will have had the very real experience
that pain does hurt, that generally it offers little of personal benefit and
much that is disadvantageous. No wonder, then, that, culturally, the
common way to manage pain is to seek help outside of ourselves. Our
society draws upon huge quantities of analgesic tablets, and a wide
range of other substances and activities aimed at numbing, minimizing
or simply distracting ourselves from pain.

A RADICAL SOLUTION

Now, expand your mind to contemplate a radical solution. Imagine what it would be like to experience pain as a sensation that does not hurt. How would that change your life? Imagine being able to take the distress out of pain, and to be able to experience pain as a sensation free of hurt. And how about that for a definition of pain? Pain is a sensation that does not hurt.

When this notion of hurt-free pain is first presented, many people experience quite a strong reaction. On the one hand there is the excitement brought about by the notion. Could it be true? Could it really be possible? Then there is the colder, harder voice of experience. Surely not. I have experienced pain. Of course it hurts; that is what pain does—it hurts.

Well, if we are going to turn this around, if we are to transform that common and very real, very undeniable experience of pain hurting, it will require some doing. Even if we can be convinced in theory of the validity of the proposition that pain does not hurt, to experience this in practice, to experience it in the reality of daily life, surely that will require a whole other level of accomplishment.

What is needed then to transform our experience of pain is a combination of understanding and practice. We will need to virtually reprogram our thinking around pain and establish a new experience of it. We need the two wings again: learning and practice.

A personal story

Back in 1970, Ian had his right leg amputated as a consequence of developing osteogenic sarcoma, reputedly one of the most painful of cancers. His personal experience with pain, along with nearly thirty years of clinical experience assisting others in managing their pain, makes for an interesting story.

Ian writes: It would seem that I grew up with a very low pain threshold. In other words, I was adversely sensitive to pain. Like most things in life it was probably the result of a complex mixture of genetics, unconscious forces and life experiences, but personally, I like to blame a formative dental experience for this. When I was eleven years old a tooth needed to be extracted. A local anesthetic was injected into my gum, whereupon the dentist left the room for a few moments, and then returned and removed the tooth. Unfortunately, the anesthetic had not taken effect and the pain seemed excruciating. The impact of this incident may well have been compounded by the dentist's apparent dispassionate dismissal of my muffled protestations. Needless to say, future visits to the dentist involved some trepidation.

In my late teens and early twenties, a major part of my life was taken up with competing in decathlons—ten diverse athletic events completed over two days, finishing with a 1500-meter run. Virtually every decathlon athlete loves to hate the 1500 meters; the other nine events require speed and strength, whereas the 1500 meters requires endurance, and it comes at the end of the two days. The physical pain it causes most decathletes tends to bind them as a group even more than the sheer craziness of attempting to train and perform well in such a wide range of events. But for me, the 1500 meters was a real problem. To run a good 1500 meters it is not enough to be fit. To achieve even a reasonable time you need to be able to push on through the pain barrier. I never ran a reasonable 1500 meters. I was too sensitive to the pain.

It would be no surprise then for me to say that when my right leg was amputated it was painful. Heavy analgesic narcotics provided very welcome relief. Even having the stitches removed about ten days after the operation was, for me, acutely painful. My complaints came long and hard with virtually every stitch, so much so that my surgeon became quite distressed by the exercise. While he did refuse my genuine request for a general anesthetic to complete the procedure, he did say that, in his clinical experience, my reaction placed me in the top 1 or 2 percent of people most sensitive to pain. The subsequent rehabilitation and convalescence following the surgery was long, slow and marked by a reliance on heavy analgesics.

All this is mentioned to highlight the transformation that was to come. Within a few years I was able to have major dental work performed free of analgesics, to personally sew up two significant skin wounds on my body without the use of local anesthetic, and to find a way of comfortably managing the chronic pain experienced from having to walk on one leg with the aid of crutches. There is no doubt this was a radical transformation; this change fuels the motivation to share this knowledge and experience with you.

Turning theory into practice

This personal account of transforming pain leads us to the obvious question: How is this possible? How is it possible to radically transform our personal experience of pain? For those working in a clinical setting or supporting family and friends, how can we help others to transform their experience?

Back to theory and practice. We need to develop our understanding of the theory behind this transformed experience of pain in such a way that we begin to believe it is possible. The stronger this belief, the more likely we will get there. But, crucially, we must go further than this and reexperience pain in a way that transforms the theory from being just a good idea into a real experience. The transformation comes when we are able to have the direct and personal experience of pain without hurt.

Pain's important message

Before we embark on learning a new theory of pain, there is the need for a caution. Pain is a warning signal. In daily life, pain serves the very useful function of alerting us to the fact that something is amiss and needs attending to. When we pick up a really hot saucepan, it is pain that helps us to release it quickly and to minimize any burns. When we break a bone, it is pain that signals us to keep it still and, in doing so, to minimize the damage. If we have a bad headache, we need to be aware of it and pay attention to what is behind it. So always with pain it is important to understand its message. What is causing it? What is wrong? What needs attending to? Therefore, whenever faced with pain, always make sure that it is adequately and properly investigated.

What we are discussing in this chapter is how to take the hurt out of pain, while at the same time still following through with a sensible and sufficient response to what pain implies.

THE NATURE OF PAIN

As we develop our theory then, let us go on to consider the nature of pain and what we understand about it. These explanations are intended to provide a good working model for what pain is, how it develops and how we might experience it in a radically different way.

Here is a commonly quoted definition for pain, provided by the International Association for the Study of Pain:

> Pain is an unpleasant sensory and emotional experience associated with actual or potential tissue damage, or described in terms of such damage, and when there is no available remedy for its cause, a disease of its own.[1]

The key to our new understanding of pain comes in addressing the two elements of pain alluded to in this definition. These are the *sensory* and the *emotional* experiences associated with pain.

The sensory aspect of pain can be even more simply explained by saying there is usually a physical reality to pain. Pain commonly starts with some sort of tissue damage, which in turn leads to nerve receptors being activated. Messages are then transmitted along nerve fibers, leading to the release of neurotransmitters in the brain that we experience as pain. These days a good deal is understood about how, in a physical sense, tissue damage is experienced as painful stimulus.

However, once a sensory stimulus is recorded in the brain, a secondary response to that stimulus is then activated. This secondary response is psychological—that is, our emotional and mental reaction to the stimulus. The emotion can run through a wide gamut of distressing feelings, from simple fear and surprise to distaste, confusion, outrage and extreme aversion, and on to more complex emotions of shock, anger, blame, self-pity, guilt, horror and, for some, even distorted pleasure. The mental responses, the way we think about pain, can be many and varied, and will be shaped by our knowledge, beliefs, habits and culture. These mental responses have a lot to do with how we interpret and react to the sensation. We may have voices in our head that say, "Grin and bear it," "No pain, no gain," "Big boys don't cry," and so on.

So, while the first element of pain is made up of the physical sensation, the second element involves a psychological response to that sensation. The radical approach to pain management is based upon the notion that the physical sensations associated with pain are just that, sensations. Of themselves, these sensations do not hurt; they are not distressing, they are just sensations. However, the psychological reaction to pain can be deeply hurtful and distressing. Physical sensations do not hurt; psychological reactions do!

Psychological reactions hurt

To repeat, the theory is that the physical experience of pain is not of itself hurtful, it is our psychological response that makes it so. When we take the psychological response out of our experience of pain, what we are left with is the raw sensation of pain. The theory is that the pure physical sensation of pain does not hurt; it is just a sensation. Paul talked earlier of this being like "a beautiful intensity"; but maybe it does have a sense of being unpleasant, and perhaps, all things being equal, we would prefer to be without it, but still, it is not hurtful, it is not distressing.

Ian began his working life as a veterinarian. He remembers well how animals respond to pain: Working as a country vet, it used to amaze me to observe working farm dogs brought to the surgery with broken legs. They would come in appearing quite happy, with what seemed to be a smile on their face and definitely a wag in their tail. It was as though the excitement of a ride in the car and a trip into town more than compensated for the injury. Sure, they took the message of the pain they must have felt. If they could sit they would. If they could lie down they would. If it was necessary for me to manipulate the break a little to determine the nature and the extent of the injury, they would object but generally only modestly. Then, as soon as the procedure had finished, the smile would return and the tail recommence its wagging.

It seems to me that they got the message. Broken leg: painful. Move it around: more pain. Keep it still: less pain. Simple solution: keep it as still as possible. However, if there is something interesting on offer to do, might as well make the most of it and do it.

This rather simplistic dog philosophy is somewhat reminiscent of the Serenity Prayer:

God grant me the serenity
to accept the things I cannot change,
the courage to change the things that I can,
and the wisdom to know the difference.

There is something simple, elegant and compelling in this. Take the message, do what you can, accept what is left.

But even in veterinary practice there was a contrast worth thinking about. Unfortunately town dogs can break their legs too. Now, quite a few town dogs can be described as being highly socialized, almost humanized. When one of these dogs breaks a leg, you often hear their screams coming from blocks away. Their pain and distress is obvious to all.

Consider for a moment what might happen were we to be in that regrettable situation of breaking a leg. Say we are lost in a moment of mindlessness and step out in front of a passing car. A glancing blow, a crack, a strong sensation, falling to the ground. In the instant of the impact, a realization that the leg is probably broken. In the same instant, shock and fear. Perhaps even panic. A range of strong emotions. And then the thinking starts. *Is it broken? Will I need surgery? Will I ever walk again? Is the health insurance up to date? Who will look after the kids? What about work? What about the state of my underwear?* A range of strong and anxious thoughts. Perfectly natural. Perfectly reasonable. All too common. Altogether, a big dose of psychological reaction.

Changing the way we experience pain

But what if we could be more like the farm dog and just accept the reality of life as it is unfolding? What if we could just accept how mindlessness has brought us a tough experience, and in that acceptance experience the accident free of judgment, free of reaction? What would that be like? And how could we learn to do that? And what of the types of pain other than that to do with our physical body? What of emotional pain?

Mental pain? Even spiritual pain? How realistic is it to suggest that all these types of pain can be experienced in a radically different and non-distressing way? We need to convert the theory into practice. We need to consider how we can train our mind and our body to relate and respond to pain in this new and revolutionary way.

But first, another important step. It needs to be acknowledged that pain, particularly chronic pain, can be debilitating and can lead to quite understandable suffering and depression. It makes sense, therefore, to manage any pain you may experience in the best way you can. If the ideas and techniques explained here work for you, then you will have a very natural, reliable and side-effect-free method of self-regulating pain. However, maybe these principles just make life a little easier, a little more bearable. Or perhaps you cannot relate to them at all, or try them with little benefit.

The key point here is to do the best you can, free of guilt or recrimination. Take comfort in the fact that these days pain management is a well-developed medical specialty that is very effective. Pain-management clinics and specialists draw on the services of a wide range of clinicians and employ a variety of treatments. Holistic or integrative pain management may use various combinations of drugs, surgery, physiotherapy, psychology, acupuncture, judicious exercise, massage and so on. There are also a wide range of self-help supports for pain management available in the home. There is the trusty hot-water bottle, cold packs, music, humor, distraction and lots more. In Ian's book *You Can Conquer Cancer* and a CD called *Effective Pain Management*, these self-help aspects are described in more detail. Here, however, we aim to focus on the mind's role in transforming pain.

For completeness, it needs to be pointed out that there are two main ways in which the mind can change our perception of pain. They are dissociation and a version of mindfulness. Before we go on to develop the radical one we have been discussing so far, which is to do with being more mindful of pain, let us consider the usefulness of the other option, which is dissociation.

DISSOCIATION

Dissociation (dis-association) is where we move our attention away from the pain and on to something more pleasant, more manageable. We may do this in an almost unconscious way by simply becoming distracted, or we may dissociate quite deliberately using a technique based on imagery or hypnosis. Distraction is a reliable way of minimizing, avoiding or even forgetting the pain.

Vera attended a meditation group seeking relief from her painful scoliosis, a chronic recurrent back condition marked by persistent pain. Vera reported how important being busy was to her:

> When I go to work and have to interact with people, it takes my mind off my back. The more involved I am, the quicker the time passes. The busier it is the better. The worst part of the day is when I go to bed. I spend ages trying to find a comfortable position. That is when the pain is strongest.

This experience is a common one. Being busy, especially when we are engrossed in the busyness, or being distracted, like when we go to a good movie, are both ways of dissociating. What we are giving our attention to comes into the foreground of our mind, and it is as if the pain slips into the background.

It is last thing at night, with all the activities of the day completed and with nothing else for our mind to dwell on, that pain often comes to the fore. There are no more distractions and our mind is free to fantasize. *How long will the pain go on for? Will it be better or worse tomorrow? What if it gets worse?* And so on. With no distractions, no dissociation, the psychological reactions of the mind and emotions are free to run riot. The pain seems more obvious, stronger and more distressing.

Understanding how this works, how the impact of dissociation and distraction affects our perception of pain, gives us more confidence to manage it. Clearly it can be useful to use dissociation. When we partake in a pleasant and engaging activity we can experience genuine pain relief. Also, we can use the principle of dissociation in some very good mind-body medicine techniques that provide effective pain relief.

It is not the intention of this book to discuss techniques like hypnosis and self-hypnosis. It is enough to acknowledge that these are also useful applications and to say that, commonly, when hypnosis is used for pain, the principle that makes it work is often dissociation. The mind is distracted from the pain. It is paying attention elsewhere.

Imagery for pain relief

For ourselves, we can apply the principle of dissociation through the use of imagery. One of the most reliable ways we have found is a technique where we create a mental image of a place where we feel particularly peaceful and comfortable. This place becomes an Inner Sanctuary, a place we can retreat to, give all our attention to and rest in the feeling of its space and comfort. In this exercise we move the focus of our attention quite deliberately from the pain to this Inner Sanctuary.

The whole intention of this exercise is to imagine yourself as fully as possible to be in your Inner Sanctuary. Aim to use all of your senses—see the place through your own eyes as if you were actually there, hear the sounds, notice whatever there is to smell, and feel the physical sensations. Perhaps there may even be something to taste (for example, when people imagine themselves to be in the ocean). The intention is to transport yourself from your normal conscious reality to this place of inner peace and comfort.

Here, then, is the exercise. You might like to read it and learn it well enough so that you can lead yourself through it, or you might find it useful to have someone else read it to you in a slow, steady and relaxed tone of voice. Spend at least twenty minutes on this exercise.

THE INNER SANCTUARY

Settle into your posture and take a few moments to relax your body in your own way.

Allow an image to form in your mind of a place where you feel particularly peaceful and comfortable. . . . It may be a place

---

you have been to before, or it may be a fantasy place . . . just allow an image to form in your mind in a way that you can explore it in more detail.

What can you see in this place . . . ? What is close by . . . ? What is farther off in the distance . . . ? What can you see . . . ? What shapes . . . ? What sizes . . . ? What colors . . . ? What shades of color . . . ? What time of day is it . . . ? If you can see the sky, are there clouds, or is it clear . . . ? You may notice some movement. . . . Or is it quite still . . . ? What can you see in this place?

Now notice what sounds you can hear in this place. . . . Are there any sounds coming from nearby . . . ? Are there any sounds coming from farther away . . . ? What sounds can you hear in this place?

Give your attention now to noticing what you may be able to smell in this place. . . . What fragrance . . . ? What odor . . . ? Perhaps just the quality of the air itself. . . . What can you smell in this place?

What sensations can you feel in this place . . . ? You will probably be aware of the temperature. . . . Is it warm . . . ? Or cool . . . ? Or neutral . . . ? Can you feel a breeze on your skin . . . ? Or the warmth of the sun on your face . . . ? Notice too your position and what you are in contact with. . . . Is it hard or soft . . . ? Damp or dry . . . ? What physical sensations are you aware of in this place?

Is there anything you might like to change to make this place even more peaceful and comfortable . . . ? If so, you could do that now.

Now dwell on the feelings that come with being in this place. . . . Allow these feelings to build within you and rest with those feelings. . . . Just simply letting go . . . relaxing . . . releasing . . . letting go.

Many people find this exercise gives them a reliable way to dissociate from pain and find a comfortable inner haven. Children are particularly good at it, and as a technique it is very useful when the need for pain relief is short-term.

Marty was a nine-year-old boy who needed repeated injections for cancer tests and treatment. The most challenging were lumbar punctures, where Marty would have to lie still while a needle was passed between the bones of his lower spine and into his spinal canal to collect fluid. Just one of these procedures would have been harrowing enough, but as more and more were required he began to react with great distress.

Two techniques transformed Marty's experience. First, Marty was taught how to "go all floppy." This is child-speak for relaxing the body. In a few moments, Marty was taught to make his body all stiff, and then to relax it, to make it go all floppy. Children are terrific at learning the essence of the Progressive Muscle Relaxation exercise in this very quick, simple and effective way. Second, Marty was taught to go to his own personal Inner Sanctuary. No real-life place for him; Marty created a Disney-like castle full of interesting and fun characters and animals. There was plenty to entertain and distract him.

Marty's medical staff cooperated by giving him time to do his preparations before each new procedure was performed. When Marty was advised that the procedure was about to begin, he made his body go all floppy; then it was as if he left his body there on the table while the procedure was carried out. Instead of being present for the harsh realities of what was going on, Marty was happily off in his own magical space. When the procedure was completed, he quite readily and easily took leave of his Inner Sanctuary and brought his attention more particularly back to his body. These relatively simple steps transformed Marty's experience.

Therese was an older woman who had chronic rheumatic pain that had distressed her and restricted her movement for many years. When Therese attempted to meditate she found the hurdle of her pain was too much to manage. She simply could not relax or find any peace. Even in the group setting, she made little progress. However, with this Inner

Sanctuary imagery exercise, Therese found instant relief. After her first experience of it she explained: "It was wonderful. I went to a tropical beach that I visited not long after I was married. We were so happy there. I could feel the warmth and relax on the sand. I just seemed to drift off in that place. It is the most relief I can remember experiencing for so long."

What Therese did next was even more useful for her. She was able to remember the feeling of her Inner Sanctuary and to keep that feeling with her.

While this Inner Sanctuary exercise can be a great way to dissociate from pain, by its nature it involves dissociating from life itself. To do it, we need to move our attention from our present moment, worldly reality to an inner fantasy, an inner reality. Many people like Marty find this really useful for short-term pain relief. Some, like Therese, use it to work out a method that brings long-term relief.

> What I did was to find such comfort in that Inner Sanctuary, such peace and relief, that it really left its mark. I did not want to forget it. So in some way after I come out of the experience, the feeling stays with me. It is like I remember that feeling and it becomes a new part of what I experience during the day. Perhaps it is the comfort of knowing I can go back to that lovely beach anytime I want to. It is like it is always there. And I feel it. I really feel it and it gives me a lot of comfort. My pain is much easier to manage than it used to be.

Another valuable use for the Inner Sanctuary imagery exercise is in first aid. If someone is involved in an accident, sustains a painful injury and has little or no experience with managing their own pain, leading them through this exercise can help them to dissociate from the pain and to find great relief. Ian had a dramatic experience with this some years ago when he was the first to come across a young motorcyclist who had fallen and broken his leg. Using a conversational style, Ian invited the young man, who was in marked distress, to think of his favorite, most peaceful and safe place. Then he was invited to describe it in detail and to talk about what he liked about this place, what made it so special for him. By the time the ambulance arrived, the young man was calm and able to talk to the paramedics in a level tone.

Dissociation then has its place and can be quite useful. But it does involve dis-associating—losing our association with what is actually happening in our current moment experience.

MINDFULNESS-BASED PAIN MANAGEMENT

So what of the other possibility? What if, rather than avoid the pain, we give it our full attention? What happens then?

This brings us back to the proposition of learning how to feel the pain as a raw physical sensation, and take the psychological reaction out of it. This brings us to learning what we call mindfulness-based pain management.

This is a comprehensive system of pain management that does take a little while to learn, understand and practice. However, the time we spend doing this will be repaid when we have acquired a radical way of managing both acute and chronic pain. While, as the name suggests, this technique does draw on mindfulness, there is more to it. In fact, this style of pain management draws on the same four elements as the main MBSM practice—preparation, relaxation, mindfulness and stillness.

Preparation

We prepare by getting our head right. We need a good theoretical understanding of why and how it is possible to transform our experience of pain. Then we need to cultivate our own belief system so we can begin to let go of fear and negative expectations, and to build confidence in our own ability to actually do it. This has been the aim of the chapter so far—to build the concepts and to inspire you with the potential you have. There are so many remarkable stories to tell.

Arthur had advanced prostate cancer. He had painful secondary cancers in many bones throughout his body. Arthur came to the cancer groups in the early days, not long after Ian's book *You Can Conquer*

Cancer was released. Somewhat diffident, even skeptical to start with, Arthur decided to give "this meditation thing" a go. He felt desperate and could think of nowhere else to turn.

This was in the early days when Ian was teaching meditation based solely on the techniques of Dr. Ainslie Meares. Arthur learned how to relax his body, calm his mind and to experience some inner peace. His pain diminished rapidly. Arthur explained later:

> The pain relief was proof of what I was doing. When I started, my bones were really sore. They ached all day and were close to unbearable at night. Painkillers did give some relief, but they made my head feel terrible and I didn't like taking them unless things got really bad. Within a few days of starting the meditation, I noticed some difference. That gave me the confidence to try the dietary changes. Then, as my attitude became more positive, I found it easier to talk with my family and things steadily improved.

Arthur went on to have a full, long-term recovery without any medical treatment for his cancer. It was the pain relief he achieved that gave him confidence to really begin to believe he could make a difference, and to persevere. Over the years, we have noticed this for many people who have been able to use meditation to relieve their pain. The relief is so dramatic, so real, that it inspires real confidence in meditation's wider possibilities for healing and well-being.

In the late 1980s, Ian learned more about the mindfulness of pain technique we will discuss soon. During a workshop in Queensland he gave around that time, a woman named Andrea reported that she had been suffering from severe, debilitating back pain for the past eighteen years. She explained she had tried many self-help techniques, visited many doctors and naturopaths, and while some things had provided temporary relief, nothing had really helped the problem in the long term.

Andrea took up an offer to try the mindfulness of pain technique in front of the workshop group, and, to everyone's amazement—including Ian's, it must be said—the pain completely left her. On request, this lady wrote to Ian three months later and reported that the pain had not returned. A radical transformation indeed!

This, then, is something worth taking seriously. Whether you have pain at present or not, the nature of life seems to be that from time to time we will all experience pain in one form or another. And some of us will encounter more severe and perhaps longer-term chronic pain. These techniques of personal pain management are a life skill we can all benefit from learning, even children.

The starting point, the preparation, is to open yourself to the new possibilities. Then be prepared to train and experiment with pain and develop pain management as a personal skill.

Relaxation

One of the body's natural, instinctual reactions to pain is to tense up. However, you may have noticed—for example, if you need to have an injection—that when you tense up, the pain is much stronger. If you can relax, the pain diminishes, even disappears.

Pain relief is greatly helped by learning how to relax the body generally and how to release tension locally. In other words, we actually impose relaxation on any tension the body may have produced, and then we take this all the way so that our body is not only free of tension but is deeply relaxed.

How? We start by using the Progressive Muscle Relaxation (see pages 90–92) exercise to relax the body generally. Then we release any localized tension using the techniques we learned for relaxing the body in greater detail, as explained on pages 99–100. This is really simple and it makes a rapid and significant difference. All we need to be cautioned about is that, initially, the sensations of pain may become a little more noticeable for a short while. The explanation for this short-term increase in pain is twofold. First, by relaxing our body and the area around the pain, we are bringing our attention to the pain itself. This is the opposite of dissociation, so it is logical that at first we notice things a bit more. Also, when we relax the localized area around the pain, it can be a bit like releasing a cramp. You can probably notice quite easily for yourself that when you have a pain, the body tries to wall it off by creating tension around it. This is an instinctual reaction aimed at both protecting the area from further damage resulting from movement, blood loss or swelling, and protecting us from the hurt. Unfortunately, this is one of those bodily reactions that come at a cost. The cost is that the tension then exacerbates the pain. And when we release that tension, just like a cramp, it can seem worse before it gets better. With this caution, and a little patience and practice, most people do find that physical relaxation does bring significant relief to their pain.

To put these concepts regarding relaxation into practice, start by learning the PMR and then practice it in increasingly uncomfortable and challenging positions and situations.

To develop your pain-management skills specifically, you may like to experiment more deliberately with potentially painful (but not harmful) experiences. Try lying down with a pebble or pencil under your back. A bulldog paperclip is terrific for practicing as you can attach the clip to a piece of skin—perhaps the back or front of the wrist area, or the webbing between thumb and index finger—and you can control the clip. So while it does create a reasonable sensation for you to experiment and practice with, when you choose to, you can simply unclip it and the sensation stops.

Restating the key point, you do need to put the theory into practice. The notion of training with pain is no more bizarre than pushing yourself to train for a sport or enduring hours of study to learn a new subject. Here the benefit is pain relief; in fact, a whole new way of experiencing pain. So take the time to experiment with gradually more painful experiences. The aim is to let go of any instinctual reflex tension, to learn how to be able to relax, to develop the capacity to allow the sensation to be there, and then to use mindfulness.

Mindfulness of pain

Remember the definition of mindfulness is paying attention to our present moment experience, deliberately and nonjudgmentally. Mindfulness of pain, therefore, is paying attention to our present moment experience of pain, deliberately and nonjudgmentally. However, in practice—again both personally and in our clinical experience—what we have found to be even more effective is a very special type of mindfulness based on stillness. We will explore both possibilities in detail.

Pure mindfulness of pain would say that we give our attention to the pain, deliberately and nonjudgmentally. This approach is very similar to elements of the traditional Buddhist practice "the Four Foundations of Mindfulness." Hopefully, having read and practiced some of the mindfulness-based exercises earlier in this book, you understand quite well what mindfulness does mean. There is no attempt to distract ourselves or to dissociate. There is no attempt to change the pain. We do not make more or less of it. We do, however, give it our full attention.

The aim is to not judge it. We let go of any commentary that the pain is a bad thing or that someone is to blame for it. We have to let go of the story or stories that go with the pain. Let go of our past experience and reactions to it. Let go of fantasizing in any way about how the future might be. Let go of any notion we may have as to whether the pain may get better or worse. Just focus on how it is right now. What does it feel like today? This hour. This minute. Right now. What sensations am I feeling? Let go of the reaction. Take up a curious, nonjudgmental state of inquiry. What does it feel like? Now, in this very moment.

In a practical sense we take up a curious interest in the pain. What does this particular pain feel like at this particular moment? Just feel it. No need to go into it, no need to go away from it. Do not make more or less of it. No need to attempt to change it. Resist the temptation to bemoan it ever existed, or to hope that it passes. Just be present to what it is like in this very moment. A courageous, open curiosity. Nonjudgmental and nonreactive. The experience of pain as a pure physical sensation, free of any psychological reaction. There is almost a sense of relaxing into it; moving from tension to relaxation. And as we do this, as we aim to be present and not to react, most commonly everything changes and often the sensation of pain even dissolves.

When we can do this purely, it does work. Just as when we can look at our thoughts with pure mindfulness they dissolve, so too does pain dissolve when it is given full, mindful attention.

There is a very effective exercise that helps to develop this mindfulness of pain. This is the same technique that dissolved Andrea's pain, as described earlier. It combines mindfully examining the sensory experience of pain, really going into the perceived reality of the pain, with a simple breathing exercise.

This is another exercise where you can learn the script first, listen to it on CD or an mp3 player, or have a friend or family member read it out to you. If you have the equipment, you can make your own recording based upon the script that follows. Or you could obtain Ian's CD on pain management, which includes him leading the exercise. If you are listening to a CD or having someone read it to you, actually speak your answers to the questions out loud. This helps to focus your mind and concentrate. If you do the exercise for yourself, then you do need to do all the steps in it, including asking the questions! This may be stating the obvious, but the exercise works best when you concentrate and move steadily through the steps described.

Many people have found this exercise changes their perception of pain dramatically. However, when you come to do it, it is best to aim to let go of expectations and to try this exercise as an experiment. This direction probably sounds very familiar by now. We use it because it works! Aim to give the exercise your full attention, free of judgment or expectation. Aim to have that open, curious approach and be really interested in and aware of what happens. Remember, speaking your responses to all the questions in this exercise can help it to be even more effective.

Allow twenty minutes for this exercise.

MINDFULNESS-BASED PAIN MANAGEMENT

If you need to adjust the way you are sitting or lying, get your body settled . . . and, in your own way, take a few moments to feel your body relaxing once again. . . . The feeling of the muscles softening a little . . . and loosening . . . relaxing and releasing . . . just simply letting go. . . . Perhaps a deeper breath or two helps . . . and that feeling of letting go a little on the out breath. . . . Just feeling the ease of it all . . . quite effortlessly . . . effortlessly.

Now scan your attention through your body and notice if there is a particular sensation . . . concentrated in a particular area . . . an area of discomfort or pain. . . . Now focus your attention on that part of your body . . . and first notice which part of the body this sensation is located in . . . and just imagine you are speaking, describing where that area is located . . . and giving attention to whether it is close to the surface of the body . . . or deeper into the tissue. . . . Just notice exactly where it is located.

And then, in your mind, notice what shape this sensation has. . . . Whether it is round like a ball . . . or oval . . . or long like a rod . . . or a flat sheet. . . . What shape does it have . . . ? Just notice what particular shape the sensation has.

And then be aware of what size it is. . . . How long is it . . . ? How wide is it . . . ? How deep is it . . . ? How many centimeters or inches . . . ? What size is it?

And what density does it have . . . ? Is it hard like a rock . . . ? Or soft like a sponge . . . ? And is it the same all the way through . . . ? Or is it harder on the outside . . . ? Or harder on the inside . . . ? What density does it have . . . ? And what is its surface texture like . . . ? Is it smooth or rough?

And what temperature is it . . . ? Does it feel warm . . . ? Or cool . . . ? Or neutral . . . ? What temperature is it?

And what about color . . . ? If it had a color, what color would it be?

Now hold this area in your attention. . . . As you breathe in next time, imagine you are traveling with the breath . . . right to that area you are focusing your attention on. . . . And that the breath then gently washes around the outside of it. . . . And as you breathe out, the breath just gently ebbs away again . . . a bit like a wave coming into the shore, washing around something in the sand and then just going out to sea again with the out breath.

And do that for three more breaths . . . so each time you breathe in, the breath comes in and washes around the outside of the area. . . . With the out breath, the breath just gently ebbs away again.

Now the next time you breathe in, imagine that your breath flows right into the very center of this area. . . . And as you breathe out, the breath just gently ebbs away again. . . . Do that for three more breaths. . . . So breathe in and the breath goes right into the center of this area. . . . And then, with the out breath, it just gently ebbs away again.

Good . . . Now, as you breathe in again, imagine flowing with the breath as it goes to this area once again and washes around the outside of it . . . and then, as you breathe out, the breath gently ebbs away. . . . Do this again for three more breaths, breathing in and the breath goes around the outside of the area . . . breathing out and it just gently ebbs away.

Good . . . And now just gently scan your attention through the body again. . . . Notice if there is a particular sensation that your mind is drawn to. . . . And notice where that sensation is localized. . . . Which part of the body . . . ? Is it close to the surface or deeper into the tissue?

And then be aware of what shape it has. . . . Round like a ball, or oval like an egg . . ? A rod . . ? What particular shape does it have?

And then notice more particularly what size it is. . . . How long is it . . . ? How wide . . . ? How deep . . . ? How many centimeters or inches . . . ? What size is it?

And then be aware of its density. . . . Is it hard like a rock . . . ? Or soft like a sponge . . . ? And is it harder on the outside, harder on the inside or the same all the way through . . . ? What density does it have?

And then the surface. . . . Notice whether the surface is rough or smooth. . . . What is its surface like?

And what temperature is it . . . ? Is it warm . . . ? Or cool . . . ? Or neutral . . . ? What temperature is it?

And color . . . If it had a color, what color would it be?

And now, as you hold your attention on this area, the next time you breathe in, follow the breath in and around the area . . . the breath washing around the outside . . . and then with the out breath, gently ebbing away. . . . And do that for three more breaths.

Good . . . Next time you breathe in, follow the breath right into the very center of the area. . . . Then breathe out, the breath just gently ebbing away once again. . . . And do that for three more breaths.

And then as you breathe in again, follow the breath in and around the outside of the area. . . . And as you breathe out, the breath just gently ebbing away once again. . . . And do that for three more breaths.

Good . . . And now you can just rest with the feeling you have right now . . . or you can continue with this exercise . . . but you might like to just let go of the exercise and simply rest with the feeling. . . . Just simply letting go . . . going with it . . . just simply letting go . . . quite effortlessly . . . effortlessly . . . more and more . . . deeper and deeper . . . just simply letting go . . . letting go . . . letting go.

This approach involving mindfulness of pain helps many to reduce their experience of pain significantly. While for some it is difficult to do completely, and difficult to sustain on its own, for others it does provide the radical solution to pain.

Mindfulness of stillness

The special type of mindfulness we alluded to earlier involves mindfulness of stillness. Instead of paying attention deliberately to the pain, we pay attention deliberately to the stillness. Then we simply allow the pain to be there, almost disregarding it, a bit like that old metaphor of white clouds drifting across a blue sky.

Think back to the exercises with Mindfulness of Thoughts in chapters 11 and 12 when we learned how to give our attention to the stillness, learning to simply allow any thoughts to be there, just allowing them to come and go, while remaining undistracted. Similarly to that, in this truly radical way of managing pain, we give our attention to the stillness and allow the pain to be there while we remain undistracted.

This technique has a number of elements. It begins with the preparation that gives us a positive mind-set with which to approach pain. It draws huge support from the physical relaxation that we practice. Then, in a way, the stillness can be compared to the ultimate "Inner Sanctuary." This stillness is an ever-present source of peace and calm. In fact, the more we experience the stillness, the more we realize there is this part of us that is completely free of pain. In the stillness comes the direct experience of that part of us that is more permanent, more enduring and, just like the metaphor of the blue sky, unstainable, inviolable. We realize that there is this part of us that cannot be hurt.

Pain is to do with our physical, emotional and mental world. On these levels it is real enough and can be a source of very real hurt and distress. However, pain does not exist in our inner essence. And while we may theorize that this is true, when we come to experience it, when we come to know that it is true, there is a great freedom, and a knowing that pain is as impermanent as the clouds. Sure there may be cloudy days; storms may rage for a while. But that blue sky is always there, accessible, real and unstainable.

Stillness

How then do we experience this stillness in the face of pain? Maybe we can get an inkling of it when we are well and do those Mindfulness of Thoughts exercises. But what if pain is our present moment experience?

Start where you are at. Maybe analgesics are necessary to make life bearable. Maybe you can use more natural self-help methods to take the edge off. Maybe, like for Arthur, just by practicing MBSM, the pain eases and becomes more manageable. Maybe you learn courtesy of a bulldog paper clip and maybe there is something else in the range of possibilities we have covered that speaks to you more directly. It is important to be prepared to experiment a little and to find what does work best for you. Just knowing that genuine pain relief is a possibility is a starting point. For many who have worked at this, a genuine change in their experience of pain has transformed their life for the better.

Finally, maybe it is obvious, but surely the best time to learn pain-management skills is when you are pain-free. Why wait until the need is strong? This is a life skill that everyone can benefit from. Build on the techniques explained in chapter 11 on Mindfulness of Thoughts. The more reliably you experience the stillness and its deeply calm, pervasive qualities, the more confidence you will have in the face of pain.

Remember that, as your experience of stillness develops, you will experience stillness and movement. In this case what we call the movement is actually the pain. For those of advanced practice, there comes a point where the stillness and even the pain "taste" the same. Pain is just a sensation and it does not hurt. Now that is a really radical solution!

Why not experiment and find out the truth of the matter for yourself. You might just transform your experience of pain in the process.

CHAPTER 16

MEDITATION, IMAGERY AND AFFIRMATIONS

If one advances confidently in the direction of his dreams,
and endeavors to lead the life he has imagined
he will meet with success unexpected in common hours.
—HENRY DAVID THOREAU

Take a few moments to indulge in a fantasy. Imagine you have unlimited time and money for an ideal holiday. Where will you go? Which part of the world? And will you go to the beach? The mountains? Touring? How will you travel? Airplane? Train? Car? Walking? A combination? Who will you go with? Family? Friends? In a group? On your own? What will you do while you are on this holiday?

Imagine all the possibilities and then decide on your ideal holiday destination. Now, notice the feelings that go with all of this. Is there a sense of excitement, a feeling that perhaps you could do it? Is there disappointment or frustration that you feel you cannot? Is there an inner voice urging you to make a booking? Or the voice of reason saying none of this is possible? Do images of past holidays come to mind and influence the current plan? Does the thought of an ideal holiday bring to mind a long-held dream, something you have been seriously saving for and working toward? Put all this together, indulge in the fantasy and imagine you are booking your ideal holiday. Be specific in your plans.

Now for some observations. How easy was it to imagine all of this? Most people find it easy enough to create images in their mind as they imagine a fantasy like this. Next, consider all the options you had to choose from—all the places, all the people, all the details. Consider how, as you decided what to do, which holiday to opt for, you actually needed to sort through an incredible array of conscious and unconscious choices and influences.

This, then, is the process of thinking. This is what the thinking mind is good at. It starts with an intention, a plan to do something, like embark on a holiday. Then it assesses the possibilities—how much money, time and inclination we really have. Putting all this together, the mind then makes a choice, effectively setting a specific goal. I will go to that location, for this much time, with these people. Then the mind follows through, directing the actions that are required to get it all done—booking the tickets and the accommodation, getting to the airport on time and so on. So this is what the mind does.

Our mind gives us the capacity to be aware, to think, to feel and to do. And now some really interesting questions. How does the mind manage to do all of this? What process does it use? What are the actual mechanics of how we think? The answer is simple. We use imagery. As we experience life events, the mind records these events as images and stores them in our memory. Try to remember your last holiday: you will notice that you use images in your mind to recollect where you went and what you did. If you fantasize about or plan a future holiday, again you will be using mental images. Our mind functions through the active use of imagery.

There is a great deal to consider and choose from when it comes to learning and applying the techniques of imagery—for purposes more far-reaching than planning a trip. Ian has explored these possibilities quite fully in his book *The Creative Power of Imagery*. However, here we will focus on imagery exercises that complement MBSM. In this context, imagery is an active form of meditation that engages the thinking mind with its two components, the conscious and the unconscious. This is the realm of meditation that utilizes intention, and it is referred to in some traditions as visualization.

CONVERTING INTENTION INTO REALITY THROUGH IMAGERY

The word *image* is defined in the *Shorter Oxford English Dictionary* as "a mental representation of something, a simile or a metaphor." In the context of meditation we define imagery as "the conscious development and repetition of mental images for a creative purpose." Through the use of imagery we are able to tap into the potential and the power of the mind and convert an intention (to do something) into a reality (where it is actually done).

The example of how we use our mind to convert the intention of going on a holiday into a reality demonstrates how we use imagery to enable us to function in ordinary life. This gives us an insight into how the mind works generally, and with this knowledge we can then go on to use imagery for specific purposes. We can learn how to generate images that reflect the goals we have decided upon, and then repeat these images over and over in our mind so that they become established in a way that the mind follows them through to completion. Many people whom we have helped to learn to meditate have found imagery exercises a useful addition to their mind training.

Read through the exercises that follow and consider how relevant they are to your own situation and needs. If any appeal, try them as an experiment. With any imagery exercise, if you practice it regularly for a few days, maybe a week or two at most, you will get your own inner sense of whether it feels useful for you to continue and adopt as a regular exercise or whether it is of no particular use to you, in which case you can just let it go. Trust your own sense of this and be guided by your own responses.

Inner peace

When our intention is to find inner peace, we simply manufacture images in our mind that generate feelings of inner peace. This is one of the oldest techniques that use imagery in combination with meditation.

One simple way to do this is to sit as for meditation, relax, close your eyes and imagine a place where you feel particularly peaceful, comfortable and safe. One of the most reliable ways to do this is to use the Inner Sanctuary exercise that was presented in chapter 15 on transforming pain.

Inner silence

Another exercise many people find easy, useful and enjoyable is to generate images in their mind that create their own version of the Temple of Silence. Allow fifteen to twenty minutes for this exercise.

THE TEMPLE OF SILENCE

Sit as you would to meditate. . . . Adjust your position and allow your body to settle. . . . Close your eyes. . . . Take a moment and in your own way relax your body once again.

Now in your mind, imagine a place where silence has been kept for countless years, a Temple of Silence. . . . Imagine yourself to be approaching this place. . . . Notice the surrounds of this temple of silence. . . . Where is it located . . . ? In a city, town, or in the countryside?

As you draw closer to your Temple of Silence, examine its features . . . the shape of it . . . the size of it . . . the color. . . . Perhaps there is a particular fragrance you can notice. . . . As you come to the entrance of the temple, perhaps there is something you need to do. . . . Take off your shoes . . . ask permission to enter. . . . Whatever you need to do, do it . . . and then enter.

Feel the presence of this temple. . . . The silence is almost tangible. . . . There is the knowing that silence has been revered and kept here for ages past. . . . Feel yourself immersed in that silence . . . and at the same time, take in the features of the temple. . . . Perhaps it has a focal point . . . particular decorations . . . open areas. . . . Take it all in and feel yourself to be a part of it . . . as if the silence is within you. . . . Feel it all through you.

And perhaps now you move to a particular part of the Temple of Silence . . . so that you can just be in the silence for a while. . . . Take up your position, whatever posture feels appropriate for you . . . and feel the silence all through you . . . all through. . . . Just resting in the silence for as long as you care to.

And when you are ready to take your leave . . . maybe you express your gratitude . . . maybe you just feel it . . . And as you take your leave . . . do whatever you need to . . . and know you can always come back to this temple, whenever you want . . . this Temple of Silence.

You could do this type of imagery exercise regularly, or just occasionally when you feel the need for inner quiet. Like the Inner Sanctuary exercise, the Temple of Silence is an easy but effective way to use imagery as a stepping-stone into meditation.

Spiritual presence, connectedness and invocation

As well as intention, there is another traditional use of imagery, often called invocation. With this method we invoke or draw to ourselves inspiration, strength, wisdom or the energy needed to support us to achieve whatever we need to do.

Traditionally, of course, this has been a spiritual practice. Religious people have invoked the presence of Christ, or Mother Mary, or the Buddha; whatever represents and embodies their own spiritual truth. If you find this practice useful, the key is to bring to life the spiritual figure you invoke. So rather than just dispassionately imagining a picture or a two-dimensional figure, invoke Christ or the Buddha as if he were actually standing there in front of you. You aim to generate as much detail as possible as well as the sense of actually being in that figure's presence. By doing so you open to that presence, really feel it, absorb it and aim to be at one with it. You aim to let go of any thoughts to do with the past or future, and rest in the present moment, your mind merged with that of the spiritual figure you have invoked.

This type of imagery can lead to very powerful experiences and the deepening of your meditation. It can also be an excellent prelude to more formal prayer or MBSM. It is a way of infusing a spiritual presence and sense of connectedness into meditation and, if you hold the feeling, into daily life. This exercise can be done regularly if it has meaning for you.

In native cultures, totems and power animals served a similar purpose, providing another level of strength, inspiration, wisdom and direction. For example, a young warrior in Africa in need of strength and courage might invoke the presence and spirit of a lion.

We too can use these principles by consciously imagining whatever embodies the qualities we seek or need. Ask yourself who inspires you. Who do you draw energy from? Who is your best role model? Who embodies your spiritual aspirations? Then imagine them as if they were standing in front of you. Feel their presence. Invoke their qualities. This technique is very reliable, very effective, very potent!

REINFORCING INTENTIONS

Bev was one of those women who was going to meditate next week, maybe tomorrow, but almost certainly not today! Chronically busy, stressed and a little anxious, Bev was keen to find some balance in her busy working and family life. She came up with a plan, a good intention; she would learn to meditate and then get into a routine. However, her attendance at one of our groups rapidly became a source of some good-natured mirth. Bev would usually arrive a little late, all apologetic and somewhat in a fluster. When she settled, Bev really enjoyed the groups and the moments of peace as we meditated together. Then when the group discussed how much meditation was being done at home, Bev would say week after week, "Well, not much last week, but I'm going to start this week."

Each time she said this she really believed it, but somehow the weeks rolled by and the busyness continued to get the better of her. The good thing was that Bev was not put off by her difficulties. Some people in her situation become embarrassed or feel guilty, and stop coming to the group. Bev responded by asking what to do. What solved her problem was the use of imagery supported by an affirmation.

The imagery Bev practiced was to simply imagine herself meditating each day. Bev had decided that her best chance to establish a meditation routine was in the morning, and so, in her mind several times a day, Bev "saw" herself getting up, having her usual shower, meditating and then going off to breakfast. In effect, she used these images to program herself to carry out her good intention. Then Bev reinforced this imagery with the use of the affirmation, "I really enjoy getting up early to meditate each day."

Affirmations

Affirmations are another simple and effective way to imprint a goal onto the mind in a way that the mind can recognize and commit to, and then drive the choices and actions to fulfill it. Affirmations are short, sharp sentences or phrases, regularly repeated, that encapsulate our intentions, our goals. So for Bev: "I really enjoy getting up early to meditate each day." For affirmations to be effective they need to be:

- expressed in the first person
- expressed in the present tense
- goal-oriented

Affirmations are something that only we can do for ourselves, therefore most affirmations begin with "I am" or "I have." Present time is the only time the mind responds to, therefore affirmations need to indicate that the goal is already achieved or reached. The aim is to give the mind a target that it can lock on to, and that target is the end goal.

Here, then, are more guidelines for making up your own affirmations.

Be positive

Indicate what is needed, rather than what is not. The mind needs a positive direction to aim for, not something to avoid. So rather than saying, "I am not going to stay in bed," say, "I really enjoy getting up early . . ."

Do not make comparisons

There is no need to say, "I am as good as . . ." Your potential may be to be better, or perhaps not as good as whatever it is you are comparing yourself to. Aim to develop affirmations that encourage the development of your own full potential.

Do not specify a time for completion

As with comparisons, specifying time may slow you down or frustrate you. Bev did not specify a time when she would start to get up to meditate; that took care of itself, as we will explain later.

Be specific, accurate and accountable

The mind needs a specific target. The more precise the goal, the greater its clarity, the more confident you can be of success.

Be realistic

It is normal to expect some reaction to using affirmations. When Bev began saying, "I really enjoy getting up early," she soon encountered an echo! The echo was her own inner voice, her experience saying, "No, you don't, you love staying in bed a little longer," and "When you do get up you are too busy to meditate anyway." If these echoes were not there, there would be no need to use the affirmations or the imagery. So do not be surprised by the echo. As long as the affirmation has more certainty, more expectation, more hope and more energy than the echo, and it is repeated, it will gradually replace it and soon become your guiding force.

However, you will need to stay within the bounds of what you believe is reasonably possible. Set realistic goals. Be gentle with yourself, and gradually you may feel ready to set increasingly higher standards and goals.

Set ongoing goals
This follows on from what was just said. As you see yourself nearing completion of one goal, look for what comes next. Extend your planning and make new resolutions.

Use action words and add a sense of excitement
The feeling that goes with an affirmation has a lot to do with how quickly it will imprint and be accepted by your mind. Affirmations, therefore, work better when said with zest and excitement. One way to do this is to add "wow!" onto the end of them. For example, "I am a positive person now—wow!" Saying "wow!" encapsulates that positive, expectant feeling.

For Bev, saying "I really enjoy . . ." was intended to establish not only that she did get up but that she actually enjoyed it, and as such she would persevere until this new habit was established.

Be precise with your choice of words
Words used as affirmations are definitely words of power. Pay particular attention to how they might be interpreted. If you need to, you can add a phrase like "in a harmonious way." However, aim to be as clear and precise as possible, consider all angles and choose your words wisely. Meditating upon your choice of affirmations before you use them is an excellent way to check their meaning and validity. The practice of contemplation, described in chapter 18, can be very helpful in developing clear goals and effective affirmations.

Keep a balance
Affirmations can have a profound effect on your direction in life. Consider the range of goals you are setting. Take account of your physical, emotional, mental and spiritual needs, and those of your family, friends and community. Affirmations are exciting tools to use. Aim to maintain a sense of balance with them.

Affirmations as agents of change

Affirmations can be used to reinforce any good intention. This may involve changing an old, unhelpful habit, like sleeping in and being late to work, establishing a new pattern like a meditation routine, improving relationships or enhancing self-esteem. For example:

- For health—"Every day in every way I am getting better and better."
- For state of mind—"I am a positive person now."
- For relationships—"I greet this person with love."
- For self-esteem—"I am worthy of being happy. I am worthy of being loved."

How to use affirmations

Bev combined her affirmation and imagery exercises. Before rising, once during her lunch break and on going to bed, Bev pictured herself getting up and meditating; at the same time she repeated her affirmation. She was advised to make no particular effort to get up early or to meditate, just to wait and see what happened.

After only two weeks a strange thing occurred. Bev reported back to the group:

> In the last few days I have found myself waking up a little earlier with a strong urge to get up. It just seems like sleep is over and I have this pleasant anticipation of meditating. The hardest thing has been that it all seems a little weird. I guess that part of me didn't expect it to work, especially so soon, but I can say that my mind feels different and I really am enjoying getting up early to meditate!

Affirmations can be used like this in conjunction with imagery, or they can be used on their own. Both practices involve the use of repetition to imprint a goal in a way that our mind recognizes and acts upon. For many people, the use of affirmations and imagery has led to really helpful breakthroughs.

Inner rehearsal

Imagine for a moment that you need to give a speech in front of a large public audience. In response, many of us probably begin to practice inner rehearsal almost straightaway. We imagine what we might say, what we will see and, often, particularly how we will feel. Many of us, contemplating something that needs to be done in the future, do a thing in our mind that is aptly described in chapter 6 as "catastrophizing." We rehearse in our mind all that could go wrong and how bad we will feel and how difficult it will be. The worst-case scenario.

With the technique of inner rehearsal we take charge of this aspect of our inner life and repeatedly rehearse the ideal outcome. Of course, this inner work is now a major part of training for many athletes and other sportspeople. But it is easy to grasp the direct relevance of this technique to business, healing and even relationships. Remember that neuroplasticity confirms that what we do more of we get better at, and new neuro pathways are formed. The good thing about rehearsing in our mind is that we can do it perfectly!

Again, all we need to do is to repeatedly picture in our mind an image of ourselves acting in an idealized way and then to support this with positive self-talk, preferably with a matching affirmation. Do not be put off by the simplicity of this. The reality is that many people have derived great benefit from these techniques.

Manifestation

This is where we use imagery to attract or draw to us the things we need. Many people use this principle to manifest parking lots! The idea is simple enough. When you drive somewhere that you know will be busy, you ask and expect a parking lot to be available close to where you need it. The lovely thing about this is that most people find manifestation does work for parking lots. So why not try it with apparently trickier things like manifesting the resources you need, the people you need or the circumstances you need for a healthy, happy life?

The principles of the laws of manifestation are simple enough. First you need to believe enough in the concept to give it a go. Then you need to differentiate between needs and wants. Manifestation is often only reliable when used for genuine needs; when it is based on wants the results are somewhat variable.

Once you are clear, ask for what you need. Ask the highest source of power you know: God, the universe, the abstract principle of abundance. A direct request to the highest source of power you know. Then let it go. Having asked, retain a positive expectation, but do not dwell on it. Ideally, you will feel a quiet confidence rather than doubt or anxiety.

Then when what you need does manifest, it is best not to be too surprised! If you say, "This is too good to be true," your disbelief will probably interfere with it happening again. Instead be grateful. Thank whoever or whatever you asked, and smile. Enjoy what you manifested, and ideally consider how it can be of most use or benefit to the most people.

USING IMAGERY TO INFLUENCE THE BODY

This is a very particular type of imagery where the intention is to influence specific functions within the body. As such, it is quite different from the types of imagery discussed so far where we have worked more directly on the mind itself. The use of imagery in healing is based on the key tenets of mind-body medicine. This type of imagery is based on the fact that the myriad physical processes that combine within the body to produce healing are regulated by the mind.

The best analogy we can provide here is that of running. Consider the question "Shall I go for a run?" When we consider this we do so with our conscious mind. If we do decide to go for a run, we do not then attempt to consciously tell our body how to run. Running is a highly complex process. We need to move a multitude of muscles in coordinated sequences, we need to elevate our heart rate and our breathing; there is a complex array of bodily functions that need to work together so we can run effectively. This complexity is beyond the scope of our conscious, thinking mind.

As a result, the process of running is controlled by that more automatic, unconscious part of our mind. Effectively, there is a part of our unconscious mind we can call "the running center" that knows how to coordinate the whole process of running. The conscious mind makes the decision to run, but then that decision is conveyed to the unconscious running center, which recognizes the instruction and directs and coordinates all the necessary elements so that the body can in fact run.

While we may be able to learn and understand all the processes involved in running, if we try to consciously direct or influence them as we run, we will soon stumble. As another example, if you have a toothache and consciously try to chew on one side of your mouth, very often you will end up biting some part of your tongue, cheeks or lips; this is because you are interfering with a complex process that is normally regulated via that automatic part of the mind.

Just as there is a "running center," each of us also has what can effectively be called a "healing center" in the mind. Through the study of mind-body medicine we now know a great deal about the physiology and biochemistry relating to the activity of that healing center. Candace Pert, the great research pioneer in this field, helped popularize this knowledge through her book *Molecules of Emotion*, first published in 1997 and still very relevant to this discussion today. Dr. Pert's work has inspired and informed a huge new field of research exploring the effect of our emotional state on mental health. This research has established that when someone is depressed their brain releases specific molecules that travel via the bloodstream, attach onto white blood cells and depress immune function. Conversely, have a good laugh and different molecules are released that in turn stimulate immune function.

The intention with imagery is to tap into this mind-body potential, to focus healing where it is needed, and to get the most out of it. Perhaps it could be said that imagery is actively working with the placebo response. However we understand it, imagery uses our mind to directly influence healing. And this is where it gets easy. What we are aiming to do is to give a conscious message to an unconscious part of our mind, in a way that it will recognize and act upon it. For this to happen we need a way to communicate between the conscious mind and the unconscious; we need a common language. And that common language is imagery. The natural language of the unconscious mind is imagery, and the conscious mind can easily learn to work with images. Therefore we can use images to convey the intention to heal from the conscious mind to the unconscious. How?

In the imagery exercises we have experimented with earlier in this chapter, the imagery used has been fairly literal. For example, we saw the Temple of Silence, and Bev literally saw herself getting up early and meditating. However, because of the complexity of healing, literal images are not useful, so we rely on symbolic and abstract methods.

While the use of personalized symbols to represent the different aspects of healing can be quite useful, the techniques involved benefit from individualized, more extensive and specialized attention. What is easier and safer to explain here is the use of abstract imagery.

Abstract imagery draws on the use of archetypal symbols. An archetype is a profound symbol that is interpreted in a common way across cultures. So when virtually all cultures are asked what their most deeply rooted, deeply significant symbols are for healing, the answer is water and light. Many cultures, therefore, use images of water and light to facilitate healing. What we have found useful over many years now is the White Light imagery exercise. This technique has its origins in traditional practices such as those found in Tibetan Buddhism, but here it has been adapted into a modern context. Due to its archetypal nature, it has the potential for wide application. While it is a major technique for healing, it is also excellent for gaining an energy boost, for preventing illness and for strengthening our connections with our spiritual roots.

This exercise is easy to follow and can be modified to incorporate your own spiritual views. Give yourself at least twenty minutes for this exercise.

WHITE LIGHT HEALING

Settle into your posture and, if you need to, adjust your position. . . . Then, in your own way, take a few moments to feel your body relaxing once again . . . that feeling of the muscles softening and loosening . . . relaxing . . . releasing. . . .

Perhaps a deeper breath or two helps. . . . Just simply letting go . . . letting go.

In your mind, imagine the highest source of power you know, as if it was in the sky above you . . . maybe a symbol that represents for you God, or maybe the figure of Christ, Mother Mary, a saint, the Buddha or a particular figure from another tradition . . . whatever it is that embodies the highest source of truth you know. . . . You may have a more abstract view and prefer to imagine a white ball like the sun that symbolizes universal life force, the source of creation . . . a source of vitality and healing . . . a source of energy and power . . . also a source of loving kindness that has your own best interest at heart . . . a source of energy that is full of all that is life-affirming.

And as that image forms in your mind as if it is in the sky above you . . . just imagine what it would be like to come into the presence of what it is that embodies your own truth . . . this source of creative energy . . . this source of spiritual or universal energy. . . . Open yourself to that feeling. . . . What would it be like to be in this presence . . . ? Feel what it would be like to approach this presence . . . to be in this presence. . . . Feel yourself coming closer and more directly into this divine presence.

And as you do that, perhaps there is something you feel you would like to say. . . . Perhaps a prayer . . . perhaps something you would like to explain . . . perhaps there is something you would like to ask for . . . perhaps forgiveness or healing or some other thing you need or would like . . . and if something does come to mind, just say it, ask it quietly. . . . And there is always the possibility of a direct response . . . of something being said to you, for you. . . . So you could listen for that . . . be open to the possibility of an exchange or a dialogue developing.

And then, when you are ready, imagine coming from the

very heart of this symbol, from the heart of the figure or the very center of the white light of the sun, a beam of white light flowing down toward you . . . a beam of light like a searchlight . . . but this light also has liquid properties . . . a bit like a shower or a waterfall . . . warm, liquid, white light. . . . And as this warm, liquid, white light flows down toward you and reaches your head, it quite gently, slowly, softly flows not only over and around your body, but actually through it . . . a bit like water filtering down through dry sand . . . quite slowly . . . slowly . . . down through your head and down through your body . . . warm, liquid, white light . . . almost like having a wash on the inside . . . washing away anything that is old, worn or unwanted . . . and bringing with it a new sense of energy . . . healing . . . vitality.

So, as this white light continues to flow from that divine source in a steady stream . . . feel it coming from that infinite source and flowing gently down through your head . . . out across the shoulders . . . down through the arms . . . into the chest . . . gently flowing down through the body. . . . And as it continues to flow down through your body . . . feel your body fill with this warm, liquid, white light . . . feel a warm glow spreading throughout your body.

And as that light reaches down to your fingers . . . you will find it flows down and out through the fingers. . . . And when it reaches your feet . . . you will find it flows out through your feet.

So a stream of warm, liquid, white light . . . flowing from that infinite source . . . and steadily flowing on down through your body . . . washing through your body . . . and taking with it anything that is old or worn or unwanted. . . . You may see anything that you want to be free of as a stain . . . just being gently washed out through your body . . . out of your body . . . flowing out through the hands and the feet.

And if you sense there is any part of your body that needs more of this warm, liquid, white light . . . you can imagine a concentrated stream of the warm light going to that area . . . warm, liquid, white light . . . flowing into that area . . . flowing through that area . . . washing . . . cleansing . . . invigorating . . . revitalizing . . . healing.

And as the light continues to flow down through your body, it is almost like turning up a dimmer switch . . . the light getting stronger and clearer . . . all through your body . . . radiant light . . . warm . . . clear . . . flowing all through and becoming clearer and stronger . . . through every part of your body. . . . Sometimes you may notice a warmth or tingling flowing with it. . . . You can sense its energy . . . its vitality . . . its healing quality . . . its radiance. . . . There is a new vitality and energy that comes with it.

And as it gets stronger and clearer it is almost like this light flows from your body into your mind. . . . It is almost like, with your mind, you can merge into that light . . . merging and uniting with it . . . feeling its presence all through you . . . through the body . . . and the mind . . . the sense of just going with it . . . resting in that divine presence . . . just going with it . . . welcoming . . . relaxing . . . releasing . . . expanding . . . flowing . . . merging.

Rest in that divine presence for a few moments now . . . just naturally resting . . . feeling a part of it all . . . feeling the ease of it all . . . just simply letting go. . . . Just rest in the presence of that light for as long as you are comfortable.

Remember you can come back to this exercise at any time you like . . . and each time you do, you will find it will feel easier and even more complete. . . . You will be able to go with it more thoroughly and rest in the presence even more completely.

Also remember you can have a sense of this energy, this

presence, being with you all through the day. . . . Even while you sleep . . . This is an infinite energy you are drawing upon. It is always there. It is limitless. . . . So have a sense of taking this energy, this quality, with you throughout the day and even while you sleep.

When you are ready to finish the exercise, move your feet a little . . . feel your hands move a little, and then, when you are ready, just let your eyes gently open again.

As with other imagery techniques, this exercise can be used daily or whenever you feel the need. It is best to be guided by your own instincts.

In our experience this exercise is the simplest, the most potent and the most reliable form of healing imagery. It is also an excellent exercise for healthy people who are interested in preventing illness, maintaining good health and strengthening their spiritual connection. In other words, it is an ideal exercise for most people and, like the other imagery techniques described in this chapter, well worth experimenting with.

CHAPTER 17

MEDITATION USING INTENTION—FORGIVENESS, GRATITUDE AND LOVING KINDNESS

From intention springs the deed, from the deed springs the habit.
From the habit grows the character, from the character develops destiny.
—OLD CHINESE SAYING

Mindfulness-Based Stillness Meditation uses attention to bring us into the experience of the present moment. Just through this simple act of being present, many qualities and virtues are developed. Giving non-judgmental attention to our present moment experience begins the development of:

- acceptance—as we let go of the struggle to achieve, attain, change, fix, improve;
- humility and simplicity—as we cease extending ourselves to do more, be more and have more;

- patience—as we give up trying to make something happen or get somewhere;
- presence—as we let go of imagining the future or recalling the past;
- trust—as we let go of our controlling ways;
- compassion—as we bring nonjudgmental attention to our pain, our suffering and all of our emotions; and
- right action—as we become more accepting, more present and our minds become clearer. We become more caring and more efficient, more effective and useful in daily life.

These qualities grow naturally from the regular practice of MBSM. Quite often, friends, neighbors, family and work colleagues notice the emergence of these qualities before the meditator notices them. These qualities are the fruits of meditation.

These qualities, and others, can be enhanced and developed further by the use of intentional meditation. Intentional meditation is more active than mindfulness in that it carries a wish/hope/goal and uses conscious creative thinking to realize that goal. Meditation using intention utilizes images, words and emotions to attract the desired outcome. In chapter 16 we described the use of intentional meditation (affirmations and imagery) for health, healing and well-being. In this chapter we will explain how intentional meditation can be used to cultivate the qualities of forgiveness, gratitude and loving kindness.

The seeds of these qualities are planted through the practice of MBSM, and now we will describe how those seeds can be nurtured to sprout and grow using intentional meditation.

FORGIVENESS

If you let go a little,
you will have a little happiness.
If you let go a lot,
you will have a lot of happiness.

If you let go completely,
you will be free.
          —Ajahn Chah

Meditation using intention can be used to cultivate forgiveness. Forgiveness is about completing unfinished business and making a new start. Forgiveness enables us to put down the heavy burden of the past by releasing our hostages. Our hostages are all those people to whom we remain tied by an ongoing complaint, demand or judgment. The complaint may be conscious or subconscious. We may include ourselves in the list of hostages tied to us by any complaints we have against ourselves. By releasing our hostages, including ourselves, we set ourselves free.

For a few moments take your own inventory. Are you still carrying any hostages with you? Do you still carry any grudges, resentments, complaints against anyone from your past or present? Your mother, father, sister, brother? An ex-lover, friend, neighbor, work colleague? Anyone else? Do you carry ongoing complaints against yourself? Any old guilt or shame? Now check in with yourself again. Are you tired of carrying the load of blame, resentment, guilt or self-criticism? Are you ready to let it go? To do so can take some courage, although the reward is that it can be incredibly healing and liberating.

Forgiveness does not forget nor does it condone the past. Forgiveness is not an act of weakness or giving in, nor does it mean we would allow ourselves to be used or abused again. There is strength to forgiveness. We take back our power rather than give it to someone else or to the past. As we choose to forgive, we can also say, "Never again will I allow these things to happen" or "Never again will I do these things."

Through forgiveness we step away from being the victim of our past and become the creator of our present and future. We stop waiting for something to happen to resolve the past and complete unfinished business. We stop waiting for the other to change, or to say they are sorry. We stop waiting for something to change the past. After all, we could be waiting forever, and in the meantime we carry the burden of unfinished business. So, we give up all hope of a better past. In this way we take back our power and make a fresh start.

Before we describe the process of letting go of the past, we will look at how we hold on to it and how we continue to hurt ourselves by holding on. We get hurt when someone does something harmful, aggressive or abusive. We get hurt when someone does not meet our expectations, hopes or dreams. We get hurt by change, loss and disappointment. When we get hurt, we commonly experience shock, sadness, fear and anger. If we do not have the support or personal resources to move through the hurt, we move away from it by using repression and excessive thinking. (It may be useful here to review the sections on repression and limiting beliefs in chapter 10.) Or we move away from the hurt by using denial.

The Blame Story and Awareness

One way people often attempt to deal with hurt or disappointment is to create a story of blame or resentment. We try to move our attention away from the pain and vulnerability of the hurt and control it by consciously or subconsciously constructing a story of blame or resentment. We create the complaint against the other person, which might be: "They shouldn't have done that," "They shouldn't be like that," "They always do that," "It shouldn't have happened," "They should be more loving/supportive/honest," "I'm right, they're wrong," "They should do something to fix it." As we construct the complaint we also assemble all the justifications that prove we are right and they are wrong. We can interpret anything they say or do as further evidence to prove our case. We take a position of self-righteousness and we stubbornly dig our heels in. We expect or demand the other to change.

The blame story is a cognitive construction used to defend our hurt, our wound. It is a construction of judgment, complaints and justifications. However, the blame story does not allow the wound to heal. Blame does not allow healthy grieving. Bitterness, resentment, self-righteousness, stubbornness and pride smolder away. Or else it creates emotional numbness. Some people hold on to the blame story for many years and continue to hurt themselves by maintaining it. With the holding on comes a contraction inside, a defensiveness. The resentment and defensiveness creep out and affect other relationships. Holding on in this way can create isolation. The first step in the process of forgiveness of others is to become aware of any blame stories you may be holding on to.

Letting go of guilt and self-criticism

The other way of hurting ourselves by holding on to the past is through guilt and ongoing self-criticism. Self-criticism can become a habitual voice in our internal dialogue. We can create an ongoing complaint against ourselves; this inner criticism might be: "I shouldn't have done that," "I shouldn't be like that," "I always do that," "I'm dumb," "I should be more intelligent/kind/successful," "I should be more/do more/have more," "I'm not good enough." The story of guilt and self-criticism is different from healthy regret. Regret recognizes a mistake or shortcoming, learns from it and then lets it go. Unhealthy guilt and self-criticism can be relentless and insidious. It creates self-doubt.

The story of guilt can also take the form of being driven to prove ourselves, to prove we are worthy and capable. The drive actually confirms the guilt. Many people have a conditional relationship with themselves. They like themselves when they are successful and winning but abandon themselves when the going gets rough, at just the time when we need our own unconditional love.

The first step in the process of forgiveness of self is to become aware of any guilt stories you may be holding on to. Knowingly or unknowingly, we have all hurt others and been hurt by others. Some of the hurts may be quite small, some may be bigger. Every hurt is an opportunity for practicing forgiveness. Forgiveness enables us to accept this truth, to learn from the hurts we have inflicted and those that have been inflicted on us. We can grow from our wounds and heal them, not hold on to them.

In Chinese medicine, the lungs and breathing are associated with healthy grief. Breathing out represents the ability to let go of the past. If we do not breathe out fully, our lungs hold on to old stale air. By breathing out fully and letting go, we make space for fresh air and new life to come in. By letting go of the past we make space for a new start.

After recognizing any stories of blame or guilt, the next step in the forgiveness process is to consciously let go of the story of blame or guilt. After all, it is a mental construction, so we can choose to dismantle it. We can let go of the complaint, let go of the justifications, let go of the pride, self-righteousness and stubbornness. We can let go of the need to win, be right and have the last word. We can let go of the self-criticism. As we dismantle the story, it may be appropriate to say, "I am sorry for my part in this."

Feeling the pain and moving on

The next step after letting go of the story of blame or guilt is to feel the hurt, pain and sadness that have been hiding behind the story. Let any feelings of sadness or hurt arise so they can be accepted and experienced. Once the story has been released, then the feelings commonly arise to be completed. The feelings may be small or big. At times people can be surprised to find there are no feelings hiding behind the story; the feelings have already been healed. It may be only the story of blame and guilt that remains.

Whenever blame and guilt are released there is an accompanying sense of liberation. Having let go of the story of blame and guilt, and accepted any emotions that arise, the next step is to wish yourself well and to wish others well. This is not always easy. You do not have to do all of the steps of forgiveness at one time. Timing is important. Do not force yourself to do anything that does not feel genuine or sincere. Forgiveness cannot be hurried. However, by continuing to meditate with the intention to forgive, in time even the deepest hurts can be healed. Forgiveness is about giving up the struggle with yourself, with others and with life.

The forgiveness meditation is very useful for completing unfinished business and making a new start.

A FORGIVENESS MEDITATION

Prepare yourself for this meditation by practicing Mindfulness-Based Stillness Meditation for five to ten minutes.

Forgiveness from others

Say to yourself: *I know that in many ways, sometimes without my knowing, I have hurt others. Out of ignorance, pain, fear and anger I have caused suffering to others.*

Now let yourself remember or imagine the ways in which you have hurt others. . . . In your mind see the ones you have hurt, see the sorts of incidents, see yourself. . . . Let any unfinished business arise from your heart. . . . Feel your own sorrow or remorse.

If it feels appropriate, place your palms together in front of your chest in a prayer position. . . . As you remember the ones you have hurt, gently say: *I am sorry for any hurt I have caused you. I ask your forgiveness. I am sorry.*

Breathe consciously. . . . Direct the breath to your heart. . . . As you breathe out, let your heart soften.

Forgiveness of others

Say to yourself: *I know that in many ways I have been hurt by others, sometimes without their knowing. Out of their ignorance, pain, fear and anger they have hurt me. They have abused, betrayed or abandoned me.*

Let yourself remember or imagine all the ways in which you have been hurt by others. . . . In your mind see the times you have been abused, betrayed and abandoned. Let any unfinished business arise from your heart. . . . Feel any hurt, fear or anger you have been carrying.

If it feels appropriate, make soft fists with your hands and place the backs of your hands on your thighs. . . . As each person, memory and incident comes to mind, slowly allow your fists to open, in a gesture of letting go, and gently say: *I forgive you for the hurt you have caused me. I release you and set you free. I set myself free.* If the time feels right you might also say: *I wish you well.*

Breathe consciously. . . . Direct the breath to your heart. . . . As you breathe out, let your heart soften as you let go of any blame, resentment or bitterness.

Forgiveness of yourself
Say to yourself: *I know that in many ways, sometimes without even knowing, I have hurt myself. Out of my ignorance, pain, fear and anger I have caused suffering to myself. I have abused, betrayed and abandoned myself.*

Let yourself remember or imagine the ways in which you have hurt yourself. . . . In your mind see the times you have abused, betrayed and abandoned yourself. . . . See the times you have been too hard on yourself or too self-critical. . . . Let any unfinished business arise from your heart. . . . Feel any sorrow and compassion.

If it feels appropriate, place your hands, one on top of the other, over your heart. . . . As each memory or incident comes to mind, gently say to yourself: *I am sorry for any hurt I have caused myself. I forgive myself and step forward with kindness and compassion for myself.*

Breathe consciously. . . . Direct the breath to your heart and feel the touch of your hands over your heart. . . . As you breathe out, let your heart soften as you let go of any guilt or self-criticism.

Jennifer had never forgiven her husband for missing the birth of their first child. Instead of being by her side, her husband had gone overseas for a business conference and a series of meetings with his company's executives. The birth was very traumatic for Jennifer and she felt alone and unsupported. The resentment lingered on for years and soured their marriage. Subtle power struggles developed in their relationship.

Nothing her husband did for her or the children was ever enough. She continued to subtly blame and distrust him; he continued to feel guilty and tried to make it up to her. On the verge of separation, they sought counseling. They were told that before any new relationship skills and commitments could be developed, they had to address their unfinished business. In order to make a new start, they had to first let go of the past.

They were given the forgiveness meditation to practice. Jennifer needed·a lot of support as she began to practice forgiveness. The "abandonment" by her husband had opened some old, deep wounds from her family of origin. In time she began to again see in her husband all the qualities that she had loved in him. She realized how much her resentment had blinded her, and she and her husband were able to steadily rebuild their relationship.

The forgiveness meditation is a powerful tool for healing the heart and liberating the mind and spirit. We can strongly recommend it.

GRATITUDE

Just as resentment can blind us to love, the "more syndrome"—or, as it is commonly called, greed—can blind us to all the gifts and blessings we already have in our lives. Gratitude is an acknowledgment of all that sustains us, nourishes us, inspires us and touches our heart. Gratitude gives thanks for all our blessings, great and small, and gives appreciation for all those people and things that support and carry us through each day.

In chapters 5–10, we described how some of the habits of excessive thinking include "problem saturation" and the "more syndrome." These habits keep us hoping for and running toward some future happiness. They can keep us believing that the glass is only half full. Cultivating gratitude helps to heal those habits of excessive thinking by reminding us of the good in life, and the good in ourselves and in other people. Through sensationalist media reports we receive enough exposure to the bad in life. It is easy to forget about the good. There are so many good people in the world and in our lives, and there is so much good inside each individual. In the simple words of Walt Whitman:

"I am larger and better than I thought. I did not think I held so much goodness."

Admittedly, at times our perception of our own worth may be clouded by ignorance, pain, fear or anger. But still, the good exists. Cultivating gratitude is not about putting on rose-colored glasses and a false smile. Paradoxically, as we accept and acknowledge our pain, vulnerability and suffering, and feel compassion for ourselves and others, we can naturally begin to sense the sweetness and goodness in life. The seeds of gratitude appear from the practice of MBSM.

When we stop struggling with ourselves and others, we give ourselves more space. By letting go of expectations and judgments, we give ourselves more space. Out of that spaciousness, gratitude can begin to emerge quite naturally. Intentional meditation on the quality of gratitude can enhance this emergence.

Like forgiveness, gratitude cannot be forced but it can be developed by choosing to practice and cultivate it. MBSM can prepare the way. Once gratitude starts to touch your heart and mind, you may well find it arising spontaneously at any time or place. Just by momentarily pausing the forward momentum of the utilitarian mind, a space for gratitude can open up. Mindfulness can create the space.

Paul recalls sitting on a bench in the Mount Tomah Botanical Gardens in the Blue Mountains: I was sitting quietly admiring the view when a small bird landed on a branch just above my head. The bird began to sing the sweetest song. It seemed to be singing just to me. Some part of my mind whimsically asked the question, "What did I do to deserve that?" My inner knowing replied, "You did nothing to deserve it. It was a gift, a blessing!" My heart and my whole body filled with such a deep sense of gratitude, it brought tears of joy to my eyes.

When gratitude appears, it humbles the mind, gladdens the heart and leads to joy. We do not have to earn or fight for everything life brings to support, challenge and inspire us. We receive so many blessings that are not earned but are freely given by life. It behooves us to give thanks.

A GRATITUDE MEDITATION

Prepare yourself for this meditation by practicing MBSM for five to ten minutes.

Bring to mind all of the **material things** in your life that sustain and comfort you . . . the food you eat, the clothes you wear, your home. . . . Bring to mind the material things that entertain and inspire you . . . your books, garden, television, furnishings, artworks. . . . In your mind, begin to recall and name all those material things.

As you dwell on these things, say to yourself: *Thank you. Thank you for all these things that support and comfort me, that amuse and inspire me. Thank you very much.*

Breathe consciously. . . . Direct the breath toward your heart. . . . As you breathe out, let your heart be touched with the feeling of gratitude.

Now bring to mind all of your **teachers** . . . all those who have encouraged, inspired or otherwise helped you to grow. . . . Some of your teachers may have been kind, some more confronting. . . . In your mind, begin to recall, picture and name all of your teachers.

Then say to yourself: *Thank you. Thank you to all of my teachers. Thank you for the lessons you have given me. Thank you very much.*

Breathe consciously. . . . Direct the breath toward your heart. . . . As you breathe out, let your heart be touched with the feeling of gratitude.

Now bring to mind all of your **friends** . . . all of the people who have shared fun, challenges and love with you . . . all of the people who have supported you. . . . It may be a small select group or a larger group. . . . In your mind, begin to recall, picture and name all of your friends.

Then say to yourself: *Thank you. Thank you to all of my friends. Thank you for your love and support. Thank you very much.*

Breathe consciously. . . . Direct the breath toward your heart. . . . As you breathe out, let your heart be touched with the feeling of gratitude.

Now bring to mind all of your **family members** . . . your parents, grandparents and ancestors who stand behind you . . . your brothers and sisters who stand beside you . . . perhaps your children who stand in front of you. . . . All of your family members. . . . In your mind, begin to recall, picture and bring to mind all of your family members.

Then say to yourself: *Thank you. Thank you to all of my family members. Thank you for all the fun, challenges and love that we have shared. Thank you for your love and support. Thank you very much.*

Breathe consciously. . . . Direct the breath toward your heart. . . . As you breathe out, let your heart be touched with the feeling of gratitude.

Now bring to mind the **people with whom you have shared intimate love** . . . your lovers, partners, spouse . . . all of the people who have touched your heart as you have touched theirs. . . . It may be a small select group or just one person. . . . In your mind, begin to recall, picture and name your beloved ones.

Then say to yourself: *Thank you. Thank you to my loved ones. Thank you for the love that we have shared. Thank you very much.*

Breathe consciously. . . . Direct the breath toward your heart. . . . As you breathe out, let your heart be touched with the feeling of gratitude.

Now bring to mind **your own unique and precious self**. . . .
In your mind, begin to recall times in your life, see your face at
various ages, and say your own name.

Then say to yourself: *Thank you. Thank you to my own true
self. Thank you for this precious life. Thank you very much.*

Breathe consciously. . . . Direct the breath toward your
heart. . . . As you breathe out, let your heart be touched with
the feeling of gratitude.

Let the feeling of gratitude spread to every part of your
body. Let every cell of your body say: *Thank you. Thank you very
much. Thank you for this life.* If it feels appropriate, place your
palms together in front of your chest in a prayer position. You
may even like to bow your head a little as you continue to say to
yourself and to all of Life: *Thank you. Thank you very much.*

LOVING KINDNESS

Loving kindness, or *metta* in the Pali language, is a traditional form of
meditation in Buddhism. However, many spiritual and religious traditions teach practices that cultivate compassion and loving kindness
toward self and others. Jesus was a great teacher and embodiment of
loving kindness.

As we have already recommended regarding forgiveness and gratitude, MBSM is a great foundation for developing such beneficial qualities. Mindfulness practice is also a solid foundation for developing the
intention of loving kindness. Through mindfulness practice we sit in
our own company with nonjudgmental awareness. Rather than judging and struggling with ourselves, we practice acceptance, patience and
compassion. We steadily create a deep sense of connectedness with
ourselves.

Through mindfulness practice we also grow increasingly aware of
what we are thinking and feeling. This enables us to make more conscious choices and to act more in accordance with our personal values.

Mindfulness gives us the freedom to pause and reflect. We can extend compassion to others and develop our sense of connectedness by cultivating thoughts and feelings of loving kindness.

Loving kindness is the intention to do no harm to others through our thoughts, words or deeds. Coupled with this intention is the heartfelt wish that all beings enjoy happiness and peace in their lives. The intention to do no harm and the wish for happiness and peace extends to ourselves and to all beings. The intention of loving kindness reminds us of the interconnectedness of all living beings. No man or woman is an island. We all live in, depend on and are sustained by some form of community.

Contemporary biologists are beginning to challenge Darwin's theory of natural selection or "survival of the fittest," at least as far as it does not explain the natural altruism of many animal species, such as wolves who will bring back food to members of the pack that have taken no part in the hunt. Rather than "survival of the fittest," which supports beliefs in individualism and competing for scarce resources, biologists are beginning to formulate theories about "survival of the cooperative," where the members of certain species work together and support each other.

As we described in chapter 6, overuse of the fight-or-flight response creates a habit of contraction and defensiveness. This habit of chronic contraction can promote competitiveness, aggression, greed, jealousy and resentment. This habit reinforces beliefs in "survival of the fittest" and helps people to justify their perceived need to struggle to survive and fight over scarce resources. These beliefs create separation and distrust. They erode our sense of community. We see the world through the tunnel vision of our own personal concerns.

These contracted and defensive habits are destroying our health, our well-being and our planet. Cultivating the intention of loving kindness is an antidote for a contracted body-mind and a defended heart. Sending out thoughts of loving kindness can open our hearts and minds, and enable us to grow in connectedness. If life circumstances have shut down our heart, we can intentionally open up and reconnect again. We can train ourselves to see that others are not so different from us. We can train ourselves to care for others and to wish them well. We can practice loving kindness through our thoughts, words and deeds.

The practice of Mindfulness of Emotions described in chapters 9 and 10 greatly supports the intentional meditation on loving kindness. We need to be able to take responsibility for our own unpleasant emotions and pain to clear the way before we can begin to practice compassion for ourselves and then for others. This willingness enables us to stop projecting our expectations, demands, hopes, wishes and dreams on to others. Freed from these projections, we can begin to see and feel for others just as they are. Just like us.

The meditation on loving kindness is a healing practice. Once you familiarize yourself with this intention through a formal meditative practice, you can take the openness of heart out into everyday life. Begin by cultivating thoughts of loving kindness in situations where it is fairly easy to extend your compassion, and then stretch yourself in more challenging situations.

The loving kindness meditation begins by sending thoughts of friendliness and kindness to yourself, then to a friend, then to a neutral person, then to someone with whom you experience difficulty and, last, to all beings and all life. As you bring each person to mind, you visualize them as if they were sitting or standing in front of you, and then you reflect on your relationship with them and allow any unpleasant feelings to arise. Express words of loving kindness and then open your heart with feelings of loving kindness.

A LOVING KINDNESS MEDITATION

Prepare yourself for this meditation by practicing MBSM for five to ten minutes.

Bring to mind **yourself**. Visualize yourself and say your own name. . . . Briefly reflect on your life's journey. . . . Say to yourself: *May I be well. May my life be filled with loving kindness. May I enjoy true peace in my life.* Feel the loving

---

kindness carried in these words. . . . Repeat to yourself: *May I be well. May my life be filled with loving kindness. May I enjoy true peace in my life.*

Breathe consciously. . . . Direct the breath to your heart. . . . Fill your heart with loving kindness on the in breath, and send loving kindness to every part of your being on the out breath.

Bring to mind a **friend or family member** whom you love. . . . Visualize them as if they were sitting or standing in front of you and say their name. . . . Briefly reflect on your relationship with them. . . . Say to your loved friend or family member: *May you be well. May your life be filled with loving kindness. May you enjoy true peace in your life.* Feel the loving kindness carried in these words. . . . Repeat to your loved friend or family member: *May you be well. May your life be filled with loving kindness. May you enjoy true peace in your life.*

Breathe consciously. . . . Direct the breath to your heart. . . . Fill your heart with loving kindness on the in breath, and send loving kindness to your loved friend or family member on the out breath.

Bring to mind a **stranger** or a **neutral person**. It may be a shopkeeper, taxi driver or a sales assistant. . . . Visualize them as if they were sitting or standing in front of you and briefly reflect on your contact with them. . . . Say to this person: *May you be well. May your life be filled with loving kindness. May you enjoy true peace in your life.* Feel the loving kindness in these words. . . . Repeat to this person: *May you be well. May your life be filled with loving kindness. May you enjoy true peace in your life.*

Breathe consciously. . . . Direct the breath to your heart. . . . Fill your heart with loving kindness on the in breath, and send loving kindness to this person on the out breath.

Bring to mind a **person with whom you have difficulty**. Perhaps someone who has hurt or disappointed you. . . . Visualize them as if they were sitting or standing in front of you and say their name. . . . Feel any unpleasant feelings that may arise in your center. . . . Say to this person: *May you be well. May your life be filled with loving kindness. May you enjoy true peace in your life.* Feel any unpleasant feelings in your center and feel the loving kindness carried in these words. . . . Repeat to this person: *May you be well. May your life be filled with loving kindness. May you enjoy true peace in your life.*

Breathe consciously. . . . Direct the breath to your heart. . . . Fill your heart with loving kindness on the in breath, and send loving kindness to this person as you breathe out.

And now let feelings of loving kindness spread from your heart to **all beings** and to **all of life**, saying: *May all beings be well. May all beings be filled with loving kindness. May all beings enjoy true peace.*

Just rest in the feeling of loving kindness as it spreads to all beings and to all of life.

Instead of focusing on the differences between us, loving kindness opens us to knowing ourselves to be part of the intricately interconnected web of life. We begin to see ourselves, our strengths and weaknesses, our beauty and our frailty reflected back to us from others, from nature and from all of life. We share the breath of life with all beings. May the practice of loving kindness touch your heart!

CHAPTER 18

MEDITATION USING INQUIRY—CONTEMPLATION

The unexamined life is not worth living.
—SOCRATES

Do you ever take time to reflect on your life? To reflect on how you are going, what is important for you and what it is that you need?

The busyness and distractions of modern times often lead to "unexamined lives." Unfortunately, we do not take enough time to pause, to digest our experience and to reflect on life lessons, directions, meaning and purpose. Meditation using inquiry is a method for such reflection.

Meditation using inquiry is more active and more directed than mindfulness meditation. Other names for this form of meditation include contemplation, insight meditation, analytical meditation or even just reflection. We will use the terms *contemplation* and *inquiry* to refer to this form of meditation.

Contemplation is an age-old technique that goes beyond the rational, scientific mind in a way that provides access to the intuitive wisdom of the inner self. Contemplation can begin with inquiry and lead to insight. In this context, *inquiry* means to "question within," and *insight* suggests "seeing from within."

The word *inquiry* implies that questions are an important part of this contemplative process. The ancient Greek philosopher Socrates was renowned for his method of questioning. Socratic questioning is a form of inquiry that has been used for centuries to pursue thought in many directions and for many purposes, including:

- to explore issues and problems
- to get to the truth of things
- to analyze concepts
- to discover important values

Questioning is thus a powerful investigative tool that is part of the methodology of science and philosophy. However, you could also see questioning as simply thinking things through in a structured and focused way. Contemplation begins with the left-brain, scientific activity of questioning, and then takes us beyond the thinking mind into the right-brain, intuitive process of listening to our inner wisdom. The questions are directed toward the inner self, fully expecting some valuable insight.

Through a combination of questioning and listening, contemplation can be useful for:

- exploring the emotions associated with a challenging issue
- making decisions and setting goals
- gaining philosophical and spiritual insight
- inquiring into the nature of "who we are"

Contemplation is a way of pausing and reflecting on our life. It allows us to find our sense of discrimination about what is right, appropriate and true for us. Contemplation can be extremely empowering; through it we can become more the creator and author of our life and less the victim of it.

In our busy lives, we seldom take time to pause and reflect. Contemplation is like stopping the engines of a motorboat and dropping anchor. Once we drop the anchor, we can bait the hook (by asking a question), drop in a line (by reflecting) and lure a fish (by listening and waiting). At times, what emerges from the depths of our inner wisdom can be quite surprising and profound. At other times, what emerges may be a simple, practical truth. One meditator, when contemplating what she needed to do in her life, received the message, "Clean out your closet!" . . . and she did.

First we will look at the steps of a generic contemplation process, and then we will describe some specific applications for contemplation.

TWELVE STEPS FOR CONTEMPLATION

Steps 1–3 can be done sometime before you actually sit to contemplate.

1. In your mind or by writing in a journal, clearly define the issue and your question. Clarify what part of the issue needs your specific attention, or simply ask a direct question. Ask a question that is likely to evoke a useful response. Questions like "Why does this always happen to me?" or "How can I make him change?" are likely to lead to a dead end. Be prepared to spend some time allowing the question to become clear. Useful questions are likely to begin "What will I do about . . . ?" or "What is the answer to . . . ?" or be like "What is this all about?"

2. Do any relevant research. Use your active thinking mind, your intellect and your intelligence to gather information. Read books, speak to experts, discuss it with friends, dip into the Internet. Make notes. This may include making lists of the advantages and disadvantages of various options. If the question does not require any external research, it may help to write about it in your journal. You can use a process like brainstorming or mindmapping, allowing yourself to develop an uncensored, free association of ideas and feelings to explore the issue. Just write whatever comes into your mind about the issue or question.

3. Set a time for the actual contemplation and put some limits on

the amount of research you do. You cannot know everything about any subject, nor do you need to. Decide at what point in time you will begin your contemplation.

4. Give yourself enough time for the contemplation—half an hour to an hour is ideal—and some space. You might like to use the place where you meditate regularly or any other quiet area. Have a pen and paper available in case you want to write down any insights you gain.

5. When you sit down, begin by reviewing your research or journal material. Refresh all the information you have on the issue/ question.

6. Consciously relax your body and practice Mindfulness-Based Stillness Meditation for five to ten minutes. This step is important as it will clear some of the distracting chatter of the thinking mind and create more openness and receptivity to the question. The MBSM is like tilling the soil before planting the seeds; the seeds are more likely to germinate.

7. Bring the issue to mind and begin by acknowledging your feelings about the issue. Feel into your body and its emotional centerline (see chapter 9). For example, the issue may be concerning your employment. Is it time to leave your job? Is it time to develop some new skills? Is it time to renegotiate conditions? If your mind wanders or becomes distracted, gently bring your attention back to the issue and your feeling or sense of it.

8. Slowly and mindfully ask your question or questions. This is like throwing in your fishing line or dropping a pebble into a pond. Allow the question to create subtle ripples inside you. Think on it, dwell on it, think it through. Allow it to silently resonate inside you. Be patient, listen and wait, while continuing the mindfulness practice.

9. Repeat your question or questions several times, allowing it to sink inside you. Be patient, listen and wait. Ask any other questions relevant to this issue.

10. Allow any relevant thoughts, memories, symbols or associations

to come to mind. If the memories or associations stray too far from your inquiry, come back and restate your question.

11. A response may come in words or images, or it may come in another form. The response may come as a feeling-sense that takes time to find its way into words or images. The response may not come while you are sitting; it may come when you least expect it.

    Whenever a response comes, you can test it against your own sensibilities. If you doubt what comes, if it is unconvincing, then it is probably just your thinking mind still at work. When you receive a real insight there will be an inner knowing that it is true for you. The response may not be profound or earth-shattering; it may be simple, short and direct. As you continue to use this practice, and as you gain useful insights, trust and value them, then more are likely to come. Insight can come in some strange and unexpected forms. Do not judge or overanalyze the response; just hold it, turn it over and give it time and space.

12. When it comes time to complete the session, give thanks for any response or insight you have received. If you feel that the contemplation is not finished and that you may need to continue in another session, you can set the intention that the contemplation continues inside, continues to percolate, until the next time you formally sit to contemplate again.

    While often one session is useful, some major questions may take many days or weeks of contemplation before clarity and insight dawns. Write down any thoughts that came to mind or draw any images or symbols that arose during the contemplation. Spontaneous drawing is a great way of enhancing the feeling-sense of the contemplation.

The more you practice this technique, the more reliable it becomes. Our intuition and inner wisdom become clearer and more accessible with regular practice. Remember to do this contemplation with pen and paper close by so that, at the appropriate time, you can record any feelings or insights. The act of writing things down actually helps to give more form and substance to even the slightest insight.

Let us consider now some specific applications of contemplation and some specific questions for inquiry.

Contemplation for decision-making

1. Do any relevant research.
2. Consciously weigh the advantages and disadvantages of each option. Make a list, write them down. Weigh the advantages of *not* making a decision.
3. Here are some possible questions to form the basis of your contemplation. Read through the list and make a note of the question or questions that feel relevant and useful for your inquiry. This list may also spark off your own ideas about useful questions.
   - *What is best for me?*
   - *What is right for me?*
   - *What do I most need?*
   - *What is my truth in this?*
   - *What is the healthiest choice for me?*
   - *Why is this issue so important to me?*
   - *What do I fear about this situation?*
   - *If I had the courage, what would I do?*
   - *What is the worst possible outcome?*
   - *What is the best possible outcome?*
   - *What would my True Self do?*
   - *Is this an either/or decision? Could my answer be both?*
   - *Do I need to seek more help? What help? From whom?*
   - *What is the first step I need to take?*
4. With your research in place and your questions in mind, go through the twelve steps for contemplation.

Contemplation for exploring difficult or stuck emotions

1. In conjunction with this contemplation, revisit chapters 9 and 10 on Mindfulness of Emotions. Resolving emotional responses can never be a purely cognitive or intellectual process; however, contemplation can help to open up emotional responses that have become stuck or inaccessible. Having opened up the emotions through contemplation, Mindfulness of Emotions can then transform and integrate them.

2. Throughout this contemplation, use the Mindfulness of Emotions in chapter 9 to stay connected with your feeling centerline. Keep your breath flowing. You can move back and forth between inquiry, contemplation and focusing on the feeling along your centerline.

3. Here are some possible questions to form the basis of your contemplation. Read through this list and make a note of the question or questions that feel relevant and useful for your inquiry. This list may also spark off your own ideas about useful questions.

   - *Where am I feeling these emotions?*
   - *What does it feel like?*
   - *What is going on here?*
   - *What am I feeling? Is it fear? Is it anger? Is it sadness? Is it grief? What name best fits this feeling?*
   - *What am I afraid of?*
   - *What might have caused these feelings?*
   - *What do I need in all of this?*
   - *What is the most difficult part of this for me?*
   - *What was I hoping for or expecting?*
   - *Why is this so important for me?*
   - *What do I need to say about this? To whom?*
   - *What do I need to do about this?*
   - *What am I afraid of saying or doing? Why?*
   - *What is the first step I need to take to address this?*

4. With your issue defined and your questions in mind, go through the twelve steps for contemplation.

5. Be gentle and connected with your feeling centerline as you ask the questions. Take plenty of time after asking a question to listen, feel and breathe. Practice compassion—this is not an examination or interrogation.
6. Make notes when appropriate. These notes can be expanded on later in your journal.

Contemplation for finding purpose and passion

1. Your research or preparation might take the form of looking through a whole series of photographs of yourself from your childhood to now. Look closely at your body posture, your face and particularly your eyes. Or your research might take the form of writing or relating the story of your life journey. Express your challenges, your disappointments, your joys, your loves, and acknowledge your teachers and your lessons. Approach this life review with a nonjudgmental, compassionate and resolute honesty.

2. When it comes time for the contemplation on purpose and passion, here are some possible questions to form the basis of your contemplation. Read through the list and make a note of the question or questions that feel relevant and useful for your inquiry. This list may also spark off your own ideas about useful questions.
   - *What gives me enthusiasm?*
   - *What excites me?*
   - *What deeply nourishes me?*
   - *What is most important to me?*
   - *What do I love, cherish and care most about?*
   - *What am I passionate about? What is the nature of that passion?*
   - *What have I needed to learn through my life journey?*
   - *What have I been trying to share/give through my life journey?*
   - *What are my best qualities, talents and gifts?*
   - *What makes me feel most true to myself?*
   - *What do I need to do more of?*

- *What qualities are most important to me? Honesty? Courage? Compassion? Peace? What others?*
- *What would I most like to be known and remembered for?*

3. With your preparation done and your questions in mind, go through the twelve steps for contemplation.
4. Dare to dream big; there is no need to be too humble, too self-critical or to keep yourself small. As you contemplate the purpose and passion in your life, allow yourself to be big, important and special.

Contemplation for gaining inspiration and insight

1. Your research or preparation might take the form of some inspirational reading, or just walking and sitting in a beautiful, natural setting.
2. Choose a theme, a quotation or a verse to contemplate. The theme could be a spiritual quality or truth, such as peace, love, truth, compassion, humility, impermanence or gratitude. As you contemplate, you can merely repeat the chosen word and listen deeply as it resonates in the core of your being. Or you may frame a question: for example, "What is love?" or "What is humility?" Repeat the question and then listen deeply as it resonates in the core of your being. As the words resonate inside, allow a feeling-sense to be evoked by the slow repetition of the words. Allow the feeling-sense to grow and spread as you continue the contemplation.

   If you have chosen an inspirational quote to contemplate, treat it in the same way. Read the quotation, then close your eyes and allow it to resonate inside. Allow a feeling-sense to be evoked by the inspirational passage. Read it again, or repeat any particularly meaningful words or phrases. Feel the resonance inside. Listen and allow any thoughts or images to be generated by the quotation. Here are a few samples:

   A single sunbeam is enough to drive away many shadows.
   —Saint Francis of Assisi

Thy will be done on earth, as it is in Heaven.
> —Lord's Prayer

I say unto you suffering is not holding you, you are holding suffering.
> —Osho

In the twilight of Life
God will not judge us
on our earthly possessions
and human success,
but rather on how much
we have loved.
> —Saint John of the Cross

Be still and know that I am God.
> —Psalms 46:10

Trust in God . . . but tie up your camel first!
> —Sufi saying

When you hear the splash
of the water drops that fall
into the stone bowl,
you will feel that all the dust
of your mind washes away.
> —Zen poem

God grant me the serenity
to accept the things I cannot change,
the courage to change the things that I can,
and the wisdom to know the difference.
> —The Serenity Prayer

3. With your inspirational word or quote in mind, go through the twelve steps for contemplation.

Who is meditating? The path of Self-Inquiry

Do not meditate—be!
Do not think that you are—be!
Do not think about being—you are!
—Sri Ramana Maharshi

Self-Inquiry is a very specific application of contemplation and inquiry. While similar to the Buddhist technique of Analytical Meditation, this method was clearly expounded by Sri Ramana Maharshi (1879–1950), who was one of the greatest spiritual teachers of India in recent times.

Sri Ramana Maharshi taught that every conscious activity of the mind and body—for example, "I think," "I remember," "I feel," "I am doing" and so on—revolves around the tacit assumption that there is an individual "I" who is thinking, feeling and doing something. He says, "Of all the thoughts that arise in the mind, the 'I' thought is the first. It is only after the rise of this thought that all the other thoughts arise."

It was Sri Ramana's basic teaching that the individual self is nothing more than a thought or an idea. He taught that the "I" thought is actually a nonexistent entity, and that it only appears to exist when it identifies itself with other thoughts and the body. Thus, the idea that one is an individual person is generated and sustained by the "I" thought. This process of misidentification and attachment produces a "mind-created me."

Sri Ramana taught that this illusion of self or "mind-created me" was the root cause of human separateness and suffering. He also taught that if we can break the attachment between the "I" thought and the other thoughts that it identifies with, the "I" thought itself will gradually subside and finally disappear. Breaking the attachment between the "I" thought and all the other thoughts that support the separate "I" leads to ultimate freedom and liberation. This is a freedom from self-conscious, excessive thinking of the "mind-created me." Freedom to just be . . . to have an aware, alert, creative and intelligent consciousness.

Sri Ramana taught a meditation technique called Self-Inquiry, which is a technique for returning our attention to the subjective feeling of "I" or "I am" that is behind all the thoughts that create the idea of a separate "I." By continuously bringing or returning our attention just to the silent beingness of "I am," the attachment to the story of the "I" thought will weaken and disappear. This is not brought about by being aware of an "I," but only by being the "I." This is the same liberating experience that is reached through the practice of Mindfulness-Based Stillness Meditation. Sri Ramana's technique for realizing the stillness of Being was the process called Self-Inquiry.

Practitioners of Self-Inquiry were taught by Sri Ramana to put their attention on the inner feeling of "I" and to sustain that feeling of just being for as long as possible. They were told that if their attention was distracted by other thoughts, they should revert to awareness of the inner feeling of "I." He suggested various aids to assist this meditative process: we could ask ourselves, "Who am I?" or "Where does this 'I' thought come from?" or "Who is this 'I'?" These questions are meant to invoke awareness of the source from which the thinking mind springs, that is, the feeling of just Being. When the inquiry "Who am I?" is persistently pursued, all other thoughts begin to lose their power, allowing the meditator to rest more fully in the silent beingness of "I am." As we inquire, "Who am I?" and "Who is this 'I'?," other thoughts will arise. Self-Inquiry also involves a second question: "From whom does this thought arise?" or "Who is thinking this thought?" Sri Ramana advised meditators to ask this question whenever their awareness was interrupted by a thought because the asking of the question causes the attention to return to the feeling of "I." None of the questions asked in the technique of Self-Inquiry are meant to elicit an answer. They are just used to guide the attention back to the feeling of "I" or *being* the "I."

Self-Inquiry should not be regarded solely as a meditative practice that takes place while formally sitting in meditation; it can be continued throughout daily life, irrespective of what we are doing. The questions "Who am I?" or "Who is doing this?" or "Who is thinking this thought?" can be used at any time to momentarily return the attention to the silent feeling of "I am." Consistent practice can weaken the story line of excessive thinking, which creates separateness and suffering.

The contemplative path of Self-Inquiry

1. Use the first three steps of MBSM—preparation, relaxation and mindfulness—to bring your attention to your present moment experience. This may take from five to fifteen minutes.
2. Ask the question "Who am I?" or "Who is this 'I'?" or "Who is meditating?" Allow the question to resonate inside and bring your attention to the silent awareness of "I am."
3. Rest in the "I am" for as long as possible, simply being.
4. When thoughts arise, without fighting them simply ask, "Who is thinking this thought?" Allow this question to resonate inside and bring your attention back to the silent awareness of "I am." Thoughts are not a problem, just see them as another opportunity to ask the question "Who is meditating?" and rest in the silent response.

There is a complementary relationship between MBSM and the contemplative path of Self-Inquiry, and they can enhance each other. While practicing mindfulness, asking the question "Who am I?" can connect you with the stillness. Also, if the thinking mind becomes distracting during the practice of MBSM, Self-Inquiry can steady the mind. And while doing Self-Inquiry, the mindfulness practice prevents it from being a purely conceptual, abstract process. Mindfulness helps to keep the Self-Inquiry experiential and present.

In conclusion, the formal practice of contemplation, like mindfulness meditation, creates a connection with your intuition, your gut feelings, your discrimination and your inner wisdom. Once the connection is made and you begin to listen to "the still, small voice inside your Heart," then you will be able to access that knowing at any time. The pause to reflect becomes a regular, informal practice; it becomes instinctive and second nature. You will come to realize that your inner wisdom is speaking to you all the time. As Mother Teresa said, "Just listen!"

You will also come to realize, through mindfulness and contemplation, that the thinking, utilitarian mind is just a vehicle for your true intelligence, not its source.

CHAPTER 19

MEDITATION AND THE SPIRITUAL PATH

The spiritual path means to come to terms with actual reality, not with the dream projection . . . [it] means encountering Existence without any desire.
—Osho

Enlightenment is a state of lasting happiness, free of suffering.
—Sogyal Rinpoche

WHAT IS SPIRITUALITY?

Meditation is often thought of as a technique for spiritual awakening. It is only in the last century that the health benefits of meditation have been researched and promoted. Traditionally, meditation has been taught as a tool for spiritual development and an important technique on any spiritual path. So, let us explore what is meant by the term *spiritual* and see how the practice of meditation has been associated with it.

In dualistic thinking, *spirit* is often defined as distinct from *matter*. Here are some of the most common definitions of spirit:

- incorporeal consciousness, as opposed to matter
- the vital principle or animating force within living beings
- the essential nature
- the immaterial intelligent or sentient part of a person
- life, will, consciousness and that which is regarded as separate from matter

The word *spirit* comes from the Latin *spirare*, meaning "to breathe into." Originally, spirit was regarded as inherent in the breath. Remember the creation stories, which recount how God formed man out of the dust of the Earth, and breathed the breath of life into his nostrils.

Matter, on the other hand, is the "dust of the Earth," and is defined as:

- something that occupies space and can be perceived by one or more senses
- a physical substance
- a more or less defined amount or quantity

The word *matter* comes from the Latin *materia*, meaning "material, stuff, wood," and *mater*, meaning "mother." So, in the creation story, Father Sky (God) breathes the breath of life (spirit) into Mother Earth (matter), and thus human life is formed from this union.

Our spirit is the subtle, formless animating force of consciousness. A spiritual path is a way of realizing and nurturing the spirit. (It may be useful here to reread chapter 6 on thinking and awareness, and chapter 12 on stillness.)

Spirituality has been defined in many ways. These include:

- a belief in a life-affirming power operating in the universe that is greater than oneself
- a sense of interconnectedness with all of creation
- a sense of belonging to the family of life
- an awareness of a purpose and meaning in life
- the development of personal values that support life

- a sense of compassion for self and others
- an experience of inner peace
- a source of hope and the will to live

Through these various definitions of spirituality there seems to run a common thread: spirituality emerges when excessive thinking and the "mind-created me" soften and relax. Excessive thinking creates separation from life and struggle with it. Struggle and separation overpower the subtler feelings of connectedness and belonging. Too much struggle and separation are aspects of "emergency mode" (refer to chapter 6), which leads to isolation and suffering. Meditation softens and relaxes excessive thinking and the "mind-created me," and this allows our spiritual nature to naturally emerge. We let go and let "God" flow.

We can find our spiritual nature in the stillness of MBSM.

The face of God
Our spirituality is our essential nature. Here is a charming story that comes "out of the mouths of babes."

Jessica was a kindergarten teacher supervising her five-year-old students at their first painting class. Each of the children was given paper, paints and brushes, and told to paint the face of their favorite person.

As Jessica was walking around the class admiring the children's efforts, she noticed an unusual shape emerging on little Katie's painting. She asked, "Whose face are you painting, Katie?"

"I'm painting the face of God," the earnest Katie replied.

"But, Katie, nobody knows what God looks like," teased the teacher.

"Well, they will in a few minutes!" said Katie.

Religion and spirituality
Fundamental religious teachings often painted an image of God as being transcendent or standing outside of the world. God was portrayed as wrathful and omnipotent. A spiritual life was lived in fear of punishment, hell and damnation. Spiritual rewards would be enjoyed in the afterlife, not in this life. In this context, a spiritual life was often a life of hardship and renunciation.

In contrast, "modern" religious teachings speak of a god that is immanent or dwelling in the world, in nature and in the hearts and spirit of men and women. This is a more accessible god, who is filled with compassion. This is the god popularized in the expression "God is love." Buddhism maintains that there is no god as an individual, separate entity, but it teaches that the qualities we associate with godliness are latent within us and form a part of the essential nature of our being.

In this context, a spiritual life is a life of connectedness and engagement with the world. Instead of renouncing life and turning away from it, modern spirituality embraces life, delights in it, is grateful for it, and accepts its challenges with courage and compassion. Spirituality has found its way out of the exclusive domain of the churches, temples, mosques and monasteries, and can be practiced anywhere by anyone. God knows we need more spirituality in our everyday life. We need more "monks without monasteries." We need more prayer and meditation "in the marketplace." In these dark times of greed, poverty and war we need more light. And the light is here, it is available. Meditation makes the light of peace and compassion more available, here and now. Peace cannot be imposed on a people, a race or a country. We will only create a more peaceful world when more people have found peace in their own hearts and minds. Meditation makes that peace directly available, and you do not have to shave your head and live in a cave in the Himalayas to experience and live it.

Just listen!

Mother Teresa's biographer heard that when she awoke in the morning she would pray for an hour or two before she went out to do her spiritual work of charitable service. The biographer asked her what she said to God when she prayed, to which Mother Teresa replied, "Oh, I don't say anything to God. I just listen."

The curious biographer then asked, "Well, when you listen to God, what does God say to you?"

Mother Teresa smiled and replied, "Oh, God doesn't say anything. He just listens too!"

It sounds like Mother Teresa was practicing something like

Mindfulness-Based Stillness Meditation, being present in a state of open and undistracted awareness. When her biographer questioned Mother Teresa further about her prayers to God, she replied: "If I ever feel the need to speak to God in prayer, there are only two words that need to be said: thank you!"[1]

NATURAL, PRACTICAL SPIRITUALITY

If we think of spirit as being immanent or dwelling in the world, then mindfulness meditation is a wonderful way of turning our attention toward spirit. Mindfulness pays attention to what exists, here and now. It shifts attention away from memory, imagination, ideas and concepts. Where excessive thinking takes our attention away from the world, mindfulness brings our attention back. The practice of MBSM steadily creates more feelings of compassion and connectedness, without even trying. Mindfulness recognizes the spirituality in simple things and in every moment of being.

The inherent myth of a purely materialistic life is the belief that if we have more, know more and do more we will be happy. Self-development and fulfillment are equated with adding things on to who we are. These things might be possessions, status, knowledge and power. This materialistic myth creates the addictive mind-set we call the "more syndrome." The more syndrome keeps alive the hope and dream that just a bit "more" will bring happiness. But this type of happiness never seems to last. It never seems to completely satisfy. It always leaves us with the sense of still needing a bit more. The more syndrome keeps us running toward an imagined happiness and away from some imagined suffering, but the constant running itself creates suffering. The running keeps us out of touch with our spirit. We probably all know of people who have everything or who have immense power but are still unhappy.

MBSM heals the addictive mind-set of the more syndrome by giving our full attention to what actually exists, rather than what could or should be. The mindful act of surrendering to what is already here slows the momentum of the more syndrome. Through this act of surrender we can begin to appreciate what we already have instead of always running toward what we do not have. The spiritual quality of gratitude awakens naturally as the more syndrome winds down. Dr. John Gray, the author of *Men Are from Mars, Women Are from Venus*, wrote an earlier book called *How to Get What You Want and Want What You Have*. What a great title, what a wonderful sentiment! The market is already flooded with books about how to get what you want. Through the practice of mindfulness, gratitude develops as we connect with the life that we already have and accept this moment, right now. Then through intentional meditation, as described in chapter 17, we can further develop the quality of gratitude.

Reconnecting to our spirit

A contracted body and a busy thinking mind keep us disconnected from our natural, inherent spirituality. The various facets of a contracted body and a busy mind are:

1. The "mind-created me," which consists of all the images, roles, conditioning, attachments and misidentifications that, together, create a fixed idea of self. As we saw in chapter 18, in Ramana Maharshi's terms these are all the other thoughts that solidify the initial "I" thought.
2. The "more syndrome," which keeps us running and struggling for a happiness that is always just out of reach. This syndrome comes from an unconscious addiction to goal-setting, itself a symptom of deeper unsatisfied cravings.
3. "Problem saturation," which comes from the habit of constantly criticizing, judging, finding fault and trying to fix or improve everything.
4. "Emergency mode" as a habit of perception, which keeps us constantly guarded, defensive and reactive.
5. "Holding on to the past," which can take many forms—all of which are derived from an attachment to the contents of memory.

MSBM gradually heals and releases these aspects of a contracted body and a busy mind. Naturally and quite effortlessly we begin to develop spiritual qualities such as:

- humility—as the "mind-created me" softens;
- gratitude—as the "more syndrome" and "problem saturation" wind down;
- patience—as the "emergency mode" and "more syndrome" lose some of their power;
- forgiveness—as "holding on to the past" is released;
- acceptance—as the "more syndrome" and "problem saturation" loosen up;
- compassion—as "problem saturation" softens;
- seeing the good in life—instead of always seeing the problems; and
- humor—as we stop taking ourselves so seriously.

These qualities arise as a natural consequence of consistent meditation practice and then begin to flow into our life so that more of our spirit is evident in our work, our play and our relationships. We may find ourselves becoming less driven, less judgmental and less reactive in each arena of our lives.

Spirit—the background of our Being

Back in chapter 6 we looked at the difference between thinking and awareness. Awareness is the background of our Being, that still and silent presence that is conscious and alert but nonjudgmental. Some call our awareness our inner essence, our true self or our spirit. Mindfulness practice, especially as it advances into stillness, frees our awareness from the domination of thinking, and so actually connects us with our spirit.

Our spirit is not hidden or distant. It is that open and undistracted awareness that silently witnesses our moment-by-moment living experience. Our spirit has always been with us; it does not have to be created or achieved. Spirit is silent and subtle, so it can quite easily be overlooked. We do not have to struggle to find our spirit—we never lost it—but the many struggles in life can prevent us from noticing and connecting with our spirit.

The horizontal and the vertical directions

It is almost as if there are two directions that our attention can follow: a horizontal direction and a vertical direction.

The horizontal direction takes our attention out into the world, scanning the horizon. It is the direction of engaging with the material world and interpersonal relationships. The horizontal direction involves activity, decision-making, goal-setting and busyness. This direction is that of self-expression and manifestation in the physical world. This is the direction of materialism. Our thinking mind, our personality and our ego are busily involved in this horizontal direction trying to maximize material comfort for ourselves, our families and, perhaps, for others. The horizontal direction presents us with many of the dramas and struggles in our lives. Much of Western civilization has focused on pursuing the values and priorities of the horizontal direction.

The vertical direction, on the other hand, takes us into our inner world. This direction gives depth and subtlety to life. When we slow down and give up some of the busyness and stimulation of the horizontal direction, then the vertical direction reveals itself. The vertical direction is more about quality than quantity. Initially, it is more about an inner focus than an external focus. It appears as we become more present in the moment. It grows from doing less and being more. As we become disillusioned by or less interested in the dramas and struggles of life, we create space for the vertical direction. We need more space to even notice this direction. Materialistic achievement becomes less important. Traditionally many of the Eastern cultures were devoted to this spiritual direction.

The horizontal and vertical directions can complement each other; they need not be antagonistic. Problems seem to arise when these directions get out of balance or become polarized—that is, when we follow one direction to the exclusion of the other.

When the vertical and horizontal directions are integrated, they form a cross, that most potent of Christian symbols. The life of Jesus embodied the integration of the sacred with the mundane, or the vertical with the horizontal. Jesus was God (spirit) made flesh (matter). Jesus, like all great teachers, modeled for us a worldly life that was infused with spiritual qualities.

Regular meditation connects us with the vertical direction, and the stillness we find in meditation can steadily transform our life on the horizontal direction. The horizontal direction on its own is neither wholly nourishing nor sustainable for the individual, the culture, the country or the planet. The vertical direction provides a deep source of nourishment that is not available from the horizontal direction. Stuck on the horizontal, we run on adrenaline until we are spiritually empty. Often it is when the batteries are drained that a physical, emotional or mental crisis alerts us to the vertical direction.

Becoming a more balanced and complete human being is the process of integrating these two aspects of our lives. This is the purpose of the spiritual path.

THE HERO'S QUEST

The famous anthropologist Joseph Campbell devoted himself to the study of myths and legends from all around the world and throughout recorded history. Campbell described myths and legends as "maps for the psyche" that have been passed on from generation to generation to provide guidance and inspiration. Storytelling, in many cultures, is used as a method of preparation and training for life's journey. Stories and parables convey some of the spiritual teachings transmitted from the elders to the younger generations.

An archetypal story line of particular interest to Joseph Campbell was the hero's quest. Whether the hero is Jason seeking the Golden Fleece, King Arthur seeking the Holy Grail, Don Quixote on his quest for chivalry or Huck Finn and his search for adventure, according to Campbell, the hero's quest has been one of the most commonly recurring maps of the psyche.

In his book *The Hero with a Thousand Faces*, Campbell explains that we are all heroes on our own personal quests. From his extensive study of classical and contemporary mythology, Campbell was able to delineate certain common stages of the hero's quest. In summary, these are:

1. the longing
2. the search
3. the struggle
4. the disillusionment
5. the homecoming

1. The longing
The longing is what motivates the hero to begin the quest. The longing might be for fame, wealth, adventure, justice, love or happiness. Quite often, of course, the longing may be defined by the hero's family or culture. The hero sets out on their quest with a heart's longing and a dream of fulfillment.

2. The search
The search begins with the hero determined to find happiness and to satisfy the longing. The search takes the hero out into the world looking to find whatever is hoped will fulfill the dream. The hero scans the terrain; this is how the horizontal direction opens before the hero. The hope is that something or someone will be found in the outside world that will satisfy the longing.

3. The struggle
Inevitably, the search in the world brings gain and loss, pleasure and pain. A moment of hope, a moment of despair. A struggle to achieve, attain, win. A struggle to avoid loss and to hold on to what has been gained. The horizontal direction brings with it unrelenting and inevitable change. Just when the dream seems to be achieved, something changes. This is the struggle.

4. The disillusionment
The disillusionment is the next stage of the hero's quest. The disillusionment comes as a crisis that shatters the hero's hopes and dreams. It is a stage of the struggle when everything seems to be falling apart. In a spiritual context, the disillusionment is called the "dark night of the soul." The disillusionment may result from the loss of employment,

the breakup of a relationship, the loss of resources, the loss of a loved one or a life-threatening, life-changing illness. The disillusionment is often a time of grieving and it can be a humbling experience. But also, for a time, the disillusionment takes the hero out of the struggle. The hero has to give up the struggle and the struggle loses some of its meaning. This disillusionment can often be a blessing in disguise; it can bring a difficult life lesson that the hero might otherwise avoid. The disillusionment gives the hero an opportunity to reassess the struggle, as well as individual priorities and values in life. The disillusionment gives the hero an opportunity to ask the questions: "What is really important in my life?" "What am I really longing for?" "Am I looking in the right places, in the right way?" The disillusionment brings the hero to a crossroad—a choice. The "black hole" that opens up as a result of the disillusionment can either reveal the vertical direction to the hero, or it can cause the person to try to fill it up before reentering the struggle.

The choice is to reenter the struggle or to embrace the home-coming. Reentering the struggle might be the panic reaction and lead to quickly finding a new job, a new lover, a new empire, or to finding temporary relief in drugs, alcohol, gambling or other addictive behaviors designed to fill the void. The disillusionment humbles the hero's pride, slows down the momentum of the struggle and allows the hero some time for self-reflection. Self-reflection can lead the hero to the homecoming.

5. The homecoming

The homecoming is the stage of the quest in which the hero stops searching and struggling toward an imagined dream of fulfillment. The homecoming is when we arrive here, now. Remember the lines we have quoted from T. S. Eliot:

> . . . And the end of all our exploring
> Will be to arrive where we started
> And know the place for the first time.

The homecoming is when we realize that the answer to real happiness is to be content with what we have, how things are, here and now, in this very moment. We stop trying to get something new, to be something else, to know something more, to prove something to ourselves or someone else. We give ourselves some space and time to connect with who we already are, "to arrive where we started and know the place for the first time."

This homecoming does not mean that we become passive or resigned. Far from it, with this profound acceptance of the present, we are truly free to act in a potent way that will ensure a healthy, vibrant future. In the clarity of the present moment, we will have the insight, confidence and the courage to do whatever is needed in the circumstances we find ourselves, moment by moment.

In the immediate sense, the homecoming is a time of healing and renewal. The vertical direction draws the hero's attention toward the spiritual qualities of acceptance, forgiveness, humility, patience, gratitude and compassion. The homecoming enables the hero to be present . . . to come home to their spirit, "and to know the place for the first time."

Many people turn to meditation as a result of some sort of disillusionment. Meditation is a skillful means for making the most of the opportunity that the disillusionment provides. Meditation has given so many people access to the healing and renewal of the homecoming. It provides some regular "time out" from the struggle.

Of course, the hero's journey does not end at the homecoming. With a renewed spirit, with some new insights and skills, the hero can return to the world, but in a different way. Having dipped into the homecoming, the hero has reflected on their values and priorities; they have in some way redefined the longing. Whereas the original longing may have been to "get something," now the longing might be to "share something."

And with ongoing access to the homecoming, through meditation or some other spiritual practice, the search and the struggle become less heavy or serious.

Engagement with the world becomes more like a *leela*. This is a Hindu concept that refers to the dance of life—the dance between spirit (Shiva) and matter (Shakti), the dance between the horizontal and the vertical directions. Having access to the homecoming, the hero can continue on the quest with a clearer sense of purpose, and with more ease, grace, freedom, trust and joy. The hero can begin to dance with life. Life itself becomes a spiritual practice—this is where the horizontal and vertical directions converge. Spirit infuses into the material world.

THE OCEAN

Let us use another metaphor to explain the relationship between the horizontal and the vertical directions, matter and spirit.

The surface of the ocean is affected by the wind, the rain, storms and the push and pull of the tides. It is on the surface of the ocean that waves appear, rise, fall, crash and disappear. The surface is where the movement and activity of the ocean are experienced, including waves, cyclones, tornadoes, typhoons and tsunamis. The surface of the ocean is like the surface of our busy lives; this is where the activity, the movement and the stimulation of our lives takes place. Tragedies, comedies, romance, all manner of dramas sweep across the surface of our lives, creating waves and storms. Fear and desire, craving and aversion, running toward something and running away from something else—all of these impulses create more movement, more waves on the surface of life.

The surface of the ocean is the horizontal direction. And it is on the surface that the search and struggle are acted out. The surface is the material, social, external, active aspect of life. This is where our ego, our personality and our social self are formed and operate. The activity on the surface keeps the thinking mind busy: "I want this, I do not want that" and "I want to be over there, not here!"

Below the surface is the still, silent, mysterious depth of the ocean. The vertical direction takes us into the stillness and depth. The depth is not affected by the storms and waves on the surface. Our spirit, our source, and stillness and silence are waiting in the depth of the vertical direction. Our spirit is whole and complete—it always has been—and it is waiting for our attention to shift away from the surface. All that is required is that at times we give up the struggle—all struggle, even spiritual struggle.

Through the practice of Mindfulness-Based Stillness Meditation, we have a method for giving up the struggle and just Being. When we stop running, stop struggling and stop judging and expecting, even for a few moments, we start to sink into the depth of stillness and spirit. Effortlessly. If the struggle has become an addiction, a habit and a source of identity, then MBSM can heal the addiction and gently guide our awareness into the vertical, the depth, the source.

An important point to understand about the movement and the stillness of the ocean is that they can both be present at the same time. We do not have to fight against the waves or try to suppress them. We just simply accept the movement, without reacting to it, without struggling against it, and then we will begin to sink into the depth. The movement is only on the surface, it does not affect the depth; let the movement be.

In his book *The Mindful Brain*, Daniel Siegel also uses the image of the ocean, in his case as a metaphor for the meditative mind:

> The mind is like the ocean. And deep in the ocean, beneath the surface, it's calm and clear. And no matter what the surface conditions are, whether it's flat or choppy or even a full gale storm, deep in the ocean it's tranquil and serene. From the depth of the ocean you can look toward the surface and just notice the activity there, as in the mind, where from the depth of the mind you can look upward toward the waves, the brainwaves at the surface of your mind, where all that activity of mind, thoughts, feelings, sensations, and memories exist. You have the incredible opportunity to just observe those activities at the surface of your mind.[2]

In the practice of MBSM we accept the movement of thoughts, emotions, sensations and breath. We accept it, we witness it. With nonjudgmental mindfulness we effortlessly begin to sink into the depth of our being. We do not run away from the movement. We do not run.

In the depth of the ocean there is a sunken treasure. The depth is the source of love, healing, creativity and wisdom. Each time we allow ourselves to sink, even for a few moments, we touch these treasures. Each time we return to the surface, we bring some of this treasure back to share. This happens effortlessly because the treasure is our true self.

The only effort required is in stopping the struggle. MBSM stops the struggle. Each time we stop the struggle, even for a few moments, we renew and refresh ourselves, and reconnect with the treasure that awaits us in each homecoming.

MEDITATION AND THE SPIRITUAL PATH

MBSM awakens our spiritual nature in these four simple ways:

1. It creates *connection* with our body, emotions, mind and spirit. It also connects us with others and with life.
2. It enables us to be aware of *the good* in ourselves, in others and in life.
3. It awakens a sense of *gratitude* for our life and for all life.
4. It opens our heart with *love* and *compassion* for ourselves, for others and for all living beings.

CONCLUSION: INTEGRATION

The purpose of meditation is to gather your mind
so it becomes strong and more conducive to virtue.
—H. H. THE DALAI LAMA

Over the course of this book we have explained a range of meditative techniques and possibilities, from mindfulness through to imagery and contemplation. Some of these techniques are more active and require the application of conscious thinking for specific goals; other techniques are less focused and are used to develop open awareness and presence.

The common thread that weaves through the fabric of all these techniques is that they provide you with more space. More space to rest in your true nature and to listen to your inner wisdom, a wisdom that sometimes speaks softly, even silently. Space to listen; space just to be. Space is an undervalued commodity in a busy, materialistic world but it is one of the greatest gifts we can give ourselves.

The practice of Mindfulness-Based Stillness Meditation, described in Part I, will steadily lead you into the experience of more stillness and spaciousness. It will give you space from an active, distracted mind and a contracted body. You will begin to experience the space that MBSM provides as peace and freedom; it will free your mind and touch your heart. Love and compassion flow from this spaciousness. Space unites us, brings us together.

The other applications of meditation, described in Part II, give you the space to listen to your inner wisdom and to access your inner healing resources. This space will enable you to trust and draw upon the intelligence of your body, mind and spirit. A knowing much deeper than taught knowledge awaits you in this spaciousness.

For us, it is truly a joy and a delight to be of service in guiding you toward more stillness, spaciousness and wisdom. Our wish is that these techniques will bring you wellness and deep peace, which will benefit not only yourself but everyone around you.

May you all be well, may you all be happy. May you all enjoy deep natural peace.

APPENDIX: DEFINITIONS OF MEDITATION

*Just as gold is tested by being burned, cut or rubbed, the learned
should accept my words only after examining them, not
simply out of faith or other such reasons.*
—THE BUDDHA

There are many different reasons why people meditate and a myriad different ways in which to meditate. The fact is that the word *meditation* is applied to a variety of activities and outcomes. As explained in the Introduction, this is akin to the way the word *travel* is used to describe how we can move from one place to another in any number of ways. For this book we chose a modern definition of meditation, as outlined in the Introduction. However, for completeness, in this appendix we have brought together some traditional and modern definitions to expand on its meaning.

THE AUTHORS' DEFINITION

In its simplest and most general sense, meditation is a mental discipline involving attention regulation. More specifically, the broad act of meditation can be subclassified according to the processes it involves or the outcomes it leads to.

The process and outcomes of meditation

The *process* of meditation is simply what we do while we are meditating. Attention regulation, which is essentially a fancy way of describing concentration, can be directed to various objects such as the breath or body, a mantra, a thought or prayer, a visualization or mental image, a physical object, a sense of being, or stillness. These in turn can be used to cultivate various *outcomes*, including therapeutic outcomes, cognitive changes such as improved concentration, nonattachment to experiences, stillness of mind and an attitude of acceptance. Other outcomes include meditative states or traits, undistracted awareness, transcendence of thought, oneness, spiritual insight and enlightenment. Meditation can also be identified by the physical effects it produces, such as physiological, biochemical, hormonal, immunological or neurological changes.

This definition was put together by two working parties who collaborated on it from 2006 to 2009. The impetus was to come up with an essentialized but comprehensive definition to use as a basis for two organizations. The first was for the Australian Teachers of Meditation Association (www.meditationaustralia.org.au) and involved input from Pauline McKinnon, author of *In Stillness Conquer Fear*; Dr. Craig Hassed, author of *The Essence of Healing*; and Ian Gawler. The second was for the Gawler Foundation's meditation teachers' training manual, and contributing here were the foundation's therapeutic team at that time: Paul and Maia Bedson, Dr. Ruth Gawler, Robyn Jones, Seikan Cech and Ian Gawler. Craig Hassed warrants particular recognition for crafting the final draft of the definition we all worked upon and agreed to.

CATEGORIES OF MEDITATION

These definitions were developed and are used by the Australian Teachers of Meditation Association.

1. Therapeutic meditation

Therapeutic meditation relates to the use of meditation in the health-care setting with the primary intention of the treatment of illness or the management of symptoms, whether it is used as the primary therapy or as an adjunct to other therapies. The criteria are more stringent for registration in this category because of the extra responsibilities associated with managing people's health-related problems. In this context meditation is used specifically for the purpose of physical or mental health, defined as the optimal function of both the body and the mind.

2. Meditation for personal development

Meditation for personal development relates to where meditation is being used to foster self-understanding, coping capacities, performance, behavior change, self-care skills or general well-being. In this case the meditation training may not have specific therapeutic goals and may not be taught within a spiritual context, and thus therapeutic effects or spiritual experiences are considered as secondary effects rather than the primary goal of the practice.

3. Spiritual meditation

Spiritual meditation refers to meditative and contemplative practices undertaken primarily for spiritual and/or religious development and insight. They may be undertaken according to the practices of one of the major religions, or within a recognized spiritual tradition independent of a formal religious tradition. Although the technique(s) may be the same as some varieties of therapeutic and personal-development meditation, the aim is primarily spiritual, and therapeutic or personal development goals are of secondary importance. Such aims could include, but are not limited to: oneness with Absolute Reality, Universal

Being or God; a deep experience of Self; enlightenment; or a direct experience of the nature of mind.

MODERN ENGLISH DICTIONARY DEFINITIONS

The *Shorter Oxford English Dictionary* defines *meditation* as:

(a) "the action or practice of profound spiritual or religious reflection or mental contemplation";
(b) "continuous thought on one subject, serious and sustained reflection or mental contemplation."

The first definition speaks to the fact that until recently, meditation as a practice was largely the domain of those on a spiritual or religious path. The second definition reflects the common view that one meditates "on" something, as in one concentrates on something in particular. In our terminology we have called this "attention regulation."

Contemplation is defined by the *Shorter Oxford English Dictionary* as:

(a) "religious musing, devout meditation";
(b) "the action of thinking about or of pondering over a thing continuously; musing, meditation."

SOME TRADITIONAL DEFINITIONS

Yoga and Hinduism[1]

1. *Dhyana* is the generic Sanskrit (the ancient, sacred language of India) term for meditation that, in the yoga sutras, refers to both the act of inward contemplation in the broadest sense and, more technically, the intermediate state between mere attention to an object (*dharana*) and complete absorption in it (*samadhi*).
2. *Samadhi* is another Sanskrit word for meditation, which can be translated as "meditative absorption" but which literally means "to hold something unwaveringly, firmly, so that there is no movement." Samadhi can refer to both the practice and the state of meditation.

Tibetan Buddhism[2]

Gom is the most common Tibetan word for meditation. It is related to the word *com*, which translates as "getting used to" or "becoming accustomed to doing something so that it is a part of oneself." What one is getting used to is the true nature of our mind.

Dzogchen

In the Tibetan Dzogchen approach, meditation generally falls into one of two categories:

1. calm abiding—*shyiné* in Tibetan, or *shamatha* in Sanskrit;
2. clear seeing—*lhaktong* in Tibetan, or *vipashyana* in Sanskrit.

The Sanskrit terms are used more commonly.

Shama means "calm," "peaceful," "pacifying"; *tha* means "to abide" or "to dwell." So *shamatha* translates as "calm abiding" or "peaceful remaining," or tranquillity meditation. *Vi* is short for *vishesa*, which means "special," "superior," "particular" or "unique." *Pashayana* means "to see." So *vipashyana* translates as "clear-seeing," or seeing in a direct and especially clear way.

With vipashyana there are different approaches. As *vipassana* it is well known as "insight meditation." Vipassana comes from the Theravadin Buddhist tradition, which originated in Thailand, and is a type of shamatha practice. It is an extraordinary practice, and vipassana retreats are conducted widely, are intensive and have helped many people in many ways. Vipashyana, from the Dzogchen point of view, comes from the Mahayana and particularly Vajrayana traditions which flourished in Tibet. This vipashyana is when we go beyond the conceptual mind to reveal the true nature of our mind.

Shamatha is the one-pointed concentration of the mind. There are two types of shamatha. Shamatha with support refers to concentrating on a particular thing—the breath, a mantra, an object and so on. The "thing" supports your practice. Shamatha without support is more like holding your awareness on the stillness; it is a more advanced practice where a particular focus for your concentration is no longer required.

Vipashyana makes specific analysis of the ultimate; it can be described as perfect discernment. When we are trying to realize the nature of mind, we need both concentration (the unwavering light of shamatha) and wisdom (the unwavering flame of vipashyana). With concentration alone, we will never realize the truth of reality, but if we lack concentration it will be impossible to see reality clearly because we will constantly fall prey to distraction. This is like saying if we were in a dark room and wanted to view a painting by using a candle, we would need the flame of the candle to be bright and we would also need to hold the candle still—we would need an unwavering bright flame to see clearly.

Christianity

Christian meditation is often associated with prayer or scripture study. It is rooted in the Bible, which directs its readers to meditate. In Joshua 1:8, God commands his people to meditate on his word day and night to instill obedience and enhance relationship and fellowship. This brings us in close touch with God's reality, power, grace, faith and miracles. The psalmist says that, "his delight is in the law of the Lord, and in his law he meditates day and night" (Psalm 1:2). The Bible mentions *meditate* or *meditation* twenty times.

Judaism

In the Old Testament, there are two Hebrew words for meditation: *hāgâ*, which means "to sigh" or "to murmur," but also "to meditate," and *sîhâ*, which means "to muse" or "to rehearse in one's mind."

There is evidence that Judaism has had meditative practices that go back thousands of years. For instance, in the Torah, the patriarch, Isaac, is described as going *lasuach* in the field—a term understood by all commentators as some type of meditative practice (Genesis 24:63), probably prayer.

Islam

Meditation in the Sufi traditions is based largely on a spectrum of mystical exercises, varying from one lineage to another. Numerous Sufi traditions place emphasis upon a meditative procedure similar in its cognitive aspect to one of the two principal approaches to be found in the Buddhist traditions, and what has been described above as shamatha practice.

ACKNOWLEDGMENTS

We would like to acknowledge and thank the bookseller. And the fellow who drove the books to Allen & Unwin's warehouse. And the people who planted the trees that were pulped and used to make paper for your book. Of course, we would like to thank our editors, and all of those we work with, but mostly we would like to acknowledge the truth of interdependence. The writing, publishing, distribution and sale of this book has depended upon thousands of people. This is the truth of our interdependence. If someone had not worked out how to build a printing press and harness the energies of countless other people to manufacture and supply it to our printers, there would be no book. Therefore, while there are so many obvious people to acknowledge, we want to point out that this book, like everything else, can only exist courtesy of the good efforts of many, many people.

So, given that you bought it, or received it as a gift, if you now gain benefit from it and even more so, if you are able to use something that you learn from this book to benefit other people, then you add meaning to countless other lives. There may have been someone working away in a steel factory in China, completely oblivious to the fact that the steel they produced was shipped to Europe, transformed into a printing press, then shipped to Australia and used to produce this book.

If there was no steel, there would be no printing, no book. If there were no sailors to guide the ship, no book. The book needed the driver, the vehicle, the road, the warehouse. It needed the people who provided the money so that you could buy the book. The more you reflect upon it, the more you realize how vast interdependence is. The more we all realize this, the more it adds meaning to our lives. The steelworker in China can smile a little more contentedly, the bookseller can take a little more pride in her shop and her work. So we acknowledge all those who we are aware of, and all those who were essential but remain unknown, for making the book possible.

There are specific people who do warrant more formal acknowledgment and gratitude. First Ian and Paul wish to say what a delight it was to collaborate on the book and write it together. With our particular backgrounds and personal interests we are united in our love of studying, practicing and teaching meditation. Through this project we now know each other a little better and the process was enriching, pleasantly challenging and thoroughly enjoyable.

Then we chose Allen & Unwin because Elizabeth Weiss would be the publisher we would be working with. Elizabeth is a dedicated senior student of Sogyal Rinpoche. We knew we would be able to rely on her expert advice when it came to the use of language and theory around meditation. In fact, this confidence was well realized, and Elizabeth has been of great assistance throughout the project.

Lauren Finger has been Allen & Unwin's in-house editor, and she too has been a reliable and expert influence, answering many questions, providing guidance and overseeing the production of the book.

We were particularly fortunate to have major input from the Venerable Robina Courtin. The wonderful Robina, an Australian-born Tibetan Buddhist nun, may currently best be known for the Liberation Prison Project. This started when a Mexican-American former gangster wrote to Robina for spiritual advice and has blossomed into a mostly voluntary organization that supports the practice of thousands of prisoners each year, many in Australia. However, earlier on, Robina was the editorial director of Wisdom Publications and editor of the magazine *Mandala*. Robina offered her expertise and helped us with a major structural edit following the first draft. She then repeated this later in the process with the effect of improving the work significantly.

Pam Coussins provided expertise with typing and layout, and Misha Wakerman was a constant source of information and clarity when it came to computers!

Then Catherine Taylor and Clara Finlay carried out the detailed copyediting, going over each word and sentence, making many useful corrections and suggestions, questioning us in a constructive way and helping improve the end result.

We would like to thank Kate Lyons-Dawson for the thorough index and trust this will make using the book more useful.

Then we need to acknowledge our teachers once again. While this has been done in our personal meditation histories at the front of the book, both of us have been deeply fortunate with the teachers who have helped us personally.

For Ian, the main two teachers are Dr. Ainslie Meares and Sogyal Rinpoche. Dr. Meares came at a pivotal time, introducing meditation theoretically and experientially. His simplicity, clarity and presence provided a wonderful role model that remains embodied in how Ian lives and teaches. But even more so, Sogyal Rinpoche has elaborated those beginnings, adding the priceless benefit of a long line of authentic meditation masters. There are many echoes of Rinpoche's words in the chapters written by Ian. What benefits there are flow from his wisdom and presence; any errors or lack of clarity are clearly Ian's.

For Paul, the main two teachers are Bhagwan Shree Rajneesh (Osho) and Satya Narayan Goenka. From Osho, Paul learned that the extraordinary is found in the ordinary, and he learned that the spiritual path is paved with humor, humility and heart. Osho taught Paul to meditate with body, breath and feeling. From S. N. Goenka Paul learned to pay attention and be present. Paul also learned that everything that he was looking for is already here. For his contact with these two embodiments of truth and love, Paul will be forever grateful.

Both Ian and Paul acknowledge and thank the people they have learned from throughout their many years of teaching others. There is no better way to learn something than to teach it. If there is a sense of practical wisdom in the book, as we hope there may be, it is due to the reactions, feedback, suggestions and understanding we have received from so many committed people seeking to learn how to meditate.

Finally we both thank our wives. Both Ruth and Maia had huge inputs, helping with typing, editing, suggestions, corrections, insights and regular cups of tea. Both of us are fortunate to work with our life partners. This is a wondrous delight, and Ruth's and Maia's profoundly feminine strength, compassion and wisdom imbue all that we do.

It has been a challenging pleasure to write this book. We hope we have done something useful and we acknowledge and thank all those who, through the truth of interdependence, made it manifest.

May you live a long and happy life. May we all contribute to the happiness and well-being of as many as possible.

NOTES

Meditation Journeys: About the Authors
1. T. S. Eliot, "Four Quartets," in *The Complete Poems and Plays, 1909–1950* (New York: Harcourt Brace, 1952).
2. Jon Kabat-Zinn, *Wherever You Go, There You Are* (New York: Hyperion, 1994), 4.

1. Introducing Mindfulness-Based Stillness Meditation
1. Osho, *Meditation and the Art of Ecstasy* (Poona, India, Rebel, 1973), xviii.
2. From a radio interview available at: www.speakingoffaith.publicradio .org/programs/thichnhathanh.
3. William H. Murray, *The Scottish Himalayan Expedition* (London: J. M. Dent & Sons, 1951).

8. Knowing Your Body
1. Eckhart Tolle, *The Power of Now* (Sydney: Hodder Headline, 1999), 103.

10. Connecting with Feelings
1. M. R. Jensen, "Psychobiological Factors Predicting the Course of Cancer," *Journal of Personality* 55, no. 2 (1987): 317–42.

15. Meditation for Transforming Pain
1. This definition is derived from a 1964 thesis by Harold Merskey and was first published in the journal *Pain* 6 (1979): 250.

19. Meditation and the Spiritual Path
1. Interview with Dan Rather, published in his *Deadlines & Datelines: Essays at the Turn of the Century* (New York: William Morrow, 1999).
2. Daniel J. Siegel, *The Mindful Brain* (New York: W. W. Norton, 2007), 285.

Appendix

1. Michael Murphy and Steven Donovan, *The Physical and Psychological Effects of Meditation* (Sausalito, CA: Institute of Noetic Sciences, 1997).
2. Sogyal Rinpoche, "A Treasury of Dharma: Essential Study Material for the Rigpa Sangha from the Teachings of Sogyal Rinpoche 2000–2004" (Lodève, France: Tertön Sogyal Trust), 106–7.

BIBLIOGRAPHY

Allenby, Guy. *The Dragon's Blessing*. Sydney: Allen & Unwin, 2008.

Benson, Herbert. *The Relaxation Response*. New York: Avon Books, 1976.

Borysenko, Joan. *Minding the Body, Mending the Mind*. New York: Bantam, 1988.

Campbell, Joseph. *The Hero with a Thousand Faces*. Princeton, NJ: Princeton University Press, 1949.

Chögyam Trungpa. *Meditation in Action*. Berkeley, CA: Shambhala, 1969.

Chopra, Deepak. *Quantum Healing*. New York: Bantam, 1989.

Cousins, Norman. *Anatomy of an Illness*. New York: W. W. Norton, 1979.

H.H. the Dalai Lama. *Dzogchen: The Heart Essence of the Great Perfection*. New York: Snow Lion, 2000.

———. *Stages of Meditation*. New York: Snow Lion, 2001.

Doidge, Norman. *The Brain That Changes Itself*. Carlton North, Australia: Scribe, 2007.

Dreher, Henry. *The Immune Power Personality*. New York: Plume, 1995.

Egger, Garry. *Lifestyle Medicine*. North Ryde, Australia: McGraw-Hill, 2008.

Eliot, T. S. *The Complete Poems and Plays, 1909–1950*. New York: Harcourt, Brace, 1952.

Gawler, Ian. *The Creative Power of Imagery*. Melbourne: Hill of Content, 1997.

———. *Meditation: Pure & Simple*. Melbourne: Hill of Content, 1996.

———. *Peace of Mind*. Melbourne: Hill of Content, 1987. Revised edition, Melbourne: Michelle Anderson, 2002.

———. *You Can Conquer Cancer*. Melbourne: Hill of Content, 1984. Revised edition, Melbourne: Michelle Anderson, 2001.

Gendlin, Eugene. *Focusing*. New York: Bantam, 1981.

Goleman, Daniel. *Destructive Emotions: How Can We Overcome Them?* London: Bantam, 2003.

———. *Emotional Intelligence*. New York: Bantam, 1995.

———. *Healing Emotions*. Boston: Shambhala, 1997.

Gray, John. *How to Get What You Want and Want What You Have*. New York: HarperCollins, 1999.

Greenspan, Miriam. *Healing Through the Dark Emotions*. Boston: Shambhala, 2004.

Griffiths, Father Bede. *The Golden String*. London: Harvill Press, 1954.

———. *Return to the Center*. London: Collins, 1976.

Hart, W. *The Art of Living: Vipassana Meditation as Taught by S. N. Goenka*. New York: Harper & Row, 1987.

Hassed, Craig. *The Essence of Health*. North Sydney: Ebury Press, 2008.

Ingram, Catherine. *Passionate Presence*. New York: Gotham Books, 2003.

Jensen, M. R. "Psychobiological Factors Predicting the Course of Cancer." *Journal of Personality* 55, no. 2 (1987): 317–42.

Johnson, Raynor. *The Imprisoned Splendour*. New York: Harper & Row, 1953.

Kabat-Zinn, Jon. *Coming to Our Senses*. New York: Hyperion, 2005.

———. *Full Catastrophe Living*. New York: Delacorte, 1990.

———. *Wherever You Go, There You Are*. New York: Hyperion, 1994.

LeShan, Lawrence. *How to Meditate*. New York: Bantam, 1974.

McKinnon, Pauline. *In Stillness Conquer Fear*. Blackburn, Australia: Dove Communications, 1983.

Meares, Ainslie. *Relief Without Drugs*. Glasgow: Fontana, 1967.

———. *Strange Places and Simple Truths*. London: Souvenir Press, 1969.

———. *The Wealth Within*. Melbourne: Hill of Content, 1978.

Merskey, Harold. "Pain Terms: A List with Definitions and Notes on Usage." *Pain*, no. 6 (1979): 249–52.

Murphy, Michael, and Steven Donovan. *The Physical and Psychological Effects of Meditation*. Sausalito, CA: Institute of Noetic Sciences, 1997. Available online at www.noetic.org/research/medbiblio/biblio.htm.

Murray, William H. *The Scottish Himalayan Expedition*. London: J. M. Dent & Sons, 1951.

Ornish, Dean. *Love & Survival*. New York: HarperCollins, 1998.

Osho. *Meditation and the Art of Ecstasy*. Poona, India: Rebel, 1973.

Pema Chödrön. *The Places That Scare You*. Boston: Shambhala, 2001.

Pert, Candace. *Molecules of Emotion*. New York: Touchstone, 1997.

Ramacharaka, M. *The Hindu–Yogi Science of Breath*, 23rd edition. Romford, England: Fowler, 1960.

Ramana, Maharshi. *The Spiritual Teachings of Ramana Maharshi*. Boston: Shambhala, 1988.

Rather, Dan. *Deadlines & Datelines: Essays at the Turn of the Century*. New York: William Morrow, 1999.

Sandweiss, Samuel. *Sai Baba: The Holy Man and the Psychiatrist*. San Diego, CA: Birth Day, 1975.

Siegel, Daniel J. *The Mindful Brain*. New York: W. W. Norton, 2007.

Simonton, Carl, and Stephanie Matthews. *Getting Well Again*. New York: Bantam, 1978.

Sogyal Rinpoche. *Dzogchen and Padmasambhava*. San Diego, CA: Rigpa Fellowship, 1989.

———. *The Tibetan Book of Living and Dying*. San Francisco: HarperSanFrancisco, 1992.

———. "A Treasury of Dharma: Essential Study Material for the Rigpa Sangha from the Teachings of Sogyal Rinpoche 2000–2004." Lodève, France: Tertön Sogyal Trust, 2005.

Thich Nhat Hanh. *The Miracle of Mindfulness*. Boston: Beacon Press, 1975.

———. *Transformation & Healing*. London: Random House, 1993.

Tolle, Eckhart. *The Power of Now*. Sydney: Hodder Headline, 1999.

Watts, Alan. *Psychotherapy East and West*. New York: Vintage, 1961.

Yogananda Paramahansa. *Autobiography of a Yogi*. Bombay: Jaice, 1983.

Yongey Mingyur Rinpoche, and Eric Swanson. *The Joy of Living*. New York: Harmony, 2007.

———. *Joyful Wisdom*. New York: Harmony, 2009.

Medical case histories of Ian Gawler

Jelinek, G., and R. Gawler. "Thirty-Year Follow-Up at Pneumonectomy of a 58-Year-Old Survivor of Disseminated Osteosarcoma." *Medical Journal of Australia* 189 (2008): 663–65.

Meares, A. "Regression of Osteosarcoma Metastases Associated with Intensive Meditation." *Medical Journal of Australia* 2, no. 9 (October 1978): 433.

INDEX

imagery techniques (cont'd)
    converting intention into reality,
        306–308
    for healing, 273
    to influence the body, 315–21
    for pain relief, 289–93
    spiritual presence and invocation,
        308–309
imagination, 131, 137–38, 304–305
immune system, 23, 166, 167,
    183–84, 272
impatience, 114–15, 119, 156
India, 24, 34–35
infinite consciousness, 255–56
infinite space, 255
Inner Child, 203–205
inner light, 254–55
inner rehearsal, 314
Inner Sanctuary, 289–90, 291,
    292
inner silence, 307–308
inspiration, 68, 347–48
intentional meditation, 45–46,
    309–15, 323, 331
Interfaith Movement, 7

Jensen, Dr. Mogens R., 184–85
Jesus, 172, 191, 334, 360–61
Johnson, Dr. Raynor, 19–20
judgment
    excessive, 139
    letting go of, 148
    nonjudgmental awareness, 79,
        180, 216

Kabat-Zinn, Jon, 9, 12, 36
kindness
    loving, 334–38
    personal, 51–52, 68

leela, 364
LeShan, Larry, 8

letting go, 79, 148, 258, 324–25,
    326–27
lightening up, 51, 116–17
limiting core beliefs, 136–37
loving kindness, 334–38

McKinnon, Pauline, 9
Mahayana Buddhism, 34
manifestation, 314–15
mantras, 19, 24
marriage, 133, 329–30
materialism and matter, 354, 357,
    360
Matthews, Stephanie, 9
MBSB. see Mindfulness-Based
        Stillness Meditation (MBSB)
Meares, Dr. Ainslie, 8, 21–23, 25,
        67, 68, 251, 264
meditation. see also Mindfulness-
        Based Stillness Meditation
        (MBSB); mindfulness
        meditation
    benefits, 4, 71–73
    books, 8–10, 12, 22, 30
    commitment, 54–56
    creating a ritual, 62–64
    definition, 4–5
    direct approach, 42–43, 249
    familiarity with nature of mind,
        241–44
    gradual approach, 44–45
    healthy choices, 269–71
    history, 6–7
    length of sessions, 67–68, 120, 278
    mastery, 258, 259
    path to nature of mind, 239–40
    place for, 60–61
    posture, 64–67
    processes and outcomes, 5
    professional support, 150, 182,
        279
    regular practice, 67–68, 102, 252

nature of mind (cont'd)
  main qualities of, 240–41
  and stillness, 215, 238–40

observer, location of, 230
oneness, 230, 256
one-pointedness, 112
Orme-Johnson, David, 11
Osho. *see* Bhagwan Shree Rajneesh
    (Osho)
out-of-body experiences, 171–73

pain
  animal's response to, 285–86
  beautiful intensity, 200–201
  culturally conditioned attitudes to,
      164–65
  imagery for relief of, 289–93
  important message of, 283
  management, 21–22, 286–87,
      293–301
  nature of, 284–85
  transformation in meditation,
      159–60, 281–83
peace, 227, 302, 356
  inner, 235, 246, 289, 306–307
Pert, Dr. Candace, 316
positive thinking, 269, 275
posture, 64–67
  challenges, 71–73
  discomfort, 67
  hands, 66–67
  traditional, 65–66
presence
  being present, 52–53, 117
  creating, 52, 142–43
Progressive Muscle Relaxation
    (PMR)
  exercise script, 90–92
  in pain management, 295
  preparation for, 78–81, 88–89

technique for children, 291
projection, 189, 195
psychoneuroimmunology (PNI),
    183–84
purpose and passion, 346–47

Ramana, Maharshi, 349–50
relaxation, 3, 77–78, 80. *see
    also* Progressive Muscle
    Relaxation (PMR)
  definition, 101
  feeling light or heavy, 252
  hollow-body feeling, 253
  mind, 103–105
  in pain management, 295–96
  physical benefits, 128–29
  psychological benefits, 129
  rapid relaxation, 96–99
  regular practice, 101–103
  relaxing body scan, 93–96
  relaxing deeply, 99–100
  transitional experiences, 254
religion
  conditioning, 165–66
  conversion, 28
  invocation, 308
  view of God and spirit, 172–73,
      355–56
repression, 185–86, 187–88, 198,
    201
research, 9–10, 12–13, 177, 184, 185,
    316
  bibliography, 12–13
  Mind and Life Institute, 12
  therapeutic benefits of meditation,
      11, 13, 267
resilience, 199
restlessness, 114–15, 119, 252
retreats, 28, 35
role models, 11, 198, 309
Rolfing, 200

values, 164
visualization. *see* imagery techniques

Western interest in meditation, 7
White Light healing, 317–21
writing, 182, 341, 342, 343–44, 346

yoga, 31–32, 78
Yoga Nidra, 161

Zen practice, 26, 36, 41, 49, 54
zhikr, 33

ABOUT THE AUTHORS

Dr. Ian Gawler, OAM, BVSc, MCounsHS (left, in photo), is one of Australia's most experienced and respected authorities on mind-body medicine and meditation. He is well-known as an advocate of self-help techniques and a healthy lifestyle.

A long-term cancer survivor, Dr. Gawler was diagnosed with bone cancer and his right leg was amputated in 1975. When the disease recurred later that year, he drew upon an integrated approach and experienced a remarkable recovery.

Since 1981, when he began one of the world's first lifestyle-based cancer support groups, his work has expanded into a dual role. One aspect is the focus on healing, the other on disease prevention, health and well-being. He has helped many people in their quest for peace of mind, good health and spiritual fulfillment.

With a gift for translating ancient wisdom into a modern context, Dr. Gawler is the author of four best-selling books on self-help techniques and meditation, and has edited another seven books on mind-body medicine. He has produced a series of CDs to support his writings. His biography *Ian Gawler: The Dragon's Blessing* was written by Guy Allenby in 2008. The founder of the Gawler Foundation, Dr. Gawler has appeared widely in the media and at conferences around the world.

Dr. Gawler, who has been a student of the great Tibetan teacher Sogyal Rinpoche since 1984, holds a degree in veterinary science and a master's in counseling. In 1987 he was awarded the Order of Australia Medal for his services to the community.

Paul Bedson, B.A., BAcup, BCounsP, is a meditation teacher, somatic psychotherapist and holistic counselor working at the Gawler Foundation. He teaches Mindfulness-Based Stillness Meditation, which develops inner peace and compassion. Previously, he practiced and taught traditional Chinese medicine and myotherapy.

He has worked in the field of mind-body medicine for more than twenty years, and has pursued a passion for meditation as a spiritual path since the mid-1970s.

Bedson's approach to therapy and healing is to bring more awareness and love into the body, emotions, mind and spirit. He believes all parts of a human being are important in becoming integrated and whole. His particular interest is in helping people deal with the range of emotional issues associated with their healing journey.

Bedson also practices and teaches qi gong, a traditional Chinese form of meditative exercise. He teaches that our health and well-being are best seen in the context of our relationship with earth, sky and all of nature.

He holds bachelor degrees in philosophy, counseling and traditional Chinese medicine.